Text printed on 100% recycled paper.

The GREATER SEATTLE SUPER SHOPPER

Seventh Edition

Vicki Koeplin

with Priscilla Johnston & Dinah Stotler

ELLIOTT & FAIRWEATHER, Inc.
Post Office Box 1524 Mercer Island, Washington 98040

The **Greater Seattle Super Shopper,** Seventh Edition.

Copyright © 1990 by Vicki Koeplin, Priscilla Johnston and Dinah Stotler.

Printed in the United States of America.

ISBN: 1-8792476-00-3

This book may not be reproduced in whole or in part, by any means without written permission from the publisher. All rights reserved.

The Greater Seattle Super Shopper has been published since 1976. The listings and information appearing in this edition were current at the time of final editing but are subject to change at any time. Reports are based on store visitations, telephone interviews by the authors and recommendations received from other shoppers. Neither the authors nor anyone connected with the publishing company has a personal or financial interest in any of the companies appearing in this book, and no gratuities of any kind have been solicited or accepted from listed firms.

The text of the Greater Seattle Super Shopper is printed on recycled paper as part of a corporate commitment by Elliott & Fairweather to do its small part in preserving our natural resources.

Editor in Chief, Nan Booth Simpson.

Design and production by Ron Green/TACT.

First printing; November, 1990.

"The **Greater Seattle Super Shopper**" is one of a series of regional shopping guides published by **Elliott & Fairweather, Inc**.

Current titles from **Elliott & Fairweather:**
Discover Seattle With Kids
The Portland Guidebook
The Vancouver Super Shopper
Vancouver Rise & Shine
Vancouver Out to Lunch

Distributed in Canada by Raincoast Books, Ltd.

ELLIOTT & FAIRWEATHER, Inc.
Post Office Box 1524
Mercer Island, Washington 98040-1524 U.S.A.

Greater Seattle Super Shopper, Table of Contents iii

Contents

Clothing *1 - 48*

Factory & Manufacturer's Outlets *1*
Factory & Manufacturer's Outlets, Locator Index *220*

Off-price Stores *6*
Off-price Stores Locator Index *220*

Clearance Centers *14*
Clearance Centers Locator Index *220*

Women's Consignment Shops *16*
Women's Consignment Shops Locator Index *220*

Discount Clothing Catalogs *26*

Menswear *27*
Menswear Locator Index *221*

Maternity & Children's *30*
Maternity & Children's Locator Index *221*

Shoes & Accessories *38*
Shoes & Accessories Locator Index *221*

Formal Wear, Bridal Attire & Furs *41*
Formal Wear, Bridal Attire & Furs Locator Index *221*

Fine Jewelry *45*
Fine Jewelry Locator Index *221*

Greater Seattle Super Shopper, Table of Contents

Contents

Food   49 - 76

Food Service Warehouses   50
Food Service Warehouses, Locator Index   222

Bakery Goods   52
Bakery Goods, Locator Index   222

Eggs & Dairy Products   56
Eggs & Dairy Products, Locator Index   222

Fruits & Vegetables   58
Fruits & Vegetables, Locator Index   222

Meat, Poultry & Seafood   60
Meat, Poultry & Seafood, Locator Index   222

Beverages   63
Beverages, Locator Index   222

Sweets & Treats   67
Sweets & Treats, Locator Index   222

Ethnic Foods   70
Ethnic Foods, Locator Index   222

Natural Foods & Health Products   73
Natural Foods & Health Products, Locator Index   223

Personal Care   77 - 85

Drugs & Sundries   77
Drugs & Sundries, Locator Index   223

Cosmetics & Grooming Products   80
Cosmetics & Grooming Products, Locator Index   223

Grooming Services   83
Grooming Services, Locator Index   223

Greater Seattle Super Shopper, Table of Contents v

Contents

Home Building and Remodeling 86 - 103

Building Materials, Hardware & Tools 86
Building Materials, Hardware & Tools, Locator Index 223

Floor Coverings 93
Floor Coverings, Locator Index 223

Paint & Wallpaper 98
Paint & Wallpaper, Locator Index 224

Window Coverings 101
Window Coverings, Locator Index 224

Home Furnishings 104 - 124

Furniture 104
Furniture, Locator Index 224

Household Appliances 110
Household Appliances, Locator Index 224

Kitchen Equipment 114
Kitchen Equipment, Locator Index 224

Bedding & Linens 116
Bedding & Linens, Locator Index 225

China, Crystal & Silver 121
China, Crystal & Silver, Locator Index 225

Decorative Accessories 123
Decorative Accessories, Locator Index 225

Contents

Plants, Flowers and Greenery   126 - 131

Nurseries   126
Nurseries, Locator Index   225

Garden Ornaments   129
Garden Ornaments, Locator Index   225

Florists   129
Florists, Locator Index   225

Holiday Greenery   131
Holiday Greenery, Locator Index   225

Office Needs   132 - 148

Office Furniture, Machines & Supplies   132
Office Furniture, Machines & Supplies, Locator Index   225

Computer Hardware & Software   137
Computer Hardware & Software, Locator Index   226

Paper Products for Home & Office   145
Paper Products for Home & Office, Locator Index   226

Recreation and Hobbies   149 - 193

Sporting Goods & Recreational Clothing   149
Sporting Goods & Recreational Clothing, Locator Index   226

Audio & Video Equipment   160
Audio & Video Equipment, Locator Index   226

Audio & Video Recordings   162
Audio & Video Recordings, Locator Index   226

Photographic Equipment & Supplies   169
Photographic Equipment & Supplies, Locator Index   227

Greater Seattle Super Shopper, Table of Contents vi

Contents

Arts and Crafts & Sewing 172
Arts and Crafts & Sewing, Locator Index 227

Used Books 179
Used Books, Locator Index 227

Museums, Films & Performing Arts 184
Museums, Films & Performing Arts, Locator Index 227

Dining Out 185
Dining Out, Locator Index 227

Coupon Books 187

Luggage 190
Luggage, Locator Index 227

Children's Toys 190
Children's Toys, Locator Index 227

Automotive 194 - 201

New & Used Automobiles 194
New & Used Automobiles, Locator Index 228

Parts & Accessories 197
Parts & Accessories, Locator Index 228

Road Services 200

Something for Everyone 202 - 217

Factory Outlet Malls 202
Factory Outlet Malls, Locator Index 228

Mass Merchandise Discounters 206
Mass Merchandise Discounters, Locator Index 228

Membership Buying Clubs 211
Membership Buying Clubs, Locator Index 228

Contents

Thrift Shops, Swap Meets & Auctions   *213*
Thrift Shops, Swap Meets & Auctions, Locator Index   *228*

Shopping Tours   *217*

Locator Map & Indexes   *218 - 228*

Shopping Center Locations   *229*

General Index   *231*

Acknowledgements

As an avid user of the Seattle Super Shopper for many years, I never dreamed that one day I would actually be writing the Seventh edition. It all started when I requested copies of the book to sell in my Cheap Chic classes and the rest is history. After a year and a half of research, hundreds of hours talking on the telephone and burning the midnight oil, there are dozens of people who deserve credit for helping me out: Dinah Stotler and Priscilla Johnston, the former publishers, for hiring me sight unseen to write my first book; Linda Martinson, a fellow author (cookbooks) for her advice on how to take that giant step into the world of publishing; Karen Walton, my typist who helped me meet my deadlines and corrected a lot of my grammatical errors; my husband and daughter, who for over a year put up with a house strewn with papers; and the many sales clerks, store managers, and owners who took the time to tell me about their stores, whether they were a small factory outlet or a 12-store chain.

Vicki Koeplin

The Greater Seattle Super Shopper

Introduction

If you adhere to the following guidelines, garnered during months of research, we guarantee you'll save on everything from automobiles to zippers!

- Use the index to find specific items you're interested in buying. Many businesses sell products other than those related to the heading under which they appear.
- Be open-minded when it comes to visiting low-overhead outlets that may not live up to your standards of service or housekeeping. Remember, that's how they keep their prices so low.
- Don't be afraid to negotiate a lower price, especially if the item is damaged or you're buying in quantity.
- Ask if you can get a discount by paying in cash.
- Comparison shop to get the best value for your money. We suggest using the Sears, Best and J.C. Penney's catalogs as starting points. Sunday Supplements put out by mass merchandisers are also great resources.
- Whenever possible, use the telephone to comparison shop and to verify that the item you want is in stock.
- Read newspaper advertisements, get on mailing lists, and talk to sales clerks to find out about weekly, monthly and seasonal sales.
- To save time, shop in an area that has a lot of discounters or several stores that sell the same product. In the north end, Alderwood Mall is surrounded by dozens of stores listed in the Seattle Super Shopper. In the south end, Andover Park and the Southcenter Parkway strip are home to a multitude of manufacturers, warehouse distributors and off-price retailers.
- Pick up a free copy of "Little Nickel Want Ads" or pay 75¢ for "Buy & Sell" at convenience stores and grocery stores for access to over a thousand classifieds that list every product and service imaginable.

Consumer Protection

- There is no state law that says stores must take merchandise back unless goods sold as first-quality do not perform as advertised or a flaw is discovered after purchasing an item. Every business sets its own return policy, which should be clearly visible somewhere in the store or printed on the sales receipt. If you don't see a sign, ask.
- Check all warranties, guarantees and delivery charges before making your purchase.

Mail-order Shopping

We've included several discount mail-order catalogs, all of which are free upon request. Once you get your name on their mailing list, chances are you'll receive unsolicited catalogs since many companies sell or trade mailing lists. If you don't purchase something within a year, you're usually taken off the lists.

Here are a few tips to keep in mind when shopping by mail:

- The best catalogs offer detailed descriptions, toll-free ordering service, satisfaction or your money back guarantees, and refunds on postage for returns.

Greater Seattle Super Shopper, Introduction

- Every year in October, Seattle Times consumer advocate Shelby Gilje publishes a readers' poll of the top ten catalogs. Her column frequently resolves readers' complaints and includes tips on how to deal with the problems inherent in mail order.

- Laws enacted by the Federal Trade Commission and U.S. Postal Service protect consumers from mail-order fraud. If you have a problem, write a letter to the Seattle Times Troubleshooter, the Post-Intelligencer action column, or file a complaint with the Attorney General's office and the Better Business Bureau.

- If you pay for your mail-order purchase with a credit card, orders will arrive much sooner than if you send a check. If you're in a big hurry, many companies will ship Federal Express, but you pay for the service.

Definitions of Terms Used Throughout This Book

- **Close-outs**, **overruns** and **discontinued styles** are first-quality merchandise that factories sell at big discounts to whomever offers the best deal. These are sometimes goods that were returned by retail stores because the products weren't shipped on time or didn't sell.

- **Private-label** merchandise is manufactured especially for a store. Specialty clothing chains use private-label merchandise to project a distinctive fashion image and offer their customers styles that are not available elsewhere. It's difficult to comparison shop when you're dealing with private-label goods. Private-labeling allows retailers to cut out the middle men, so prices may naturally be lower. Or, the products may be copies of more expensive items, which sell for less because the manufacturer used a different material or altered the style slightly to cut costs.

- **Samples** are prototypes used by sales reps when showing a line to prospective retail buyers. They're usually one-of-a-kind items.

- **Irregulars** or **Seconds** are flawed merchandise that should be marked **"as is"**, which means the item cannot be returned! Drastically reduced prices often indicate something is seriously wrong with the item. Check carefully for flaws! Sometimes the defects are barely noticeable or can be easily repaired.

And Finally

- As we go to press, we're aware that some businesses will have moved, closed, changed their hours or changed their names by the time you read this book. Call before you head out on a cross-town shopping adventure.

- Prices quoted in various listings are to serve as guidelines and may fluctuate with economic and seasonal changes.

- If you shop in one of the stores we've listed and find it disappointing, please let us know. If, on the other hand, you think a certain store is bargain-hunter's heaven tell your friends. We want these stores to stay in business!

- If we've failed to list your favorite bargain spot and you are willing to share it with us, drop us a line. We're continually updating our files to make the Eighth Edition bigger and better than ever!

Clothing

Never pay full price for clothing again! As the cost of apparel continues to rise, it's increasingly difficult to limit spending to the 7% or 8% usually suggested for clothing in family budgets. By shopping the many resources listed in this section, you can buy more for less and still get current-style, high-quality merchandise.

Factory & Manufacturer's Outlets

Seattle's nationally known manufacturers of outerwear and casual sportswear for young adults— labels like *Union Bay, Shah Safari, Brittania, Generra* and *Pacific Trail*— have put us on the fashion map. If you don't see your favorite lines listed in this section, it's because the company either ships its overstock, samples and seconds to an out-of-state outlet or sells piecemeal to discounters. Factory outlets will be bare-bones operations, frequently located at big distribution centers because a lot of the actual production is offshore. Some manufacturers maintain outlets separate from the factory that operate more like retail stores, selling other brand names, offering better service and having more lenient return policies. Others, including wholesale distributors, open their doors to the public only during annual or periodic sales to clear out inventory.

Merchandise in this category will also turn up at Wholesale Heaven's periodic sales. (See Index). Shop carefully because sales are final at most factory outlets. Call to get on mailing lists for periodic sales.

AMERICOAST *Fraje & 2022* NEW LISTING
Renton: 820 Thomas Ave. S.W. ☎ 255-6677
Periodic sales

Americoast imports and wholesales a variety of products made in the Orient. Merchandise is mainly moderately priced clothing for men, women and children. The last flyer we received listed printed T-shirts, lambs wool sweaters, fashion knit tops and children's Shaker knit sweaters for $2 to $10. The company also distributes an exclusive line of jewelry boxes and fashion accessories made of Thai silk.

Checks

BEL-BOUTIQUE
Tacoma: 2300 S. Washington ☎ 752-7701
Periodic sales

In May, July, September and December, the Bellarmine Preparatory High School Mothers' Club sponsors terrific sales of sample clothes, which include a lot of Junior sizes and young mens' wear. Prices are wholesale plus 10%. Giftware, jewelry and holiday-related items are sometimes available.

Checks, Credit cards

2 Clothing, Factory & Manufacturer's Outlets

BRB MANUFACTURING INC.
Puyallup: 320 Spring ☎ 622-2881
Hours: Mon-Sat 11-5

Since BRB makes private-label outerwear and sportswear for retail stores, left-over merchandise varies from job to job. To keep the employees busy between contracts, many items are made especially for this factory outlet. Nylon windbreakers, tights, sweatshirts, Lycra shorts and polar fleece jackets were in stock the day we called. Styles are basic, sizes XS-XXXL. The most expensive jacket was $32. Children's sizes were as low as $12.

Checks

CASCADIAN SPORTSWEAR
Everett: 2701B Colby ☎ 252-0555
Hours: Mon-Fri 8-4

This small outerwear subcontractor produces functional items for men, women and older children. The garments may not make a strong fashion statement, but they're good quality, and prices range from $12 to $25. Inventory is mainly lightweight poplin or nylon jackets and coats and vests with fleece or acrylic linings.

Cash only

CURRIER & CO. *Demi-Sport*   NEW LISTING
Seattle: ☎ 782-4545
Periodic sales

Petite sizes take note! If cotton knits and woven separates in the $14 to $25 price range sound appealing, shop the private sales sponsored by this small local manufacturer. The same garments sell for twice the price at Nordstrom's and Barisof's.

Checks

EIGHTH AVENUE WOOLENS *Collectibles*   NEW LISTING
Seattle: 711 Virginia ☎ 448-7422 *Downtown*
Periodic sales

Great buys on traditional styles for the working woman with discerning taste. Inventory fluctuates from trench coats and blazers to dresses and coordinates in beautiful fabrics manufactured for department stores all over the country. Retail prices average $40 to $200. You pay half that, and sometimes less. Enter at the foot of the driveway.

Checks, Credit cards

EXIT WEST CLOTHING CO.   NEW LISTING
Seattle: 119 S. Main, 4th floor ☎ 340-2265 *Pioneer Square*
Hours: Mon-Sat 8-5

This showroom distribution center stocks unisex T-shirts, pants, shorts and imprinted tops, most of which are made in California.

continued >

Clothing, Factory & Manufacturer's Outlets

They open a small off-price shop at street level during the tourist season. Major department stores from Macy's to Fred Meyer to The Bon carry their goods. A lot of the sale merchandise is first-quality, and prices are fantastic.

Checks, Credit cards

FASHION FACTORY LIQUIDATORS *D.D. Sloane*
Bothell: 22627 Bothell Way S.E. ☎ 486-7135 *Canyon Park*
Eastgate: 3080 148th S.E. ☎ 641-1261 *Sunset Village*
Hours: Bothell, Mon-Fri 10-8; Eastgate, Mon-Fri 10-8; Both stores Sat 10-6, Sun 12-5

D.D. Sloan's outlets always elicit rave reviews. No frills decor and out-of-the-way locations ensure great buys on contemporary and junior fashions by this well-known local manufacturer. Jeans, woven separates, knit sportswear and sweaters average $15 to $25. Leather skirts and jackets show up occasionally, as well as samples from other manufacturers. Because department stores all over the country carry these wares, labels are clipped at the time of purchase to prevent full-price returns at local stores.

Checks, Credit cards

INTERNATIONAL NEWS JUNIORS
Seattle: ☎ 682-9130
Periodic sales

You can't walk into a major department store locally without spotting this popular manufacturer's fun, distinctive apparel for Juniors and Young Men. If you're unable to attend the periodic sales at the distribution center, try Nu Yu Fashions or Morning Sun Outlet, which sell overstock and discontinued styles from *International News*.

Checks

ITEM HOUSE *Ferncrest, Christine Riley*
Tacoma: 2920 S. Steele St. ☎ 627-7068
Periodic sales

Prices are fantastic on fashionable outerwear, suits, blouses and coordinates manufactured at this factory whose merchandise is sold all over the country. Many garments are made exclusively for department stores. (Nordstrom Towne Square is a big account.) Raincoats are their best selling items, but you'll also find coats for dress and leisure in Misses, Petite and Half-sizes.

Checks, Credit cards

JUMP SPORTSWEAR   NEW LISTING
Seattle: 3131 Western #513 ☎ 282-3713 *South of Seattle Center*
Hours: By appointment only

There's always a rack of discounted samples and overstock to pick through at this small manufacturer of flashy Lycra activewear, sweat tops and trendy Spandex knit fashions.

continued >

4 Clothing, Factory & Manufacturer's Outlets

Their clothing is normally sold with aerobic and biking apparel or in boutiques like Local Brilliance. You'll find a limited quantity of Children's sizes.

Checks, Credit cards

M. GENAUER & CO. *Seattle Blues* — NEW LISTING
Seattle: 2005 8th Ave., 2nd floor ☎ 624-5351 *Downtown*
Periodic sales

This local manufacturer has been in business since 1917. Their inexpensive casual separates for the whole family appear in major department stores across the country (J.C. Penney is a big account). Acid-wash jeans, denim skirts and jackets, woven cotton shirts and pants go for $10 to $15. Sizes include Women's, Junior's, Petite's and Girl's, age 4-14. Jeans, sweatshirts and jackets for the guys. Located on top of Capitol Music.

Checks, Credit cards

MORNING SUN OUTLET
Fife: 3500-D 20th St. E. ☎ 926-0801
Hours: Mon-Fri 10-9, Sat 10-5, Sun 11-5

Morning Sun is a garment imprinting company in Tacoma that silkscreens motifs onto sweatshirts, T-shirts, nightshirts and jogging suits. Much of the printing is done with puff paints, a popular item in the apparel market today. Their fun sweatshirts retail for $28-$45 in women's apparel stores, but this outlet sells slight irregulars for only $16.99. Prices start even lower for plain cotton knits. Morning Sun also offers first-quality clothing for men and children from other manufacturers.

Checks, Credit cards

MOTTO and ONLY STUFF — NEW LISTING
Kent: 1222 N. 6th ☎ 622-9888
Periodic sales

Two of the hottest new names in the young men's and women's contemporary sportswear market should be added to your list. Their warehouse sales offer some great buys on cotton printed shirts, pants and accessories in the latest styles.

Checks

NORMANDEE ROSE — NEW LISTING
Seattle: 620 Aurora Ave. N. ☎ 284-3295 *Seattle Center*
Hours: By appointment only

Merchandise by one of Seattle's better-known manufacturers of moderately priced jeans, woven twill pants and cotton tops is produced offshore and sold nationwide. Close-outs, irregulars and first-quality goods in Misses, Junior and Girl's sizes can be purchased at the warehouse.

Checks

Clothing, Factory & Manufacturer's Outlets

NOWELL & ASSOCIATES SAMPLE SALE — NEW LISTING
Seattle: ☎ 728-9673
Periodic sales

Three or four times a year these clothing salesmen host a private sale to dispose of samples from the many lines they represent. Prices are wholesale or below on moderately-priced, contemporary style dresses and sportswear sold mainly in specialty stores. Two of their well-known import lines are *Star of India* and *Satyuga*, the latter noted for cut-work embroidery. Their samples also end up in Kathy's Kloset, Razz m'Tazz and Take Two, popular Northend consignment shops.

Checks

PACIFIC TRAIL SPORTSWEAR *Weather Watch, Pacific Trail, Inside Edge*
Seattle: 608 Yale Ave. N ☎ 682-8196 *East of Seattle Center*
Hours: Mon-Fri 9-5, Sat 10-5

Pacific Trail was one of the first local manufacturers of outerwear; forty years later their clothing is popular all over the country. Their manufacturer's outlet carries good buys on nylon wind breakers, twill jackets, down parkas and ski apparel for the whole family. Men's lightweight jackets were priced from $11.95 to $29.95 when we visited. Irregulars are not always marked, so check carefully for flaws. They also stock clothing by *Woolrich*.

Checks, Credit cards

QUALITY CLASSICS SPORTSWEAR
Seattle: 26 S. Dawson ☎ 763-8526 *Georgetown*
Hours: Tues-Fri 10-5, Sat 10-6

This warehouse distributor sells better-quality sportswear in classic styles to stores like Eddie Bauer and Frederick and Nelson. Overstock and discontinued styles go on sale at unbelievably low prices. Merchandise is mainly unisex style T-shirts, sweatshirts and sweaters. Some items have been silk screened or embroidered. *Hanes and Russell* T-shirts start at $6. When we checked, rugby and polo shirts, oxford dress shirts and jackets were also available.

Checks, Credit cards

SAMUEL MARTIN LTD.
Seattle: 2013 4th Ave. ☎ 448-8406 *Downtown*
Hours: Mon-Fri 10-3:30

Where else but Seattle would you find a factory that's been making raincoats for 65 years? Inventory also includes traditionally styled coats and jackets for dress and casual wear. Since Samuel Martin private-labels for department stores, only first-quality fabrics are used. Expect to pay $35 to $90 for production overruns, samples and seconds.

Prices are lowest in January and February during their big warehouse liquidation sales. On-the-spot alterations are available.

Checks, Credit cards

6 Clothing, Off-price Stores

SEATTLE PACIFIC INDUSTRIES *Heet, Union Bay, Sync, ReUnion, Ary Cooper, UB Kids* **NEW LISTING**

Kent: 21216 72nd Ave. S. ☎ 872-2946
Hours: Mon-Sat 10-5

The Pacific Northwest's largest clothing manufacturer is one of the hottest resources nationwide for young men and women's contemporary fashions. Styles cover a broad spectrum from casual separates to trendy active wear. Goods are manufactured offshore and shipped to this huge distribution center where the factory outlet sells overstock and close-outs at 30% or more below retail. Irregulars and past-season goods end up in the Bargain Backroom where prices plummet. You must go into the store to get on the mailing list for periodic clearance sales of first-quality goods.

Checks, Credit cards

WEARABLE ART SALE

Mercer Island: 3723 90th Ave. S.E. ☎ 232-8521
Periodic sales

Attend a private sale of handcrafted items sold in galleries, museums and boutiques across the country. Samples include sterling silver and brass jewelry, hand-painted silk accessories, clothing, wall hangings, and handwoven garments by local artists.

Cash

Off-price Stores

Off-price chains and specialty stores are the fastest growing segment of the apparel market nationwide. They offer quality merchandise for the whole family at 20% to 70% below retail. Most manufacture their own lines or use volume buying power to guarantee low prices. Many supplement their inventory with close-outs, overruns and discontinued styles. Price tags usually show both the retail price and the discounted price to give you an idea of what you are saving.

Off-price stores locate in lower-rent areas like strip shopping centers. Often several discounters cluster in one place, which is a real time-saver for the consumer. (Alderwood Towne Center, Aurora Fashion Plaza, Factoria Square, Northgate Village and Pavilion Mall, the largest, are good examples.) Big chains rely on a fast turnover, which means an ever-changing array of sale merchandise— a boon for hard-core bargain hunters interested only in items priced at 70% or more below retail.

Return policies at off-price stores can be stricter than at full-price retailers, so be sure to inquire before you pull out your checkbook.

Clothing, Off-price Stores

BI-LO CLOTHING, JOSEPH M'S & THE NEW LOOK
Tacoma: Bi-Lo; 6400 S. Yakima ☎ 473-6457
Joseph M's; 2208 N. 30th ☎ 272-7071
The New Look; 1108 S. K St. ☎ 272-1701
Hours: Mon-Sat 10-6; Sun 12-5; Bi-Lo open Fri 10-9

The owner, a former wholesale clothing rep, picks up overruns, close-outs and samples at factories in Los Angeles. Contemporary women's apparel for casual, career and dressy occasions includes such labels as *Casatia, Climax, Arpejia, TD4 and Rachelli* in Misses, Junior and Large sizes. You'll discover lots of costume jewelry and accessories. Prices range from $2 to $200, and savings vary. More expensive items are sold at the Joseph M store.

Checks, Credit cards

BURLINGTON COAT FACTORY NEW LISTING
Edmonds: 24111 Hwy. 99 ☎ 776-2221
Tukwila: 17900 Southcenter Pkwy. ☎ 575-3995 *Pavilion Mall*
Hours: Edmonds Mon-Sat 10-9, Sun 11-6; Tukwila Mon-Fri 9:30-9:30, Sat 9:30-8, Sun 11-6

With the largest inventory of outerwear in the Pacific Northwest (over 12,000 coats per store), this chain offers raincoats, lightweight jackets and dressy wool coats for every member of the family. Look for such famous names as *London Fog, Misty Lane, Perry Ellis and Larry Levine*, plus special racks for furs and leathers. You may even find a full-length mink coat at half-price. Career-oriented suits, dresses and coordinates can be found in Misses, Petite and Large sizes. Contemporary separates by *Liz Claiborne, Carole Little, Chaus and Bonnie Bill* appear regularly, as well as dresses for special occasions. The men's department offers an outstanding selection of suits, sport jackets, dress shirts and slacks by such quality manufacturers as *Colours, Henry Grethel, Pierre Cardin and Jordache* in sizes 38 to 54. Casual wear includes Big and Tall sizes up to 4XX. And, you'll find well-stocked departments for Juniors, Young Men and Children.

Some merchandise is specially-manufactured and sold under Burlington's own label, so it's hard to compare prices. While they certainly offer the largest variety of goods under one roof, their discounts are not always as great as some other off-price chains', nor are markdowns as large or as frequent. Try to hold out for special promotions, seasonal sales and the gigantic coat sale in January.

Checks, Credit cards

CLOTHESTIME
Factoria: 4074 128th Ave. S.E. ☎ 643-1235 *Factoria Square*
Federal Way: Pacific Hwy S. at 320th S. ☎ 946-0511

continued >

8 Clothing, Off-price Stores

Lynnwood: 3105 Alderwood Mall Blvd. ☎ 774-7961 Alderwood Towne Ctr.
Redmond: 2172 148th N.E. ☎ 644-8312 *Overlake Fashion Plaza*
Seattle: 325 Broadway E. ☎ 325-7803 *Capitol Hill*
    4501 Roosevelt Way N.E. ☎ 632-0820 *U-District*
    160th & Aurora Ave. N. ☎ 362-3571 *Aurora Fashion Plaza*
    832 N.E. Northgate Way ☎ 362-9480 *Northgate Village*
Silverdale: Silverdale Way & Bucklin Hill Road ☎ 698-1223 *Ross Plaza*
Tacoma: S. Steele at 38th ☎ 473-4279
Tukwila: 17900 Southcenter Parkway ☎ 575-8110 *Pavilion Mall*
Hours: Generally, Mon-Fri 10-9, Sat 10-6, Sun 12-5

With over 350 stores nationwide, Clothestime is one of the leading off-price chains for junior sportswear and trendy fashions. Although the majority of the inventory is manufactured especially for the stores, they also sell such name-brands as *Judy Knapp, Kitty Hawk, Guess, Limited Express and Condor* at discounted prices. To keep the goods moving, clearance racks are always jammed with terrific buys.

Checks, Credit cards

DRESS BARN

Redmond: 2126 148th N.E. ☎ 643-9164 *Overlake Fashion Plaza*
Tukwila: 17900 Southcenter Pkwy. ☎ 575-1916 *Pavilion Mall*
Hours: Tukwila Mon-Fri 9:30-9:30, Sat 9:30-8, Sun 11-6;
    Redmond Mon-Fri 10-9, Sat 10-6, Sun 12-5

Career women who want to maintain a professional appearance shop at the Dress Barn, where fashionable and classic dresses, suits and coordinates fill the racks. Prices on such leading brands as *Jonathan Martin, Sasson, Casper, Leslie Fay and Jones of New York* are 20% to 50% lower than department store's. Lines made especially for the stores are knock-offs of best-selling styles. You can always find a good-looking suit for around $100. Sign up to get postcards announcing the suit sales in February and August. The Pavilion Mall store has an excellent selection of sale merchandise year-round because it is the clearance center for all the West Coast stores.

Checks, Credit cards

FASHION DIRECTIONS

Factoria: I-90 & I-405 ☎ 641-6708 *Factoria Square*
Seattle: 1530 5th Ave. ☎ 622-5400) *Downtown*
Hours: Factoria Mon-Fri 10-9; Seattle Mon-Fri 10-8; Sat 10-6, Sun 12-5

Fashion Directions is Jay Jacobs's budget department. Thrifty moms encourage teenagers to shop here for trendy clothes and accessories at half the price. Some of the inventory is clearance merchandise from the retail stores, but the majority is special-purchase items and factory overruns. In-store promotions bring prices down even more on both moderate and better-quality labels, occasionally including *Calvin Klein, Jordache and D.D. Sloan*. The downtown store is located in Jay Jacobs's basement.

Checks, Credit cards

Clothing, Off-price Stores

J. THOMPSON NEW LISTING

Factoria: I-90 & I-405 ☎ 643-5210 *Factoria Square*
Seattle: 1501 4th Ave ☎ 623-5780 *Century Square, Downtown*
Silverdale: 10315 Silverdale Way N.W. ☎ 698-1341 *Kitsap Mall*
Hours: Factoria & Silverdale Mon-Fri 10-9, Sat 10-6, Sun 12-5; Seattle
  Mon-Fri 9:30-6:30, Sat 10-6

The owner of this small local off-price chain spent 13 years as a buyer for Nordstrom's Rack. Focusing on career women 30 to 45 years old, sizes 6 to 16, he offers the same service and selection as retail stores, but at discounted prices. You'll find mainly separates and coordinates, so you can put together your own look. Classic styles by *Georgio St. Angelo, Oscar de la Renta, Evan Picone* and *Rafael* fill the racks. We saw some great buys on basics, as well as fashionable items like wool gabardine skirts for only $29. Raincoats and dressier garments are available in season. Get on the mailing list for advance notice of monthly sales.
Checks, Credit cards

JACLYN'S NEW LISTING

Bellevue: 201 Bellevue Way ☎ 454-6343 *Park Row*
Hours: Mon-Fri 10-7, Sat 10-6, Sun 12-5

Here's a terrific new resource for dressing in style on a budget! The owner buys close-outs and overstock from Spiegel and leading department stores' mail-order catalogs. The stock varies from leather jackets to linen dresses, silk blouses and cotton sportswear, often limited to one size or style. Designer labels keep prices relatively high, but you're paying 40% to 60% less than catalog prices. Updated coordinates by *Together*, made especially for Spiegel, are less expensive. Sign up today for discount coupons and notices of special promotions.
Checks, Credit cards

JEANS TO GO

Bellevue: 11822 N.E. 8th ☎ 453-9517
Hours: Mon-Fri 10-9, Sat 10-6, Sun 12-5

Bargains galore on jeans by such well-known manufacturers as *Lee, Levi* and *Lawman* fill this bare-bones warehouse. Women's sizes go up to 18, men's range from 24 to 42, and there's a limited selection for children. Prices are low because most of the inventory is overruns and close-outs. Average cost for a pair of jeans is $19.95. Casual tops, sweaters, lightweight jackets and denim separates are also discounted.
Checks, Credit cards

See area locator index for this section on page 220

Clothing, Off-price Stores

L.A. CONNECTION

Factoria: I-90 & I-405 ☎ 643-5755 *Factoria Square*
Everett: 12818 4th Ave. W. ☎ 348-4883 *Puget Park*
    1001 N Broadway ☎ 259-4598 *College Plaza*
Kent: 25824 104th Ave S.E. ☎ 859-4973 *Kent Hill Plaza*
Renton: Rainier Ave. S. at Sunset ☎ 226-6641 *Renton Shopping Center*
Tacoma: 8720 S. Tacoma ☎ 581-4933
West Seattle: 8989 Barton & 25th Ave S.W. ☎ 935-6609 *Westwood Village*
Hours: Generally, Mon-Fri 10-9, Sat 10-6, Sun 12-5

Shipped factory-direct from manufacturers in California, the Junior-oriented overruns and close-outs here are priced 20% to 30% below retail. The inventory, which includes styles not carried by other local retailers, is a mixture of both fun and sophisticated sportswear, separates, dresses, costume jewelry, belts and hair ornaments. Look for such names as *L.A. Gear, Stella and New Times.*

Checks, Credit cards

LOEHMANN'S

Factoria: I-90 at I-405 ☎ 641-7596 *Loehmann's Plaza*
Hours: Mon, Tues, Sat 10-5:30, Wed & Fri 10-9, Sun 12-5

A pioneer in the concept of off-price marketing and the first big chain to open an outlet in the Pacific Northwest, Loehmann's has long been famous for stylish merchandise. Some women make weekly treks to ensure first choice on haute couture labels. Even the sportswear tends to be sophisticated. Sizes range from 4-16 with a few Juniors mixed in. Petites are displayed separately.

The main room holds long racks filled with sweaters, skirts, blouses, dresses, jackets, suits and coats. Look for sensational buys on leather, suede and ultrasuede garments originally valued at $200 to $600. Belts, handbags and scarves reflect the same quality. The Back Room features expensive coordinates, dresses and evening wear by such top American designers as *Donna Karen and Anne Klein.*

Wear your best undies when you shop at Loehmann's because you'll be trying on clothes in a large communal dressing room or on the sales floor of the Back Room, since garments are not allowed out of the room.

Loehmann's mailing list promotes special sales and events like their annual fall fashion preview, which includes informal modeling.

Checks, Credit cards

Clothing, Off-price Stores

MARSHALL'S

Redmond: 2150 148th Ave. ☎ 644-2429 *Overlake Fashion Plaza*
Lynnwood: 3205 Alderwood Mall Blvd. ☎ 771-6045 *Alderwood Towne Center*
Seattle: 160th & Aurora Ave. N. ☎ 367-8520 *Aurora Fashion Plaza*
Tukwila: 17900 Southcenter Parkway ☎ 575-0141 *Pavilion Mall*
Hours: Mon-Fri 9:30-9:30, Sat 9:30-8, Sun 11-6

Marshall's, one of the oldest off-price chains in the country, carries a full range of clothing for every member of the family, along with housewares and gift items. Less expensive brands share space with better quality goods. Women's apparel features the usual array of Junior and Misses fashions, plus excellent Petite and Large-size departments. Working women will find stylish suits, dresses and coordinates by contemporary designers like *Chaus and Evan Picone*. Beautiful silk dresses by *Arjenti* are staples in the dress department. Maternity wear is also available. Costume jewelry, belts, handbags, shoes and scarves complete your wardrobe. Mens apparel tends to be oriented towards the casual, although dress shirts and pants are stocked. Children's departments outfit toddlers through teenagers. The Redmond store is the largest.

Checks, Credit cards

MODERN WOMAN

Factoria: I-90 & I-405 ☎ 643-2274 *Factoria Square*
Everett: 1402 S E. Everett Mall Way ☎ 355-7808 *Everett Mall*
Lynnwood: 3105 Alderwood Mall Blvd. ☎ 774-3550 *Alderwood Towne Center*
Redmond: 2130 N.E. 148th Ave ☎ 643-1555 *Overlake Fashion Plaza*
Seattle: 160th & Aurora Ave. N. ☎ 361-1812 *Aurora Fashion Plaza*
Silverdale: 10406 Silverdale Way N.W. ☎ 698-1805 *Ross Plaza*
Tacoma: 3304 S. 23rd St. ☎ 572-4309 *Tacoma Center*
Hours: Mon-Fri 10-9, Sat 10-6, Sun 12-5; Redmond Mon-Fri 10-6;
Lynnwood & Bellevue Sun 11-6; Everett Sun 10-6

Formerly known as XXtra Special, this huge off-price chain caters to the full-figured woman with a taste for fashionable apparel and accessories. The customer's average age is 35, and sizes range from 16W-24W. Current-style merchandise from *Young Stuff, Bonnie and Bill, and Eao Too* shares space with goods manufactured especially for the store. Modern Woman has frequent sales, so visit often, get on the mailing list, or watch for newspaper ads.

Checks, Credit cards

12 Clothing, Off-price Stores

ROSS DRESS FOR LESS
Bellevue: 14327 N.E. 20th ☎ 644-2433
Federal Way: 320th & Hwy. 99 ☎ *Century Square*
Lynnwood: 18930 29th Ave W. ☎ 778-9706
Seattle: 13201 Aurora N. ☎ 367-6030 *Haller Lake*
Silverdale: 10406 Silverdale Way N.W. ☎ 698-3180 *Ross Plaza*
Tacoma: 2931 S. 38th ☎ 474-3888 *Cascade Plaza*
Tukwila: 17672 Southcenter Parkway ☎ 575-0510 *Parkway Plaza*
Hours: Mon-Fri 9:30-9, Sat 9:30-6, Sun 11-7

Apparel at this popular off-price chain focuses more on basics than fashion-oriented merchandise, so prices are going to be on the low side. Women's clothing includes Junior, Petite and Large sizes, mainly separates for career and casual wear (especially pants and tops), plus lingerie, sleepwear and outerwear. Costume jewelry, scarves, belts and handbags are plentiful. Ross has the largest selection of women's hosiery around and their shoe department features moderately priced dress, casual and athletic footwear for men, women and children. Casual wear is the main focus in the men's department, but Ross stocks a terrific selection of dress shirts and accessories. And, don't forget to check out the children's department.

Assorted giftwares are displayed near check out stands. Sterling silver and 14K gold jewelry is sold at the Seattle, Bellevue and Tacoma stores. Ross is the only off-price chain with a fragrance and cosmetic counter, mostly drugstore brands. Direct-mail advertising also sets Ross apart from its big competitors. Fill out a preferred customer card at any store to receive beautiful color brochures, advance notices of sales, and discount coupons.

Checks, Credit cards

SAMPLE FASHIONS
Seattle: 613 Queen Anne N. ☎ 282-8780 *North of Seattle Center*
Hours: Mon-Sat 10-6

Samples purchased from manufacturers in New York and California offer you one-of-a-kind garments not available anywhere else. Inventory is mainly dresses and separates in sizes 6-16, which appeal to the professional woman. Look for moderately priced dresses and sportswear in synthetics at 40% to 60% below retail. Sample costume jewelry includes over 5,000 pairs of earrings. A big sidewalk sale held every July draws avid shoppers.

Checks, Credit cards

SMART SIZES
Everett: 1402 S.E. Everett Mall Way ☎ 347-2629 *Everett Mall*
Renton: 36 S. Grady Way ☎ 228-7827
Seattle: 10005 Holman Road at 6th N.W. ☎ 784-0537 *Greenwood*
Tacoma: 10401 Gravelly Lake Drive S.W. ☎ 582-5929 *Villa Plaza*
Hours: Generally, Mon-Fri 10-9, Sat 10-7, Sun 12-5

continued >

Good news for the full-figured woman! An off-price chain that specializes in sizes 32W-52W. The focus is on basics and casual styles for work and play. Lingerie and accessories also available. The Tacoma store, which still goes by the name "Lerner Woman", stocks more fashion-oriented merchandise for career and dressy occasions. All stores have clearance sections, but Renton offers the biggest selection. The Seattle store maintains a mailing list.

Checks, Credit cards

SPORTSWEAR EXPRESS DISCOUNT JEANS & TOPS — NEW LISTING

Auburn: 416 E. Main ☎ 833-3100
Kent: 326 W. Meeker ☎ 354-4774
Puyallup: 106 S. Meridian ☎ 840-1018
Sumner: 1008 Main St. ☎ 863-6864
Hours: Mon-Sat 10-6; Puyallup & Kent, Sun 12-5

The merchandise is a combination of first-quality goods from factory close-outs, plus some irregulars by such manufacturers as *Lawman, Taboo, Fade-In and Seattle Blues*. Lots of jeans, sweatshirts, T-shirts and tops for Girls through Large sizes. A limited selection of men's clothing includes *Levi* jackets. The average price for a pair of jeans is only $20!

Checks, Credit cards

T.J. MAXX

Lynnwood: 184th St. S.W. & Alderwood Mall Blvd. ☎ 776-8814
Seattle: 11029 Roosevelt Way N.E. ☎ 363-9511 *Northgate Village*
Tacoma: 3216 S. Center ☎ 272-4422 *Tacoma Central Plaza*
Hours: Mon-Sat 9:30-9:30, Sun 12-6

T.J. Maxx delivers the max for the minimum! Although the store offers apparel for the whole family, women's fashions in Junior, Misses and Large sizes are the main focus, with lots of separates for career and casual wear. Gorgeous sweaters that originally retailed for $50 to $100 go for half-price. Dress racks are a mixed bag of better-quality and moderately priced goods; occasionally you'll find a *Perry Ellis, Ellen Tracy, or Liz Claiborne* buried in the racks. Sleepwear, activewear, lingerie and accessories are also carried, and during the holidays, party dresses.

The children's departments feature quality name-brand clothing. Menswear is mostly casual. Dress shirts and slacks are available year-round, but sport coats and overcoats only show up occasionally. We spotted a *Members Only* jacket for $20 less than the going retail price.

In the past, T.J. Maxx has brought in clearance merchandise from Saks Fifth Avenue; watch the newspaper for ads announcing these special sales. All stores include giftware and domestics. Lynnwood and Tacoma feature a limited, but fashionable, selection of shoes. Sterling silver and 14K gold jewelry is sold only in the Seattle store. T.J. Maxx sale racks offer some of the best buys in town.

Checks, Credit cards

Clothing, Clearance Centers

VALERIE'S
Seattle: 4738 University Way N.E. ☎ 524-0073 *U-District*
Hours: Mon-Sat 10-6, Thurs 10-8

Students love Valerie's, and so will you. Prices are 35% to 50% off on fun, easy-to-wear sportswear by well-known California manufacturers like *Judy Knapp, Limited Express, Condor and Max Studio*. Inventory is mostly Junior sizes, cotton knits in S-M-L and inexpensive accessories. During the U-District Street Fair (third weekend in May), all swimsuits get marked down to $10. There's a mailing list for biannual sales.

Checks, Credit cards

Clearance Centers

When stores have to make room for new merchandise, clothing that's been on the sale racks for a long time is usually donated to a charity, sold to a discounter, or shipped to a clearance center. The advantages of shopping clearance centers, if you are a faithful retail customer, are that you know the merchandise and prices start at 50% off. The drawbacks are one-of-a-kind styles and sizes, broken groupings, shop-worn or damaged goods, and out-of-season or year-old merchandise.

THE BON CLEARANCE STORE
Everett: 2804 Whitmore ☎ 252-1143
Hours: Mon-Fri 10-6, Sun 12-5

Just as the first floor offers rock-bottom prices on home furnishings, the second story is a bargain hunter's paradise for outfitting the whole family. Merchandise, which sometimes includes shoes and accessories, may be damaged, discontinued styles or returns, but prices are super-low. Markdowns are fantastic because everything starts at 40% off the already-reduced price. Much of the clothing is off-season, but who cares at these prices! (Clearance merchandise from the Bon's better Women's Sportswear departments ends up in a corner of the basement at their Northgate store.)

Checks, Credit cards

FREDERICK AND NELSON RED TAG CLEARANCE CENTER
Kirkland: 529 Park Place Center ☎ 827-3100 *Parkland Mall*
Tacoma: 5401 6th Ave. ☎ 759-4200 *Sixth Avenue Plaza*
Hours: Mon-Fri 10-9, Sat 10-6, Sun 12-5

Frederick & Nelson Clearance Centers look more like retail stores than repositories for leftover merchandise. Inventory is sparse, but in good shape and neatly displayed. Stock is mainly clothing, much of it value-priced items purchased especially for these outlets, plus some shoes and accessories. Misses, Junior, Petite and Large sizes for the ladies. The Kirkland store has the largest selection of designer labels, which go fast. Mailing list for periodic sales.

Checks, Credit cards

Clothing, Clearance Centers

J.G. STYLES   NEW LISTING

Everett: 1402 S.E. Everett Mall Way ☎ 353-4233 *Everett Mall*
Hours: Mon-Sat 9:30-9:30, Sun 11-6

Jeans Galore sends clearance merchandise from their three stores to this outlet. All mens' styles are by *Levi*, sizes 27-38. Women's sizes 2-17 include *Seattle Blues, Guess, Lawman and Essex*. Sundry tops and sweatshirts are also discounted.

Checks, Credit cards

NORDSTROM RACK

Lynnwood: 3115 Alderwood Mall Blvd. ☎ 628-2915 *Alderwood Towne Center*
Seattle: 1601 2nd Ave. ☎ 448-8522 *Downtown*
Tukwila: 17900 Southcenter Pkwy. ☎ 575-1058 *Pavilion Mall*
Hours: Tukwila and Lynnwood; Mon-Fri 9:30-9:30, Sat 9:30-7, Sun 11-6;
  Seattle; Mon-Sat 9:30-7, Sun 12-6

We know Nordie fans who shop the retail stores, decide what they want to buy, wait the three to four months it takes for their favorite items to reach The Rack, then snatch them up for a fraction of the original cost. Prices start at 50% off, but progressive markdowns and tag sales create unbelievable savings. Fashion addicts zero-in on top American and European labels. The downtown store is the largest and easiest to shop since its four levels divide merchandise into separate areas. Not everything comes from Nordstrom's department stores. Over a third of the merchandise is purchased off-price to round out the selection, and these prices start at 30% off retail. Once a month The Rack has a sensational sale, during which specific items get marked down 30% to 50%. Get on the mailing list for advance notice, and come early to cherry pick the racks. Every once in a while an "as is" rack will show up, and prices are rock bottom. Nordstrom's service extends to their clearance operation— all Racks have a personal shopper.

Checks, Credit cards

QUEEN SIZE BOUTIQUE

Bellevue: 2102 140th N.E. ☎ 747-8881
Hours: Mon-Sat 10-6, Sun 12-5

Sale merchandise from Queen Size Boutiques' three stores ends up in this location in a corner, dubbed "Trudi's Back Room". Shoppers sized 14W-54W snap up stylish separates, coordinates, dresses and coats for 30% to 50% below retail. Join over 25,000 people and add your name to their mailing list. The annual sidewalk sale in the Renton store is a must.

Checks, Credit cards

Women's Consignment Shops

Consignment shops are the crème de la crème of used clothing stores. They offer a fun, easy way to upgrade the whole family's wardrobe or to make money recycling your "gently worn" clothing and accessories. People who would never set foot in a thrift shop feel right at home in consignment shops because most of them look and operate just like retail stores. You don't have to spend hours sifting through marginal cast-offs to find the good stuff.

The variety, quality and prices can be astounding. Most stores are very selective about what they accept. Many items have hardly been worn, some never. (Who among us hasn't purchased something that ends up hanging in the closet unloved?) You'll sometimes find samples, factory overstock, clearance leftovers and inventory purchased from retail stores going out of business.

Prices average 1/3 of the original retail value, but expensive items often go for less. Prices will vary from store to store, depending upon the clientele, location and inventory. Some stores keep prices low to ensure a fast turnover. Others just don't realize the value of an item. In Bellevue you'll find higher prices, but better quality and more designer labels. You can visit three or four of these shops in an afternoon since they're all concentrated in a fairly small area. The U-District to Northgate is another locale dotted with consignment shops. (Look for other, more specialized consignment shops in Menswear, Maternity & Children's and Formal Wear.) All sales are final, so inspect each item carefully before you buy. Most shops have a layaway plan and some will let you take things out on 24-hour approval. Consignment shops, just like retail stores, have seasonal clearances, special promotions and sales racks that deliver incredible bargains. Remember, the best values get snatched up fast, so visit your favorite haunts frequently. Happy hunting!

A CLASS ACT   **NEW LISTING**
Seattle: 2205 N.E. 65th ☎ 523-6750 *Ravenna*
Hours: Mon-Sat 10-5

> Prices are among the lowest in the Northend at this small shop. You never know what's going to turn up, but generally, you'll find casual separates, suits, blouses, skirts, dresses and coats. We found a terrific looking vintage fur on one of our visits. Some sportswear and accessories are new.

Checks

See area locator index for this section on page 220

ACCENT ON FASHION

Seattle: 8337 15th Ave. N W. ☎ 782-8745 *Crown Hill*
Hours: Tues-Sat 10:30-5

This shop specializes in clothing for the working woman. Better-quality labels are displayed on a separate rack. Coats and holiday dresses show up in season. Accessories, including shoes and handbags, are always available.

Checks, Credit cards

ACT II CONSIGNMENT BOUTIQUE

Federal Way: 1610 S. 341st ☎ 927-7190 *Spectrum Business Park*
Hours: Tues-Fri 10:30-6:30, Sat 10-5

Act II offers a great selection and low prices for women age 25 and up in sizes 2-24. Clothing for work or play fills the racks, much of it by well-known manufacturers. Mothers-to-be will want to check out the maternity section. Evening wear and furs are a bargain during the holiday season. Accessories, shoes, handbags, sample garments and new jewelry complete the inventory. Get on their mailing list for storewide sales.

Checks, Credit cards

ACT II CONSIGNMENTS   NEW LISTING

Bothell: 18008 Bothell-Everett Hwy. ☎ 481-4395 *North Creek Center*
Edmonds: 514 5th Ave. S., Suite C ☎ 774-1787
Hours: Bothell, Mon 12-6, Tues-Fri 11-6, Sat 11-5;
Edmonds, Mon-Sat 10-6, Sun 12-4:30

Career and casual clothing, plus accessories, can be found at these two stores. Some sportswear, sweaters, belts and jewelry may be new. Girls' clothing in sizes 10-12 are brand-new samples or current ready-to-wear that has been discounted. Look for *Byer*, a popular label for Pre-teens.

Checks, Credit cards

BETWEEN FRIENDS

Seattle: 818 3rd Ave. ☎ 624-2220 *Downtown*
Hours: Mon-Fri 10-6, Sat 11-4

The only consignment shop located in downtown Seattle carries "dress-for-success" clothing and accessories, plus sportswear and cocktail dresses for after work. Samples and off-price goods come from local manufacturers and retailers. Previously-owned merchandise, except for very expensive items, is purchased outright rather than taken on consignment. Everything is dry cleaned or laundered before it's put on the racks. Mailing list for seasonal sales.

Checks, Credit cards

BUDGET BOUTIQUE

Everett: 1830 Broadway ☎ 259-1285
Hours: Mon-Sat 10-5

continued >

Clothing, Women's Consignment Shops

With over 3,000 consignees on the books, Budget Boutique has been supplying families in Everett with consignment clothing at affordable prices since 1975. You'll find quality work attire, lingerie, party dresses, bridal gowns and coats. Sizes 3-52. Infants through size 14 for children. Casual styles for men. Lots of accessories.

Checks

CHAMPAGNE TASTE NEW LISTING
Kirkland: 111 Main St. ☎ 828-4502
Hours: Mon-Sat 10-6

Seasoned shoppers ferret out designer labels from among racks of suits, dresses, sportswear and lingerie, some in large sizes. New clothing and jewelry in bold, attractive styles contribute to the boutique atmosphere, along with consigned accessories, shoes and handbags. Seasonal sales and special promotions announced via mailings. The annual holiday apparel preview is a must.

Checks, Credit cards

CINDERELLA'S CLOSET
Tacoma: 3812 Steilacoom Blvd. S.W. ☎ 581-4472
Hours: Mon-Sat 12-5:30

Buy Cinderella's recycled riches and save on attire for every occasion—work clothes, cocktail dresses and even wedding gowns. Such well-known labels as *Liz Claiborne, St. John Knits and Oscar de la Renta* turn up frequently. They acquire close-outs from specialty shops and samples too. Pick up a monthly calendar to find out about special events and sales. Don't miss the fall preview for working women and the Christmas open house.

Checks, Credit cards

THE CLASS ACT CONSIGNMENT BOUTIQUE NEW LISTING
Tacoma: 2405 N. Pearl ☎ 759-5918 *Westgate Shopping Center*
Hours: Mon-Fri 10-8, Sat 10-7, Sun 12-5

This small, exclusive shop stocks only the best when it comes to consignment goods. The working woman will find *Anne Klein, Liz Claiborne and Trahari* at a fraction of the original cost. We found a cashmere coat that retailed for $900 priced at only $125. About 35% of the inventory is new, some of it by local designers.

Checks, Credit cards

CLOSET TRANSFER
Bainbridge Island: 562 Bejune Drive ☎ 842-1515
Hours: Mon-Sat 10:30-4

The owner of this shop is very selective. Clothing for men, women and children must be in mint condition and natural fibers are preferred. Shop for everything from casual to formal wear, accessories and jewelry. New merchandise from India includes basic as well as ethnic-looking dresses, hats, socks and mittens. Located below the Streamliner Diner.

Checks

Clothing, Women's Consignment Shops

THE CLOTHES CONNECTION
Bellevue: 11026 N.E. 11th Street ☎ 453-2055
Hours: Mon-Sat 10-5

The quiet neighborhood and cozy white house will make you feel like you're visiting a friend instead of shopping! Every room contains fashionable clothing and accessories, all in tip-top condition. Inventory is career-oriented, but you'll also find casual wear, lingerie, cocktail dresses and some men's apparel. We found a poplin raincoat that still had the tags on it for $35!

Checks, Credit cards

CONSIGNMENT CLOSET
Renton: 140 Rainier S. ☎ 228-7054
Hours: Mon-Fri 10-5, Sat 10-4:30

You'll find Petite through Large sizes for career and casual wear, along with gently used maternity clothing, lingerie, party dresses, coats and fun furs. Look for well-known labels like *Leslie Fay*. Shoes, handbags and jewelry are also available. Prices are negotiable on some items.

Checks

CRYSTAL THREADS   NEW LISTING
Issaquah: 1660 N.W. Gilman Blvd. ☎ 392-9456
Hours: Mon-Fri 11-6, Sat 10-6

Customers come from Kirkland, Mercer Island and Seattle to replenish their wardrobes with contemporary fashions by *Rothchild, Karen Kane and Marisa Christine*. There are special racks for maternity wear, Large sizes, evening wear and lingerie. Furs in season. Samples are sold at wholesale prices, and new ready-to-wear is discounted below department store prices. Accessories and estate jewelry complement the inventory. Children's clothing available up to size 7/8. Mailings announce seasonal sales.

Checks, Credit cards

THE DARK HORSE
Bellevue: 11810 N.E. 8th ☎ 454-0990 *Bellevue Lake Mall*
Hours: Mon-Fri 10:30-6, Thurs 10:30-8, Sat 10:30-5

The Dark Horse is the oldest and one of the largest consignment shops in the Pacific Northwest. Glamorous cocktail dresses are in stock year-round, ski and tennis wear in season. Look for expensive designer labels in the center of the store. Sizes range from 2-24, with the accessories, shoes and handbags to complete any wardrobe. New earrings, necklaces and hair ornaments are sold at tempting prices. An outstanding selection of men's apparel in sizes 36-50 hangs on one wall. The store is located behind the Hunan Garden Restaurant.

Checks, Credit cards

Clothing, Women's Consignment Shops

ENCORE CONSIGNMENTS
Lynnwood: 17602 Hwy. 99 ☎ 745-0768
Hours: Tues-Fri 10-6, Sat 11-6

The whole family can shop economically at this store, which has been in business 20 years. Ladies apparel ranges from Junior to a "Big and Beautiful" rack that goes up to size 50. You'll find clothes for the bride-to-be, the mother-to-be and accessories to polish any look. Men can buy jackets, suits, slacks, shirts and sweaters. Encore stocks children's clothing from Newborn through Pre-teen. Merchandise not picked up by consignees goes on the $1.00 rack. What a deal!
Checks

FASHION QUEST   NEW LISTING
Renton: 123 Wells Ave. S. ☎ 271-2886
Hours: Tues-Fri 11-6:30, Sat 10-5:30

The owner is committed to quality brands. *Jones of New York, Evan Picone and Dalton* are preferred labels. Separate rooms in this converted house display casual wear, Big and Tall sizes, lingerie and coats. One room holds nothing but vintage clothing. Accessories complete a "total look". New merchandise comes from retail store liquidations and off-price goods.
Checks, Credit cards

FURIE, LTD.
Seattle: 2810 E. Madison ☎ 329-6829 *Madison Park*
Hours: Tues-Sat 10-5

Fashionable labels appear on everything from jeans to silk dresses in this upscale shop. Some merchandise is purchased from small retailers; white tags designate new items and pink tags signal consigned goods. The selection of accessories is limited, but stylish. Look for terrific buys in early August and February when everything goes on sale.
Checks, Credit cards

GENA'S RESALE FASHIONS
Tacoma: 10227 Bridgeport Way S.W. ☎ 588-6848
Hours: Mon-Sat 10-5

Although this is a small consignment shop, name-brand women's clothing, shoes and accessories in excellent condition make a visit worthwhile. Everything is discounted during annual open-houses held in the fall. Don't hang up when Gena's answers the phone, "ABC Driving School"— they share the building and business number.

Checks, Credit cards

GLAD RAGS BOUTIQUE
Bellevue: 106 102nd N.E. ☎ 454-9377
Hours: Mon-Sat 10-5:30

continued >

Clothing, Women's Consignment Shops

Known for many years as Foxy Lady, this consignment shop is located in a yellow house just south of Bellevue Square. Skirts, blouses and dresses hang in the living room; pants and sweaters in one bedroom; lingerie, nightgowns and coats in another; party clothes and furs in the kitchen; and accessories are scattered throughout. Designer labels and new samples are tucked in with classic ready-to-wear styles. Add your name to the mailing list and your specific requests to the "want book".

Checks

JJ's ON CALIFORNIA NEW LISTING
West Seattle: 5409 California S.W. ☎ 937-9731
Hours: Mon-Fri 11-6, Sat 11-4

Merchandise in the little white house with hot pink trim is so tastefully displayed you'll think you're in a specialty boutique. The owner is young, so the clothes tend to be trendy and fashionable. One room contains jewelry and clothing by local designers. What doesn't sell quickly ends up on the $10-and-under rack. Inquire about their mailing list and discount dry cleaning coupons.

Checks, Credit cards

KATHY'S KLOSET
Seattle: 4751 12th Ave. N.E. ☎ 523-3019 *U-District*
West Seattle: 4738 42nd S.W. ☎ 937-2637 *Jefferson Square*
Hours: U-District, Mon-Fri 10-6, Thurs 10-9, Sat 10-5, Sun 12-4; West Seattle, Mon-Fri 10-3, Sat 10-6, Sun 11-5

The 12th Avenue location has long been a favorite of University of Washington students and career women. This two-story red brick house overflows with clothing of all kinds, plus a plentiful array of scarfs and belts. Styles range from trendy to traditional in Junior and Misses sizes 4-14. Samples and merchandise from retail outlets or local manufacturers turn up frequently. Consignment inventory in the West Seattle store is more conservative and includes children's wear, sizes 3-14. The U-District store accepts children's clothes for re-sale in the West Seattle location.

Checks, Credit cards

NEARLY NEW CONSIGNMENT SHOP
Tacoma: 2814 6th ☎ 627-0312
Hours: Mon-Sat 10-5

A variety of "gently used" apparel and accessories for women and children fill this large shop, along with toys, kitchen wares and decorative items. Children's wear is available for Infant through size 14. Larger sizes and special sections for maternity, furs, leather and evening wear makes this shop popular with everyone.

Checks

THE OTHER PLACE
Seattle: 8410 5th N.E. ☎ 527-0766 *Northgate*
Hours: Mon-Fri 10:00-5:30, Thurs 10-8, Sat. 10-5

continued >

Clothing, Women's Consignment Shops

This spacious store delivers low prices on current-style career and casual apparel. Dressy clothes are displayed in an antique armoire. Lots of coats and jackets in the fall. Some sportswear basics are new and clearance merchandise comes from a well-known local specialty shop. Lingerie, shoes and handbags are always good buys. The Other Place also stocks a limited selection of clothing for men and expectant moms.

Checks, Credit cards

PANDORA'S BOX
Bellevue: 10867 N.E. 2nd Pl. ☎ 455-3883
Hours: Mon-Sat 10-5

Nestled in a small yellow house on a residential side street, the most chic of Bellevue's consignment shops contains a potpourri of designer labels for career and casual wear in perfect condition. *Karen Kane, Metropole, Escada, Bis and Harvé Bernard* are only a few of the many contemporary lines. Lingerie is carefully selected, as are the handbags, shoes, belts and jewelry. Look for beautiful evening clothes during the holidays. One room showcases quality men's apparel. We found a fabulous wool sweatercoat, alligator shoes and an Ikat blouse by *Adri* to spruce up the old wardrobe.

Checks, Credit cards

PROUD PEACOCK
Burien: 224 S.W. 153rd ☎ 433-0376
Hours: Tues-Sat 10-6

Rooms in this big house display clothing, gift items and decorative accessories. You can purchase women's and queen-size apparel for work and play, as well as lingerie and maternity wear. The day we called there were lots of sweatsuits in stock, and a *Christian Dior* suit had just come in. Inventory gets marked down 25% after 30 days and 50% after 60 days.

Checks, Credit cards

QUEEN'S CLOSET
Tacoma: 2117 Tacoma Ave. S. ☎ 627-1221
Hours: Mon-Fri 12-6, Sat 10-4

Women seeking Tall and Large sizes will find everything from career clothes to sportswear, including coats, furs, lingerie, cocktail and wedding gowns. Sizes start at 18 and can go as high as 70. Tall sizes 10-16. Shoes from size 8 are a real find. Jewelry comes from estates and consignments. New samples and off-price goods are purchased directly from manufacturers. What doesn't sell at 50% off ends up on the $2 rack out front.

Checks, Credit cards

RAGAMOFFYN'S
Kirkland: 127 Park Lane ☎ 828-0396
Hours: Mon-Fri 10-5:30, Sat 10-5

continued >

Clothing, Women's Consignment Shops

The most exclusive consignment shop north of San Francisco reflects the owner's European background and taste for quality. Labels read like a Who's Who of the fashion industry, so expect to find a *Perry Ellis, Ellen Tracy or Ralph Lauren*, at a fraction of its original cost. Sizes range from 2-14. Classy separates in neutral colors fill one corner of the store. Leathers and suedes hang in a separate cubicle. Glamorous furs début in January and February. (We heard a sable coat valued at $10,000 sold for $2,000!) Inventory includes elegant accessories, hats, handbags and shoes.

Checks, Credit cards

RAZZ M'TAZZ

Seattle: 623 Queen Anne Ave. N. ☎ 281-7900 *North of Seattle Center*
Hours: Tues-Fri 10-6, Sat 10-5

Apparel in this small shop is beautifully displayed and carefully selected. Contemporary career apparel and sportswear comes from well-known manufacturers in sizes 2-22. Evening clothes, furs (in season), and new and used accessories reflect the owner's commitment to value and style. Don't forget to put your name on the mailing list.

Checks

REDRESS

Bellevue: 513 156th S.E. ☎ 746-7984 *Lake Hills Shopping Center*
Hours: Mon-Sat 10:30-6, Sun 11-4

A lot of clothes are packed into this large shop, which was voted "Bellevue's Best Consignment Shop" during a contest sponsored by KIRO-TV in 1989. Low prices ensure a fast turnover, and designer labels pop up frequently. You'll find a big inventory of casual separates and gorgeous evening clothes, especially during the holidays. Redress is the only consignment shop on the Eastside that maintains a rack of wedding gowns. Bridesmaid's and mother-of-the-bride dresses are often available.

Checks, Credit cards

SATIN HANGER   NEW LISTING

Midway: 24817 Pacific Hwy. S. ☎ 941-8648
Hours: Mon-Sat 10-5, Thurs & Fri 10-6

Management claims prices are so low that enterprising shoppers ferret out the best buys and make money selling them to other consignment shops. At this large store, racks are jammed with Infant to Large sizes, including maternity, cocktail and wedding dresses. There's even a men's department. New garments for women and children are mainly samples sold at wholesale prices. Moms zero-in on *Osh-Kosh and Carter's* and consignment baby furniture. Customers on their mailing list receive 25%-off coupons during the Christmas holidays.

Checks, Credit cards

SAVVY

Redmond: 8072 160th N.E ☎ 883-6441
Hours: Mon-Fri 10:30-5:30, Sat 10:30-5

continued >

Clothing, Women's Consignment Shops

Savvy delivers bargains on women's apparel of all kinds. While the new inventory focuses on unusual clothing, jewelry and scarves at wholesale prices, the management also guarantees "fun finds" and "super prices" in the consignment department.

Checks, Credit cards

SEBASTIAN'S CLOSET
Tacoma: 1205 Regents Blvd. ☎ 565-3503 *Fircrest*
Hours: Mon-Fri 10-5:30, Sat 10-5

This shop sells top-quality women's apparel, with designer labels, formal gowns and wedding dresses as its specialties. *Evan Picone and Jones of New York* suits go for $40 to $60. Some of the garments are factory close-outs so they've never been worn, and all the jewelry is new.

Checks, Credit cards

SECOND AVENUE CONSIGNMENTS
Edmonds: 527 Main Street ☎ 771-5667
Hours: Tues-Sat 10-5

Women entering the job market can save enough on name-brand clothing and accessories to have money left for Second Avenue's evening wear and furs. Sizes range from 2 to 42. Unclaimed merchandise walks out the door at 50% off. There's a "call" list if you can't find what you want.

Checks, Credit cards

TAKE TWO
Seattle: 430 15th Ave. E. ☎ 324-2569 *Capitol Hill*
Hours: Mon-Sat 10-6, Sun 12-6

Take Two stocks more samples, close-outs and seconds than most consignment shops. We saw popular lines like *D.D. Sloane, Melrose, International News and CP Shades* discounted 30% or more. You'll be impressed with the eclectic selection of trendy to fashionable recycled sportswear and dresses. Fun jewelry and accessories, both new and used, and a small selection of casual men's clothing round out the inventory.

Checks

TINA'S   **NEW LISTING**
Seattle: 7523 Aurora Ave. N. ☎ 789-5099 *Greenwood*
Hours: Tues-Sat 11-5

Over the years this tiny shop has built up a loyal clientele that appreciates service, low prices and quality merchandise. Sizes run 4-16. Career suits and separates are the best-selling items. Samples show up occasionally, and all jewelry is new. The inventory turns over fast. Add your name to their mailing list.

Checks

TWICE IS NICE BOUTIQUE
Bothell: 19215 Bothell Way N.E. ☎ 483-1991
Hours: Mon-Fri 10-5, Sat 10-3

continued >

For more than a decade, smart shoppers have been refurbishing their wardrobes here with everything from jeans to wedding dresses. Sizes start at 34 and go up to Queen. Sports enthusiasts save on tennis, golf and ski wear. You'll even find a selection of square dance dresses.

Checks

YESTERDAY'S

Lynnwood: 7300 S.W. 196th St. ☎ 771-4225
Hours: Mon-Sat 10-5:30

Although the focus is on better labels in sizes Petite to XL for career and casual wear, wedding gowns are a featured item. At any given time, 50 to 300 styles fill the racks, all at drastically reduced prices. Samples come and go, and accessories are always available.

Checks

YOUR HIDDEN CLOSET   NEW LISTING

Bellevue: 10020 Main ☎ 453-5999
Hours: Mon-Thurs 10-6, Fri & Sat 10-5

Big is beautiful at this shop, which began in 1987 when two sisters searched in vain for transitional wardrobes during a weight loss program. Customers drive for miles to save 50% or more on career clothing, sportswear, lingerie, coats and dressy clothes in size 14 to "as high as possible." New merchandise is purchased from *Tres Bon*, a local manufacturer, and queen-size shops going out of business. The mailing list is a must.

Checks, Credit cards

☑ Consumer Tips:

Here's how to make money selling your clothes in consignment shops:

☞ The best months to sell your clothes are April and September. Clothing must be in season, clean, pressed and on hangers.

☞ Most consignment policies require that merchandise be brought in on specific days or by appointment. Garments can be no more than 3 years old unless they're designer-label or timeless styles, and no more than 20 items can be consigned at a time. Visit several consignment shops in your area to determine which one will yield the greatest return. What doesn't sell at one shop may be a hot number at another.

☞ You sign a contract agreeing to leave the clothes in the store for 6 to 8 weeks. The owner sets the price, and the usual commission is 50% of the selling price, which may be reduced 20% or more after 30 days at the discretion of the store. Some shops give you 60% if the item sells for $50 or more. Any clothing not picked up on the specified date is donated to charity or becomes the property of the store.

☞ Payment is by check on a monthly or bi-monthly basis. You can pick your check up or arrange to have it mailed in a self-addressed stamped envelope.

Discount Clothing Catalogs

Call the numbers listed below to receive free copies of our favorite discount clothing catalogs. All have operators on duty 24 hours daily, except Anthony Richards, which takes calls from 9 a.m. until 10 p.m. Mon-Fri, Sat 9-5 (Eastern time).

ANTHONY RICHARDS
Cleveland, OH ☎ 800/359-5933

Good looking, basic-style dresses and career separates in synthetic blends are designed and manufactured by Anthony Richards, so prices are below retail. Misses, Women's and Half-sizes. Some lingerie, outerwear and walking shoes.

CHADWICK'S OF BOSTON
Boston, MA ☎ 508/583-6600

The leading off-price fashion catalog in the country offers contemporary separates for work and play by such well-known names as *Mirrors, Cherokee and Jonathan Martin*. Dresses by *Nina Piccalino* and sweaters by *Jennifer Reed* that originally retailed for $100 or more are discounted 20% to 30%. Save even more on basic sportswear items if you buy in quantity. Natural and synthetic fibers. Sizes 4-16, S-M-L-XL.

DESIGNER DIRECT
Salem, VA ☎ 800/848-2929

Private-label merchandise and a few name-brands come in attractive contemporary styles for casual and career wear, in sizes 8-18 and some Half-sizes. Expect savings of 20% to 30% on most items. Shoes by *A.J. Valenci*. Some accessories.

FASHION GALAXY
Hanover, PA ☎ 800/621-5800

The savings can add up to 50% on fashionable dresses, suits, separates and evening wear, plus a good selection of lingerie and shoes. Merchandise is probably close-outs and overruns since brand names aren't listed and sizes and colors are often limited. Sizes 4-18, S-M-L-XL.

THE ULTIMATE OUTLET
Chicago, IL ☎ 800/332-6000

If you like the merchandise you see in the Spiegel Catalog, you'll love their clearance catalogs. Clothing and home furnishings include top designer labels. Men's and women's apparel, accessories and shoes vary from casual and inexpensive to high fashion. Sizes are limited to stock on hand, but the catalogs include Misses, Petite and Large sizes for ladies, Tall, Short and XL for the men. Markdowns start at 20% and can go as high as 60% off.

Menswear

Men are super shoppers too! Rather than make men and the women who buy for them (20% of the market) flip through the multitude of listings to find men's apparel, we're including this special section. But, you'll still want to track down the great bargains at some of the consignment shops that cater mainly to women, especially Bellevue's cluster of upscale boutiques. For a wardrobe worthy of Gentlemen's Quarterly, shop the men's racks at Pandora's Box, the Dark Horse and the Clothes Connection. Also check out Closet Transfer, Encore Consignments, The Other Place, Satin Hanger and Take Two.

Factory outlets are other great resources for outerwear and casual wear. Try BRB Manufacturing Inc. (outerwear and sportswear); Calvert Manufacturing Co. and Gerry Sportswear (ski and outerwear); Cascadian Sportswear, Seattle Pacific Industries, Exit West, Motto and Only Stuff (sportswear); Genauer (denims and sportswear); Pacific Trail (outerwear); and Sweats Unlimited (basic cotton knits). The major off-price chains— Ross, Marshall's and T.J. Maxx— offer great buys on dress and casual wear, shoes and accessories. Burlington has the best selection for career and outerwear, plus shoes. Check out Jeans to Go for casual wear.

See our Formal Wear section for tuxedos and Factory Outlet Malls for a variety of stores carrying off-price apparel for men. And, our Sporting Goods section is your best resource for recreational outerwear and active wear.

GENTLEMEN'S CONSIGNMENT   **NEW LISTING**

Seattle: 2809 E. Madison ☎ 328-8137 *Madison Park*
Hours: Tues-Sat 10-5

One of the few consignment shops in the Pacific Northwest devoted exclusively to men's apparel, accessories and "amusements" (games, binoculars, fishing poles, books, etc.), this store is a "must" stop. Only first-quality goods are accepted, with natural fibers preferred. You'll find a great selection of stylish suits, sport jackets, dress separates and outerwear in sizes 36-54. Suits sell for $70 to $350, including such labels as *Armani*. Tuxedos are always available, as well as casual wear to round out weekend wardrobes. Alterations for a minimal fee.

Checks, Credit cards

HIS   **NEW LISTING**

Seattle: 2226 Queen Anne Ave. N. ☎ 281-0265 *North of Seattle Center*
Hours: Tues-Fri 10-6, Sat 10-5

Good news, guys! Another men's consignment shop opened before we went to press, and the owner says her customers love recycling clothes. Business attire makes up half the inventory, so young professionals entering the job market can save on quality suits, sport coats, dress shirts, slacks and accessories. For leisure time, check out their casual wear.

Checks, Credit cards

Clothing, Menswear

KUPPENHEIMER MEN'S CLOTHIERS
Bellevue: 14405 N.E. 20th ☎ 746-8177
Lynnwood: 2701 184th S.W. ☎ 672-8378
Seattle: 10738 5th N.E. ☎ 365-4350 *Northgate*
Silverdale: 10315 Silverdale Way N.W. ☎ 692-1766 *Kitsap Mall*
Tacoma: 2520 S. 38th ☎ 473-6555
Tukwila: 17065 Southcenter Pkwy. ☎ 575-9001
Hours: Mon-Sat 10-9, Sun 12-5

This huge national chain keeps prices low by manufacturing everything it sells. The main focus is on suits, jackets, slacks, dress shirts and outerwear for professionals and businessmen. Size 36S-50XL suits range from $175 to $265. You'll pay 30% to 40% more for similar styles in regular retail stores, but always compare fabric and construction. Get on the mailing list for big sales in June and December.

Checks, Credit cards

LARGE & TALL OUTLET — NEW LISTING
Federal Way: 31313 Pacific Hwy. S. ☎ 941-0611 *Federal Way Shopping Ctr.*
Seattle: 160th & Aurora ☎ 365-5701 *Aurora Fashion Plaza*
Tacoma: 2528 S. 38th St. ☎ 472-6049
Hours: Mon-Fri 10-8, Sat 10-6, Sun 12-5

Everything from underwear to outerwear for the big guys, "portly" or "athletic." Name-brand merchandise for all occasions includes *Arrow* dress shirts, *Dockers* and *Levi* pants, *Members Only* jackets, *Four Seasons* and *Ed McMahon* suits. Prices vary from 20% to 50% below retail because these stores are part of a national off-price chain. Add your name to the mailing list for sales.

Checks, Credit cards

THE MEN'S WEARHOUSE, INC. — NEW LISTING
Federal Way: 1918 S. 320th ☎ 839-6996 *Sea-Tac Mall*
Lynnwood: 2701 184th S.W. ☎ 776-7618 *TJ Maxx Plaza*
Redmond: 2110 148th N.E. ☎ 643-0987 *Overlake Fashion Plaza*
Silverdale: 3236 N.W. Plaza Rd. ☎ 692-7770
Seattle: 4th & Union ☎ 622-0570 *Downtown*
Tacoma: 2505 S. 38th St. ☎ 474-2795 *Lincoln Center*
Tukwila: 16971 Southcenter Pkwy. ☎ 575-4393
Hours: Mon-Sat 10-9, Sun 12-6

You've seen their ads on TV, and we're happy to report that The Men's Wearhouse does indeed sell the same suits found in better department and specialty men's stores for 20% to 40% less. Styles range from European cut to banker's classics to sporty tweeds with designer labels by *Ives St. Laurent, Oscar de la Renta and Nino Cerruti*. Tuxedos run under $250. They also stock dress shirts, slacks, accessories, and a limitedselection of sportswear in a full range of sizes including Big, Tall and Short. With 80 stores on the West Coast, they keep prices low year-round through volume buying and private-label manufacturing.

Checks, Credit cards

Clothing, Menswear

MOSS BAY MERCANTILE
Kirkland: 7 Lake Shore Plaza ☎ 827-1116
Hours: Tues-Fri 10-6:30, Sat 10-5:30

Tasteful decor, outstanding service and excellent selection makes this discounter popular with Eastsiders. Classic, name-brand men's clothing sells for 10% to 30% below retail. Look for first-quality goods by *Gant, Brier and Cricketeer*. "Dress for success" suits average $200, sport coats $180 in sizes 38-46. Moss Bay stocks pants, shirts, sweaters and accessories suitable for office as well as casual wear. Seasonal sales announced via mailing list.

Checks, Credit cards

MR. TALL & BIG   NEW LISTING
Lynnwood: 2701 184th St. S.W. ☎ 672-2440
Tukwila: 339 Strander Blvd. ☎ 575-1812
Hours: Mon-Thurs 9:30-8, Fri 9:30-9, Sat 10-6, Sun 10-5

Now we know where the Sonics and Seahawks shop! Men sized X-7X, Large and Tall, will find quality name-brand clothing for casual and professional wear in conservative as well as contemporary styles. *Bill Blass* tuxedos can be custom-ordered. Prices are 20% to 30% lower than department stores because the owners take a low markup and sell close-outs and overstock. In-store promotions every day, plus a mailing list for big sales.

Checks, Credit cards

NU YU FASHIONS   NEW LISTING
Burien: 15821 1st Ave. S. ☎ 243-9968
Kent: 23440 Pacific Hwy. S. ☎ 878-0629
Hours: Mon-Fri 10:30-8:00, Sat 10:30-6, Sun 12-5

The owner started out selling surplus clothing and seconds from local manufacturers at swap meets. Now he retails over a dozen major brands that include everything from jeans to fashion-forward looks from California and New York, as well as the popular local labels *International News and Motto*. Men's sizes 28-36. Jeans, sweat shirts and T-shirts for women in S-M-L. Prices average 30% to 40% off retail, sometimes lower.

Checks, Credit cards

THE SQUIRE SHOP   NEW LISTING
Seattle: 4508 University Way N.E. ☎ 632-4500 *U-District*
Hours: Mon-Wed 10-6, Thurs 10-8, Fri 10-7, Sat 10-6, Sun 12-5

Clearance and sale merchandise from the Squire Shop's 32 young men's stores ends up in this small shop where budget-conscious students take advantage of low prices year-round on jeans, sweats and T-shirts. Look for rock bottom prices in the back section, where old and damaged goods that haven't sold in six months get marked down 90%. If you live south of the Seattle area, check out the Olympia store for similar bargains.

Checks, Credit cards

Clothing, Maternity & Children's

STRICTLY BUSINESS/CROSSINGS — NEW LISTING
Seattle: 716 N. 34th St. ☎ 547-3819 *Fremont*
Hours: Mon-Sat 10-6 or by appointment

A former sales rep for a big East Coast suit manufacturer, the owner now sells the same suits retailed by better department stores out of the back room of his boating apparel store, Crossings. Prices are close to wholesale on styles that range from fine wool to cashmere blends, basic to double breasted styles in sizes 34-60. Average cost is $150 to $170. European designs go up to $300. Inventory includes sport and dress pants, neckwear and women's tailored suits in sizes 4-16. During specific times of the year, customers can special-order from fabric swatches. Private showings for banks, corporations, insurance companies and large groups.

Checks, Credit cards

☑ **Consumer Tip:** (for women shoppers)
☞ Men's clothing is often better made and longer lasting than women's, and the same item usually costs less! Shop men's clothing outlets for casual shirts, sweaters and jackets. Tall, slender women can usually wear men's trousers. If you can wear a young man's size, teen departments offer the best bargains. And, why not accent a tailored shirt or dress with a paisley tie?

Maternity & Children's

Children's Clothing

Kids! What's the matter with kids today? For one thing, their clothes cost too much and they grow too fast. And what about all that baby gear you need during the first few years, not to mention the demand for consumer goods fueled by peer pressure and TV commercials as children get older? We hope to provide you with some solutions to these problems in the listings below. (You'll also find stores that carry maternity and children's clothes the Women's Consignment Shops section.)

When you're purchasing children's clothing, always opt for the next size up to accommodate shrinkage and growth spurts. Cotton/polyester blends hold up better than 100% cotton and textured knits won't pill as quickly. Velour is expensive, but it washes beautifully.

We suggest picking up "Northwest Baby", "Seattle's Child", "Eastside Parent" and/or "Pierce County Parent." These monthly newspapers are filled with informative articles, calendars of events and ads for products and services. Complimentary issues are distributed through children's retail and consignment clothing stores, as well as day care centers.

Clothing, Maternity & Children's 31

BURLINGTON'S BABY ROOM   NEW LISTING
Edmonds: 2411 Hwy. 99 ☎ 776-2221
Hours: Mon-Sat 10-9, Sun 11-6

Tucked away in a corner of this huge off-price chain's massive clothing inventory is a special section where there's everything you'd need for babies and toddlers, including over 35 styles of cribs. Expectant moms will also find maternity wear.

Checks, Credit cards

CARTER'S FACTORY OUTLET
Tacoma: 1415 E. 72nd ☎ 472-9340
Hours: Mon-Sat 10-6, Fri 10-8, Sun 12-5

Save on clothing for Infants to size 6X at the regional outlet for one of the most popular brands in the country. Underwear, sleepwear and socks go up to size 14. First-quality close-outs average 20% to 30% off retail. Irregulars are plentiful and clearly marked, and prices start at 50% off. (What toddler is going to complain about slight imperfections?) Discounted merchandise from other leading manufacturers includes bedding, mattress covers and layette supplies.

Checks, Credit cards

HEALTH-TEX SAMPLE SALES
Seattle: ☎ 443-1919
Periodic sales

Call to get on the mailing list for big sample sales held three or four times a year by one of country's best-known manufacturers of children's clothing. You can stock up on the latest styles at prices that average 50% below retail. Sizes are limited to 3-Month, 12-Month, Toddler, 4 and 10. Plan ahead— kids grow!

Checks

KIDS' MART   NEW LISTING
Factoria: I-90 & I-405 ☎ 562-1495 *Factoria Square*
Everett: 505 S.E. Everett Mall Way ☎ 353-7259 *Greentree Plaza*
Federal Way: 320th Pacific Hwy. S. ☎ 839-6306 *Century Square*
Lynnwood: 3105 Alderwood Mall Blvd. ☎ 672-8388 *Alderwood Towne Center*
Redmond: 2122 148th Ave. N.E. ☎ 747-1396 *Overlake Fashion Plaza*
Seattle: 160th & Aurora ☎ 368-0648 *Aurora Fashion Plaza*
Silverdale: Silverdale Way & Bucklin Hill Rd. ☎ 692-7674 *Ross Plaza*
Tacoma: 19th & Union ☎ 627-7958 *Tacoma Central Plaza*
Hours: Generally, Mon-Fri 10-9, Sat 10-6, Sun 11-5

Parents rejoiced when this national off-price chain moved into the Puget Sound area. Close-outs and volume buying keep prices low on name-brand clothing and lines manufactured exclusively for the stores. A big selection of fashionable cotton knits and denim in the 7-14 category brings in the pre-teen set. Head for the clearance rack where savings can be astounding. The mailing list is a must for back-to-school, pre-holiday and anniversary sales.

Checks, Credit cards

32 Clothing, Maternity & Children's

M & L INTERNATIONAL *Bonjour and Good Friend* NEW LISTING
Kent: 20462 84th Ave. S. ☎ 872-8041
Annual sale

Customers on M & L's mailing list flock to the Fall warehouse clearance sale for great buys on overstock, discontinued styles and samples from the West Coast distributor for several well-known infants and children's clothing lines. You'll find everything from sleepers, jeans and swimsuits to sportswear and outerwear for the whole family.

Checks, Credit cards

SAMPLE SALES NEW LISTING
Redmond: 3207 176th Ct. N.E., Redmond, WA 98052
Periodic sales

Send in your name and address for details about these terrific sample sales. The inventory, which comes from reps in four major West Coast cities, includes such well-known manufacturers as *Healthtex, Carters, Polly Flinders, Calabash, Spumoni* and *London Fog*. Prices start at wholesale plus 10%. The bargain rack offers incredible buys. Hair ornaments, small toys and books are also available. Locations vary from Everett to Fife to Issaquah, and they always book three rooms at Wholesale Heaven (See Index).

Checks, Credit cards

Maternity Clothes

BAY CREST MATERNITY FACTORY OUTLET NEW LISTING
Kirkland: 141 Park Lane ☎ 827-7062
Hours: Mon-Sat 10-6, Sun 12-5

A sure winner is this local manufacturer that sells to stores all over the country and offers its samples, overruns and discontinued styles at the factory outlet. Expectant moms will discover cotton and woven separates under the *Mother-Two-Be* label, plus an aerobic-wear line, *Heart Throb* and *Amanda Grey*, a dress line. At only 10% above wholesale, prices range from $16 to $30. Pay even less for irregulars.

Checks, Credit cards

DAN HOWARD'S MATERNITY FACTORY
Lynnwood: 3105 Alderwood Mall Blvd. ☎ 672-9300 *Alderwood Towne Center*
Tukwila: 17145 Southcenter Pkwy. ☎ 575-3255 *Centerplace*
Hours: Mon-Wed 10-6, Thurs & Fri 10-9, Sat 10-5, Sun 12-5

This nationwide off-price chain sells its own line of fashionable maternity wear, as well as clothing by other well-known manufacturers. Leisure and career apparel for sizes 4-24 and Petites includes lots of separates. Dresses average $30 to $80. Women on their mailing list receive notice of special promotions, which include periodic fashion shows.

Checks, Credit cards

PROCREATIONS MATERNITY LEASEWEAR
Portland: ☎ 800/637-0763
By appointment only

Professional career women who need a designer-quality, "dress for success" wardrobe during pregnancy will love Procreations, a company that leases garments through representatives nationwide. The main focus is hand-finished tailored suits valued at $400 and up, which rent for $7.95 a week with a 6-week minimum. Jumpers, blouses, dresses, jackets and skirts are also available, plus formal wear, bridesmaid dresses and, believe it or not, wedding gowns for expectant brides. Sizes range from 4 to 16, including Petite and Tall. Call to find a rep in your area or request a catalog for at-home shopping. Orders delivered in 72 hours. A wardrobe planning booklet can be ordered for $9.95.

Maternity & Children's Consignment

Consignment shops offer expectant moms a terrific way to economize on maternity wardrobes as well as everything imaginable for newborns through toddlers. Nursery furniture, car seats, strollers, high chairs and backpacks all sell at substantial savings. Children's clothing is stronger in the Infant to 6X range, probably due to a faster turnover. Sizes 7-14 are harder to find, especially for boys. Expensive items like coats, snow suits, party clothes and dress shoes in good condition are readily available because they don't get worn much. And what child is going to mind second-hand toys?

The art of buying and selling in children's consignment shops follows the same guidelines as those outlined in women's clothing, but merchandise usually remains longer and gets marked down faster. More stores buy outright or trade for in-store credit, which is advantageous if you're moving or need cash. In-store credit usually amounts to a better deal. These stores carry a larger percentage of new merchandise, not always discounted, which can be a real temptation. But, handmade one-of-a-kind items sold only in consignment shops often make wonderful gifts.

A to Z — NEW LISTING
Seattle: 2812 E. Madison ☎ 325-9903 *Madison Park*
Hours: Tues-Sat 10-5:30

A boutique atmosphere and stylish merchandise make this shop special. Clothing ranges from Infants through size 12 for boys and girls. Such labels as *Florence Eisemann* appear regularly, and you'll also find shoes, nursery furniture, baby gear and handcrafted items. One small room is filled with books, games and toys. Look for the picket fence painted like pencils.

Checks, Credit cards

Clothing, Maternity & Children's Consignment

ABOUT FACE — NEW LISTING
Lynnwood: 7300 196th S.W. ☎ 771-4190
Hours: Mon-Thur 10-5, Fri-Sat 10:30-4:30

About Face carries quality clothing for Infants to Size 10 and a good selection for expectant moms. One customer said they stock more maternity clothes than a leading local department store. Some furniture and toys can also be found.

Checks, Credit cards

AJ's — NEW LISTING
Kent: 16408 S.E. 256th ☎ 630-9048
Hours: Mon-Sat 11-5:30, Sun 12-4

Lots of clothing for Infants through 6X fill this store. Children's furnishings include high chairs, cribs, cradles, rockers, bikes, playpens and car seats. Some items are new.

Checks, Credit cards

ALMOST NEW — NEW LISTING
Everett: 3417 Broadway ☎ 282-9362
Hours: Tues-Sat 10:30-5

You'll discover Newborn through Pre-teen clothes on consignment, plus a few new things. Stuffed animals, children's accessories and small nursery furniture are often in stock.

Checks

CHILDREN'S ATTIC
Everett: 2013 19th ☎ 339-9058
Hours: Wed-Fri 11:30-6, Sat 11:30-5

Clothing, furniture and toys for newborns through teens can be traded, purchased outright, or sold on consignment. Trades are allowed on new clothing, which comes factory-direct, or new toys, sold mainly around Christmas at discount prices. A nearby storage space holds trikes, teeter-totters, slides, cribs and bunkbeds. Located in an apartment complex.

Checks

GRANDMOTHER'S HOUSE
Lynnwood: 7331 196th S.W. ☎ 771-4640
Hours: Mon-Sat 9:30-5:30, Sun 12-5

For over 15 years Grandmother's House has been helping families save money on toys, baby furniture and clothing for Infants through size 6X. Everything is in mint condition because the store only purchases outright or trades for in-store credit. Nothing goes on the floor until it has been cleaned and repaired. The line-up of strollers, high chairs, playpens, walkers, trikes and bikes and car seats is astounding. Over 400 cribs go out the door each year at an average price of $100.

Checks, Credit cards

Clothing, Maternity & Children's Consignment

HEAVEN SENT
Federal Way: 1200 S. 324th ☎ 946-2229
Hours: Mon-Sat 10-6

The owners are very selective about what they take, and many items look brand-new. Clothing from Newborn to size 6X and baby furniture is purchased outright. Boys sizes 7-10, Girls 7-14 and maternity clothes come in on consignment. Toys, handicrafts and assorted kiddie things fill the rest of the space. Put your name on the mailing list for spring and fall sales.

Cash only

JUST FOR YOU
Seattle: 1114 W. 183rd ☎ 542-3993 *Shoreline*
Hours: Mon-Fri 9:30-5, Sat 10-4

Expect to find a terrific selection of gently used children's clothing here, plus maternity wear, toys, books and accessories. New clothing includes samples and affordable specialty lines. Inexpensive party favors and new toys priced at $4 or below make birthdays easy on the pocketbook. An impressive array of handcrafted items includes *Cabbage Patch* doll clothes, *Barbie* furniture and darling knitted booties. Mailing list for seasonal sales.

Checks, Credit cards

KID'S KLOSET
Burien: 2034 S.W. 152nd ☎ 243-1795
Hours: Mon-Fri 10-5, Wed 10-6, Sat 11-5

If it relates to kids or expectant moms, it's sold at Kid's Kloset. Savings can add up fast. Car seats and strollers are always available, as well as toys and small handcrafted items. Occasionally you'll find cribs.

Checks

KIDS ON 45TH
Seattle: 1720 N. 45th St. ☎ 633-5437 *Wallingford*
Hours: Mon-Sat 10-6, Sun 12-4

Discover bargains on abundant, good-quality clothing for infants through pre-teens, plus used baby furniture, toys and a rack of maternity clothes. Lots of shoes, accessories and handcrafted items. Watch for sales on new cotton clothes.

Checks, Credit cards

KYM'S KIDDY CORNER   **NEW LISTING**
Seattle: 18518 Ballinger Way N.E. ☎ 365-8737 *Lake Forest Park*
          11721 15th Ave. N.E. ☎ 361-5974 *Northgate*
Hours: Mon-Sat 10-5, Sun 12-5; Lake Forest Park closed Mondays

continued >

36 Clothing, Maternity & Children's Consignment

The Northgate location is one of the largest resale stores in the area. You can't miss the colorful line-up of trikes, strollers, walkers and riding toys displayed outside. Find clothing for Infants to size 8 at Lake Forest Park, Infants to 14 at Northgate. Toys, furniture and accessories are stocked at both stores. New items by well-known manufacturers are discounted. All used items are purchased outright or traded for credit.

Checks, Credit cards

LITTLE ANGEL BOUTIQUE — NEW LISTING
Kent: 406 W. Meeker ☎ 854-5557
Hours: Mon-Sat 10-6, Sun 12-5

Expectant moms will be pleased with the gently used maternity clothes and nursery furniture. Children's clothing ranges from Infants to 6X and includes samples and close-outs from leading manufacturers.

Checks, Credit cards

MAXINE'S BABY WORLD
Tacoma: 510½ 112th S. ☎ 535-2742
Hours: Mon-Sat 10-5

Lots of kids clothes (Infants to size 10), furniture and toys pass through this store, plus a limited selection of maternity clothes. Some items are new. All merchandise is purchased outright.

Checks, Credit cards

MOM 'N ME — NEW LISTING
Kent: 26124 104th ☎ 854-7664
Hours: Mon-Sat 10-5, Sun 12-5

Here's another good source of clothing for expectant moms and their growing off-spring, newborn through pre-teen. Also find a limited selection of new and used furniture, layette items and all kinds of toys.

Checks, Credit cards

MOM'S N TOTS
Factoria: I-90 & I-405 ☎ 641-8814 *Loehmann's Plaza*
Hours: Mon & Tues 10-5, Wed-Thurs 10-7, Sat 10-5, Sun 12-6

The clothing for Infants through size 10 is stylish and in good condition here. Maternity wear includes new lingerie. Baby furniture of all kinds comes and goes, but strollers and car seats are always in stock. New clothing and furniture, which make up 30% of the inventory, is discounted.

Checks, Credit cards

MOUSE CLOSET
Bellevue: 521 156th S.E. ☎ 641-0531 *Lake Hills Shopping Center*
Hours: Mon-Sat 9:30-5:30

continued >

Clothing, Maternity & Children's Consignment

Eastsiders love the big selection of fun, trendy samples purchased from local sales reps and manufacturers. Girls sizes go up to 14, Boys to 8. Prices start at 30% below retail and drop 20% more when they hit the clearance rack. Top-quality consignment clothing for mothers-to-be, infants and children makes up half of the inventory. One-of-a-kind, handmade baby sweaters, quilts and toys are an added attraction.

Checks, Credit cards

PROCTOR'S CONSIGNMENT
Tacoma: 2726 N. Proctor ☎ 752-6434
Hours: Mon-Fri 10-6, Sat 10-5

Formerly known as Kids Exchange, Proctor's has been around for over a decade. The current owner maintains an updated image and service-oriented staff. Over 60% of the inventory is consigned, mainly toys, furniture and apparel for infants and toddlers. New clothing and accessories are discounted. This is one of the few consignment stores that stocks a big selection for sizes 6-14.

Checks, Credit cards

RAINBOW BOUTIQUE
Seattle: 9518 Roosevelt Way N.E. ☎ 522-1213 *Northgate*
Hours: Mon-Fri 10-5:30, Sat 10-4

This jam-packed store has a big selection of everything, including maternity and children's clothing, toys, books and furniture. We found cribs, strollers, swingsets and chests of drawers in stock the day we stopped by, plus wall hangings, lamps and bedding.

Checks, Credit cards

RITZY RAGS BUDGET BOUTIQUE   NEW LISTING
Tacoma: 4102 S. M Street ☎ 475-7602
Hours: Mon-Fr 11-6, Sat 11-4

Ritzy Rags carries clothes for women, sizes 4-44, and children, Infants through 6X, plus toys and baby furniture. The owner only buys outright or trades, so she is very selective about what she accepts. Babies receive a free gift on their first visit.

Checks, Credit cards

THE THREE BEARS   NEW LISTING
Edmonds: 512 5th Ave. S. #3 ☎ 776-2388
Hours: Mon-Sat 10-5

Many of the maternity garments and children's clothes (sizes Newborn-10) here look like they've never been worn. New apparel and accessories include samples and unique handcrafted items made especially for the store. No furniture.

Checks, Credit cards

See area locator index for this section on page 221

Clothing, Shoes & Accessories

THE TREE HOUSE
Redmond: 15742 Redmond Way ☎ 885-1145
Hours: Mon-Fri 9:30-6, Sat 10-5, Sun 1-5

Fifty percent of the clothing for Infants through size 14 is new at this well-established shop, but only *Osh Kosh* is discounted. Inventory includes consignment furniture, walkers, car seats and strollers. Three times a year the Tree House sends out a mailing with 20%-off coupons, good on all merchandise in the store.

Checks, Credit cards

THE UNICORN BOUTIQUE
Kirkland: 12537 116th N.E. ☎ 823-4868 *Totem Lake West*
Hours: Mon-Sat 10-8, Sun 12-5

There's lots to chose from in this well-stocked shop. Half the inventory is children's clothing, including shoes, accessories and a separate section for teens. You'll also find new and used toys, nursery furniture, layette items and gifts. Clothing in small to extra-large sizes outfits moms before and after the blessed event.

Checks, Credit cards

Shoes & Accessories

It would be impossible to cross-reference all the stores that carry shoes and accessories, but be sure to look in Off-price Stores, where chains like Ross, Marshall's, T.J. Maxx and Burlington Coat Factory offer moderately priced footwear for the whole family. Belts, hats, scarves, ties, suspenders, handbags, wallets, hosiery and costume jewelry are always priced 30% or more below retail.

Accessories are also inexpensive and plentiful in consignment shops. Take the time to plow through scarf bins and belt racks. Jewelry is often new, and we've purchased handbags and shoes that were in perfect condition.

Picway and Volume Shoe Source, with over two dozen stores each in the Puget Sound area, are the lowest priced discount footware chains around, but selection is limited to basic styles and man-made materials. Name-brand athletic shoes for the whole family are their best buys. Check the phone book for a location near you. Since athletic footwear became fashionable, prices have skyrocketed. Our Sporting Goods section offers a number of stores that discount athletic shoes, including Athletic Express, Big 5 and The Close Out.

See area locator index for this section on page 221

Clothing, Shoes & Accessories

CHRISTOPHER PALLIS & ASSOCIATES
Seattle: 161 Western Ave. W. ☎ 282-4146 *West of Seattle Center*
By appointment only

Wallets, eyeglass cases and other small leather goods are designed and manufactured here. Regular merchandise is discounted 20% or more at the U-District Street Fair (third weekend in May) and the Bellevue Art Show (last weekend in July). The workroom honors sale prices during these special events. You can shop the Western Ave. location year-round for bargains on close-outs, samples and slightly blemished goods. Leather scraps can be purchased by the pound.
Checks

COWTOWN BOOTS FACTORY STORE
Tukwila: 16880 Southcenter Parkway ☎ 575-0197 *Parkway Center*
Hours: Mon-Sat 10-6

Seattle may not be home to many cow punchers, but wannabes shop here for good buys on boots for men, women and children. This national chain originated in El Paso, and since everything is manufactured especially for the stores, prices are factory-direct. Styles range from basic work boots to fancy dressboots in exotic hides. Hand-made all-leather Ropers often go on sale for $49.95. At year's end, everything in the store is marked down 20%.
Checks, Credit Cards

FACTORY OUTLET L'EGGS BRANDS, INC.
P.O. Box 9984 Rural Hill, N.C. 27099-9984 ☎ 919 744-1170

Here's a mail order outlet for slightly imperfect pantyhose by *Hanes, L'Eggs and Just My Size* sold by the half-dozen or dozen for as little as 84¢ a pair. Tiny flaws, like a slight change in the knit or a color variation, won't affect the wearability. Call or mail in your order. There's a $15 minimum on credit card orders. Ads are often included in bulk rate coupon packets.
Checks, Credit cards

NORDSTROM SHOE RACK
Lynnwood: 3115 Alderwood Mall Blvd. ☎ 628-2915 *Alderwood Towne Ctr.*
Seattle: 1601 2nd Ave. ☎ 448-8522 *Downtown*
Tukwila: 17900 Southcenter Parkway ☎ 575-1058 *Pavilion Mall*
Hours: Tukwila & Lynnwood Mon-Fri 9:30-9:30, Sat 9:30-7, Sun 11-6;
Seattle Mon-Sat 9:30-7, Sun 12-6

Nordies is simply the best place to get fantastic bargains on quality fashionable footwear for men and women. (Children's shoes are available only in the Pavilion Mallstore.) The selection of styles and range of sizes reflects their inventory at the retail level. Some shoes are purchased just for the Rack. You can save big on expensive dress shoes, and boots are super-cheap after Christmas. Be prepared to wait on yourself as this is a clearance operation.
Checks, Credit cards

40 Clothing, Shoes & Accessories

NORTHWEST HANDBAG COMPANY
Tukwila: 17900 Southcenter Parkway ☎ 575-8887 *Pavilion Mall*
Hours: Mon-Fri 9:30-9:30, Sat 9:30-8, Sun 11-6

If you like eelskin, try this small shop, which is located on the main level across from Nordstrom's Rack. Prices average $80 to $90 for handbags that would normally retail for $150. Less-expensive items include eelskin wallets, coin purses and imitation-leather handbags and accessories.

Checks, Credit cards

PACIRIM
Seattle: 1501 Western Ave. ☎ 625-1826 *Downtown*
Hours: Mon-Sat 10-6, Sun 12-6

All eelskin products come from Korea and, since Seattle is a port of entry, this distributor sells factory-direct here and wholesales in other parts of the country. Comparison shopping verifies savings of 30% to 50%. Eelskin shoes, wallets and briefcases are also available, as well as accessoriesin other exotic leathers.

Checks, Credit cards

SHOE PAVILION
Bellevue: 14339 N.E. 20th ☎ 747-3620 *Ross Plaza*
Factoria: I-90 at I-405 ☎ 643-3828 *Loehmann's Plaza*
Renton: Rainier Ave. S. at Sunset ☎ 255-9984 *Renton Center*
Seattle: 830 N.E. Northgate Way ☎ 368-0719 *Northgate Village*
Tacoma: 2919 S. 38th ☎ 473-1473 *Cascade Plaza*
        10959 Gravelly Lake Dr. ☎ 584-9564 *Lakewood Mall*
Tukwila: 17900 Southcenter Parkway ☎ 575-0196 *Pavilion Mall*
Hours: Generally, Mon-Fri 10-9, Sat 10-6, Sun 11-5

One of our favorite resources for top-quality name-brand women's shoes, this locally-owned off-price chain has grown rapidly since it opened in 1980, a testimonial to its popularity. Dressy, as well as casual shoes, in fashionable and basic styles by *Amalfi, Anne Klein, Caressa, Florsheim, 9 West, Van Eli, Bandolino and Rockport*. Boots are always a good buy. Inventory includes a wide range of sizes. Prices start at 30% to 50% below retail and drop even more during seasonal sales. Loehmann's Plaza has the largest selection.

Checks, Credit cards

TOM CHRISTIE & ASSOCIATES
Bellevue: 3012 92nd Place N.E. ☎ 451-1574
By appointment only

Visit the factory show room and save 25% or more on discontinued styles, samples and irregulars from this local manufacturer of handbags and small leather goods sold in department and specialty stores.

Checks

WAISTED BELT CO., INC.
Lynnwood: 18609 76th Ave. W. ☎ 778-4885
Annual sale
From December 1st to the 22nd, the public can purchase overstock at wholesale prices or below from this manufacturer of women's moderately priced leather and stretch belts. You can also stock up on men's, women's and children's fashion and basic socks during this sale. *Perry Ellis and Esprit* are two of their better lines.
Checks

WASHINGTON SHOE COMPANY
Seattle: 542 1st Ave. S. ☎ 622-8517 *South of the Kingdome*
Hours: Mon-Fri 8:30-4:45
Washington Shoe is the only remaining local wholesale distributor of footwear. Visit the retail outlet adjacent to their warehouse, where the company sells regular stock, close-outs and samples for the whole family. Inventory includes athletic and recreational lines by *Aria, Converse and L.A. Gear*; casual and fashionable styles for women; loafers, crepe-sole shoes and slippers for men; boots for hiking, fishing and logging, plus styles for children. Man-made and leather goods are moderately priced. Selection and sizes will be erratic due to demand.
Credit cards

☑ Consumer Tips:
☞ When it comes to buying shoes, it's best to invest in good-quality, comfortable footwear whenever possible, which means leather uppers and a well-cushioned sole.

☞ If you find a pair of shoes that fit and the price is right, but the color isn't, consider having them dyed. This is also a great way to reclaim shoes ruined by stains or scratches.

☞ To prevent spotting, treat all new shoes with a water repellant and stain resistant spray before wearing. Rain protection is a must in Seattle!

☞ Re-heel shoes before they wear down too far, and put rubber non-skid protectors on the soles.

Formal Wear, Bridal Attire & Furs

Everyone gets dressed up now and then, whether it's New Year's Eve, a charity ball or dinner out with the boss. And don't forget cruises, class reunions, anniversaries and the most important event of all, your wedding day! Unless you have a fairy godmother to transform your rags to elegant evening wear, try the listings in this section.

Refer to the Women's Consignment Shops section for fancy "duds", especially during the holiday season. The selection of formal wear at Pandora's Box, the Dark Horse and Ragomuffyns is outstanding. Although men commonly rent formal wear, women are also discovering rental garments for special occasions. However, if you plan to wear an outfit more than 3 times, you're better off buying since rentals run 20% to

continued >

Clothing, Formal Wear, Bridal Attire & Furs

30% of the retail price, plus the cost of cleaning. Rental shops have big sales, usually in January or February, to make room for new styles. Tuxedos, many in top-notch condition, normally go on sale after they've been in service for a year.

Considering the $500 average retail cost for a wedding dress, brides-to-be will be interested in some of the rental shops listed. And we've unearthed some good resources if you want to buy your wedding gown. Also see Yesterday's, Redress and Sebastian's Closet, all listed in the Consignment section, for bridal wear. Another helpful tip is to check the women's clothing section of the newspapers' classified ads.

Manufacturers overprice furs knowing full-well that the majority will sell for 40% to 70% below their original price in January and February. Fur liquidators travel around the country renting various locations where they sell new and used furs. Watch the newspapers— savings can be unbelievable. Some consignment shops carry furs, usually less expensive pelts and vintage styles. In the fall, visit the more high-fashion-oriented stores for the best selection. Even Goodwill has a fur sale.

BLACK TIE MEN'S FORMAL WEAR
Lynnwood: 18027 Hwy. 99 #F ☎ 775-3671
Annual sale

Call to get on the mailing list for the fabulous January warehouse sale of special promotion goods and the discontinued rental garments from six retail stores in the Puget Sound area. New, all-wool tuxedos start at $199. Used designer-label tuxes average $100. Accessories, including shoes, jewelry, top hats, even canes, are sold at ridiculously low prices. Request a V.I.P. card for a 10% discount on regular merchandise at any Black Tie store.

Checks, Credit cards

DISCOUNT BRIDAL SERVICE, INC.
Bellevue: ☎ 746-1601
Kent: ☎ 630-9075
By appointment only

Save 20% to 40% on the same wedding dresses found in bridal shops and national publications by calling local reps with this nationwide franchise for a price quote. Have the manufacturer's name, the style number, and, if you saw it in a magazine, the page number. They'll help you determine size, based on charts from the various companies, and recommend someone for alterations if needed. Payment is in-full, in advance, and merchandise is shipped UPS directly to your home. You can also order dresses for bridesmaids, mother-of-the-bride and flower girls, as well as candles, jewelry, veils, accessories and wedding invitations. Order four to six months before the event to ensure on-time delivery.

Checks

Clothing, Formal Wear, Bridal Attire & Furs

EMPEROR'S NEW CLOTHES
Seattle: 1503 2nd W. ☎ 282-8878 *Queen Anne*
Hours: Mon-Fri 11-6, Sat 11-3

Fantasies come to life at the Emperor's New Clothes where you can rent both outrageous original costumes and elegant formal wear. You'll find elaborate beaded dresses suitable for beauty pageants, men's evening wear, fun costumes for the kids and lots of accessories. Bridal and evening gowns range from $100 to $400. Theme weddings from the medieval to the Great Gatsby eras are a specialty. Some garments can be purchased out-right or custom-made. A newsletter announces special events, sales, costume-making classes and new acquisitions. Call to request their small mail order catalog. New and used costumes and formal wear go on sale in February.

Checks

FORRESTER FURS
Seattle: 1424 4th ☎ 622-8785 *Downtown*
By appointment only

Based in Seattle since 1928, Forrester Furs is considered one of the leading furriers in the United States. This second-generation business recently decided to open its doors to the public, so now you can buy fashionable, luxurious fur garments at wholesale. Mink, fox and sable coats are big sellers.

Checks, Credit cards

HIGHLANDS CLEANERS
Renton: 2808 N.E. 10th ☎ 228-0858
Hours: Mon-Sat 8-6

Having specialized in wedding gown cleaning and preservation since 1948, the owner also rents wedding dresses. His price is the lowest around— $49.90 plus a $25 deposit. Choose from 60 styles, mostly sizes 6-12. Dresses can be purchased.

Cash only

INTERNATIONAL WORLD OF WEDDINGS
Seattle: ☎ 643-0135
Periodic sales

Watch for newspaper advertisements or call to find out about the spectacular sales, held every two or three months, where hundreds of beautiful name-brand wedding gowns are sold at drastically reduced prices. Most are samples, overruns, discontinued styles or clearance merchandise from local bridal shops. Some can be special-ordered. The biggest sale is in September.

Checks, Credit cards

See area locator index for this section on page 221

44 Clothing, Formal Wear, Bridal Attire & Furs

MARY'S POP-INS
Seattle: 2123 Queen Anne N. ☎ 282-5151 *Queen Anne*
Hours: Mon-Sat 11-5

The oldest consignment shop in Seattle is notable for its extensive selection of furs, which sell for 1/4th their original value. Inventory ranges from stoles and capes to mink coats and prices go as high as $5,000. If you can't afford to buy, Mary Pop-Ins rents furs and formal wear for men and women. Top-condition men's tuxedos sell for $40 to $50. Prices are kept low to ensure a fast turnover on the remaining inventory of women's apparel. Dresses average $15. Mailings announce special events, including the annual fur sale.

Checks

PANDORA'S CASTLE
Seattle: 2026 N.W. Market ☎ 782-5717 *Ballard*
Hours: Mon-Fri 11-7, Sat & Sun 12-6

Furs and estate jewelry make Pandora's Castle a popular spot for those with a taste for the finer things in life. Everything is on consignment and in first-rate condition. The majority of furs are current styles, from mink coats to fox boas. Prices can go as high as $3,000, but we spotted a great-looking coat for only $625. Jade, ivory, pearls and diamond jewelry start at $50. In business for 25 years, the store is located in the Market Street Antique Mall.

Checks, Credit cards

THE TUX SHOP
Seattle: 1509 N.W. Market ☎ 789-6047 *Ballard*
Hours: Mon-Fri 10-9, Sat 10-6, Sun 12-5

Rentals from the Tux Shop's 15 stores are shipped to their Ballard store and sold at discounted prices. Wool tuxes in good condition go for $125. Ties and cummerbunds $26. The most common sizes sell quickly. Best time to shop is November.

Checks, Credit cards

V.J.'S VINTAGE BRIDAL PARLOR
Seattle: 2811 E. Madison ☎ 325-6452 *Madison Park*
Hours: Tues-Thurs 12-4, Sat 12-5

Beautiful, one-of-a-kind wedding gowns from the late 1800's to 1950's range from $300 to $400. Veils, headpieces, gloves, petticoats, camisoles, hankies, linen and lace complete your ensemble. For those interested in selling a wedding gown, the owner buys outright or takes consignments. (Consignees make more money.)

Checks, Credit cards

☞ The following stores lease bridal gowns and formal wear. Inventory, prices and sizes will vary from store-to-store, so call first.

Clothing, Fine Jewelry 45

ARRAY OF THE RAINBOWS WEDDINGS
Kent: ☎ 630-3119
By appointment only

BEDAZZLED EVENING WEAR RENTAL
Seattle: 8745 Greenwood Ave. N. ☎ 781-1138 *Newport Square*
Hours: Tues-Fri 10-5:30, Sat 10-3

ELEGANTE FORMAL WEAR, INC.
Burien: 445 S.W. 152nd ☎ 243-7779
Hours: Mon-Fri 10-6, Thur 10-7, Sat 10-5

NEVER ENDING FANTASY
Seattle: 17718 15th N.E. ☎ 364-6731 *North City*
Hours: Wed-Fr 9-5, Tues & Sat 10-6

NOTHING TO WEAR
Tacoma: ☎ 565-6737
By appointment only

PAGE ONE DESIGNS
Lynnwood: 4001 198th S.W. ☎ 778-9020
Hours: Wed, Fri, Sat 11-5; Tues & Thur 11-7

WEDDINGS, ETC.
Seattle: 9731 Greenwood N. ☎ 783-7881
Hours: Mon 12-7, Tues-Sat 11-5, Fri 11-7

Fine Jewelry

The markup on jewelry sometimes goes as high as 300%, so beware of stores advertising 50% off sales on already inflated prices. Retail jewelry stores with low prices are usually located in out-of-the-way places. They buy direct, manufacture on the premises, and take a low mark-up. Service is as good or better than at exclusive outlets.

Wholesalers and brokers open to the public offer the best buys on quality gemstones and jewelry. Their showrooms vary from fancy to bare-bones and entry is usually by appointment only. Don't be surprised to find bars on the windows and locked doors. Here, gold, silver and gemstones are sold by weight according to market value, unlike retail stores where the cost also includes craftsmanship, design and a high profit margin. Auctions are another good place to pick up bargains on estate jewelry. (See Thrift Shops, Swap Meets & Auctions.)

It's hard to compare prices unless you have a trained eye, so insist on an independent appraisal before you purchase expensive jewelry. Returns at wholesalers are normally limited to exchange or credit.

46 Clothing, Fine Jewelry

CHIPPER'S
Tukwila: 17900 Southcenter Parkway ☎ 575-4653 Pavilion Mall
Hours: Mon-Fri 10-9, Sat 9:30-8, Sun 11-6

Chipper's carries one of the largest selections in the Pacific Northwest of Black Hills Gold, a traditional grapeleaf-design jewelry. They also stock loose or mounted gemstones, gold and silver chains, diamond jewelry, pearl strands, rings and watches. Prices run 20% or more below retail. Every year jewelry goes on sale during the Puyallup Fair at a booth on the fairgrounds and in the mall store. Mailing list for preferred customers.

Checks, Credit cards

C. RHYNE & ASSOCIATES
Seattle: 425 Pike St. #403 ☎ 623-6900 *Downtown*
Hours: Mon-Fri 8-5:30, Saturdays from Thanksgiving to Christmas

This family-owned jewelry store keeps prices low and holds frequent "legitimate" sales. Inventory includes everything from loose diamonds and colored stones to fine 18K gold jewelry made in Italy, gold and silver chain sold by weight, pearl necklaces and earrings, consignment and estate jewelry. Mounting and custom design available on the premises. The store also stocks gold coins and bars for those who like to invest in precious metals, so there's lots of coin jewelry. Sales announced via mailings.

Checks, Credit cards

DAHNKEN OF TACOMA   NEW LISTING
Tacoma: 1127 Broadway Plaza ☎ 627-7181
Hours: Mon-Fri 10-5:30, Sat 10-4

Once a large discount store with merchandise similar to Best's, Dahnken's has scaled down to fine jewelry, crystal, silver and giftware priced at 20% or more off retail. Shop for diamond earrings, wedding rings, pearls, 14K gold chains or semi-precious stones. Check out the *Oneida and Towle* silverplate, crystal, glassware and porcelain figurines for gifts.

Checks, Credit cards

THE GEMOLOGIST, INC.   NEW LISTING
Bellevue: 12000 N.E. 8th #206 ☎ 455-4653
By appointment only

This wholesaler purchases quality diamonds and precious stones from importers in Antwerp and Tel Aviv for resale to local jewelers. The general public is welcome to shop at their small retail store for fine jewelry or loose stones. Prices average 10% to 20% above wholesale. Jewelry custom-made on the premises.

Checks, Credit cards

Clothing, Fine Jewelry

KEEFER DESIGN GALLERY — NEW LISTING
Seattle: 10570 15th Ave. N.W. ☎ 364-6273 *Ballard*
By appointment only

Keefer's wholesale showroom offers diamonds, gemstones, pearls, jade and lapis, which can be purchased loose or made into jewelry. Gold chains, rings, earrings, bracelets, watches and pendants are available, plus coins and bezels.

Checks, Credit cards

MARCI JEWELRY
Bellevue: 40 Lake Bellevue #310 ☎ 455-4561
Hours: Wed 10-6. Or by appointment. Mon-Sat the three weeks before Christmas

Marci Jewelry is a girl's best friend. This wholesaler presents one of the largest collections of loose diamonds in the Northwest, plus other gemstones and fine jewelry custom-designed and manufactured on the premises. Prices range from $2,000 to $35,000 and that's half off retail! Earrings, tennis bracelets, wedding and anniversary rings are best-sellers. Mailings announce big sales in May and before Christmas.

Checks, Credit cards

SCOTT MICHAEL'S FINE JEWELRY — NEW LISTING
Tacoma: 7504 27th W. ☎ 565-7684
　　　　　10610 Bridgeport Way ☎ 582-3646
Hours: Mon-Fri 9-8, Sat 11-7, Sun 12-5

The owner advertises he'll meet or beat any price in the Northwest. His stores stock everything from loose precious stones to fine settings, custom-made and estate jewelry, coins and watches. Merchandise at the 27th West store is higher-end.

Checks, Credit cards

THE SHANE CO.
Seattle: 1902 4th Ave. ☎ 587-6200 *Downtown*
Hours: Mon & Fri 10-8, Tues-Thurs 10-6, Sat 10-5, Sun 12-5

The largest selection of wedding sets in the state can be found at this discount jewelry store. The owner sits on the Diamond Exchange, so he buys direct in volume and passes the savings on to customers, which is why prices may be 20% to 40% lower than competitors. Diamonds, rubies, emeralds and sapphires purchased loose can be set in one of many mountings on display. Or choose from jewelry in stock. The 30-day return policy is an added plus.

Checks, Credit cards

See area locator index for this section on page 221

48 Clothing, Fine Jewelry

THE VAULT — NEW LISTING
Bellevue: 500 108th Ave. N.E. #800 ☎ 646-7337 *Koll Center*
By appointment only

Inventory at this wholesale showroom includes loose diamonds, precious stones and finished jewelry comparable to what you find in the retail stores.

Checks, Credit cards

WEST COAST DIAMONDS & GEMS — NEW LISTING
Seattle: 4th & Pike Building #325 ☎ 624-8828 *Downtown*
By appointment only

You can buy costly gemstones direct from this wholesaler and save as much as 50% off retail. Select from high-quality finished jewelry in stock, or create your own unique setting from hundreds of mountings and wax models in classic or contemporary designs. Loose stones custom-set on the premises in five to seven working days.

Checks

WILLIAMS & SON, INC. — NEW LISTING
Federal Way: 19415 Pacific Hwy. S. ☎ 878-7966 or 800/24-CARAT
By appointment only

Open since 1974, this small, low-overhead diamond broker, importer and custom-goldsmith guarantees substantial discounts on quality products. All gemstones are independently certified. Using state-of-the-art equipment, staff will gladly explain what to look for in buying fine diamonds. For a small deposit, you can take home a video on the subject.

Checks, Credit cards

☑ Consumer Tips:

☞ Educated buyers sometimes turn up super bargains at pawn shops. The best stuff is usually kept in a safe, so be sure to let them know what you're looking for.

☞ If you have jewelry to sell and want to recoup as much money as possible, our sources suggest advertising in the classifieds.

Food

According to statistics put out by the U.S. Department of Labor, the average urban family of four, with a median income of $25,000 a year, spends 16.5% of its income on food. The lower the income, the higher this percentage. Current figures indicate that food costs can vary from $90 to $237 per week, so careful shopping habits and a few changes in diet may significantly reduce your annual food budget.

Read ads in the food section of the newspapers and weekly grocery store supplements. Shop at the store that is offering the best buys or plan your menus around your favorite store's specials. Watch for weekly specials on items that you use regularly and purchase them only when they're on sale. Limit your grocery shopping to once or twice a week and always go with a grocery list. This saves both time and money since most people succumb to impulse buying at the supermarket.

Collect coupons and cents-off labels to maximize your savings. Pay'N Save, Bartell's and Pay Less regularly put out coupon books that offer discounts on packaged and canned food items. By using coupons, you can save an average of 30% on cereal, cat food, snack items, cleaning products and bake mixes. Coupon-clipping takes some time, but it's worthwhile.

Buy in quantity or the largest size available. Share bulk purchases with relatives or friends. Try to consume everything you buy. Learn to be creative with leftovers. Store odds and ends in the freezer for later use as soups and stews.

A Word of Caution:

When you shop at big warehouses and distributors that usually sell by the truckload or case-lot, please respect their minimum orders and buy in volume. Some companies require that you have a business license or represent a non-profit organization. Others welcome the public— as long as customers follow wholesale procedures. Pay cash if you don't have a business check or aren't affiliated with a church or school. Many operate on a "will call" basis, which means you must call first to place your order and pick up at a specified time. Many will send price lists on request, and we suggest you use these whenever possible since browsing is not acceptable. Insisting on special services or interfering with wholesale business practices disrupts their operation, and we wouldn't like to see their doors closed to our readers.

☑ Consumer Tip:

☞ A survey of eight top grocery stores in the Seattle area in December, 1989 by the Washington Public Interest Research Group, a non-profit independent consumer advocacy organization, revealed that prices can vary as much as 11% from one store to another. The results of the survey showed that Fred Meyer had the lowest prices overall, and Stock Market came in second. Meat and eggs were cheaper at Safeway; Food Giant beat everyone's prices on fresh produce, which fluctuates more than any other category.

Food Service Warehouses

We suggest you visit a food service warehouse in your area to get an idea of how they operate and familiarize yourself with their unusual inventory. Some cater to the cooking and equipment needs of restaurants, hotels and institutions, while others stock your local supermarket or convenience store. Food runs the gamut from fresh produce to bakery goods, canned, refrigerated, or frozen items, plus specialty items not available at grocery stores. Prepared and canned mixes are best sellers. You will be buying in bulk. Cooking oil comes in 25-gallon containers, mayonnaise in tubs, ketchup in giant-sized jars, and green beans in 10-lb. cans. Bar supplies, paper products, cleaning compounds, commercial grade cookware and appliances are usually available as well. Some warehouses will break up case lots or sell in smaller quantities. Be sure to compare prices when you buy; volume does not always guarantee savings. Look for weekly or monthly sales on specific items, plus low prices on surplus or salvaged goods. Refer to Membership Buying Clubs for similar food products.

A & B FOOD MARKET
NEW LISTING

Tacoma: 608 N. Oakes ☎ 627-2011
Hours: Mon-Fri 10-6, Sat. 10-5

A & B caters to the restaurant business, but anyone can shop here. Frozen and canned goods damaged in shipping are the best buys. Some of the inventory is surplus. Glassware, plates, silverware and cleaning products are all available.

Checks

BARGREEN'S RESTAURANT SUPPLY, INC.

Everett: 3532 Smith ☎ 743-4017
Hours: Mon-Fri 8-5

Bargreen's is a big supplier of food-service products from staples to specialty items in North King County. You'll also come upon kitchen wares, china and flatware, plus just about any other type of equipment needed to run a restaurant or bar.

Checks

THE CANNED FOODS STORE

Everett: 710 S.E. Everett Mall Way ☎ 353-6224
Tacoma: 11011 Pacific Hwy. S.W. ☎ 581-5333
Hours: Everett, Mon-Sat 10-7; Tacoma, Mon-Sat 9-6. Both stores, Sun 11-6

This outlet keeps prices 20% to 40% lower than supermarkets by buying direct from the manufacturer and stocking only packaged, frozen and canned groceries. Discounts extend to most housewares, health and beauty aids. Food products can be purchased by the can, box, or case.

continued >

Food, Food Service Warehouses

This outlet keeps prices 20% to 40% lower than supermarkets by buying direct from the manufacturer and stocking only packaged, frozen and canned groceries. Discounts extend to most housewares, health and beauty aids. Food products can be purchased by the can, box, or case. Because they buy closeouts from manufacturers all over the U.S., some labels won't be familiar. Shop the small section that displays big 10-lb. cans and 5-lb. jars for the best savings. The last time we called they quoted us great prices on cereal, diapers and name-brand frozen foods. Some of the goods are surplus, but everything is 100% guaranteed.

Checks

CASH & CARRY WHOLESALERS
Seattle: 5710 Rainier Ave. S. ☎ 722-5119 *Rainier Valley*
Hours: Mon-Fri 8-5, weekends by appointment

Generally, Cash & Carry's customers are Mom and Pop grocery stores, and most items are packaged, canned, or bottled. You can't buy meats or frozen foods, but you will find a good selection of snack items, juices and beverages like those sold in vending machines. Movie houses stock up on popcorn, soda pop and candy here.

Checks

COMMISSARY CASH & CARRY, INC.
Seattle: 1155 N.W. Ballard Way ☎ 789-7242 *Ballard*
Tukwila: 404 Strander Blvd. ☎ 246-6017
Tacoma: 6626-B S. Sprague ☎ 475-3475
Hours: Mon-Fri 8-5, Sat 8-4

Rub shoulders with caterers and restaurant owners buying dry, canned and frozen foods, as well as paper products, janitorial supplies and dinnerware. You'll discover a terrific selection of deli meats, cheeses, salads and frozen hors d'oeuvres for your next party.

Checks

FOOD SERVICES TACOMA
Fife: 2001 48th Ave., Court E ☎ 922-8100
Hours: Mon-Fri 8-5

The inventory of over 5,000 products at Food Services Tacoma includes food, paper products and janitorial supplies. There's an extensive selection of frozen food, with breaded fish and prime rib the best-selling items.

Checks

MONTE VISTA DISTRIBUTORS BULK WAREHOUSE SALES
Snoqualmie: 140 North Falls Ave. ☎ 888-1811, 747-6701
Hours: Mon-Fri 9-5

Here's a great place to check out when your church, school, social or business organization is looking for fast food items for a fund raiser or picnic. Hamburger patties, fish, potatoes, corn dogs, hot dogs, onion rings and dairy products are sold by the case or carton. Prices will be quoted and orders taken over the phone. Will call only.

Checks

Food, Bakery Goods

NORTHWEST GROCERS   NEW LISTING
Everett: 2500 Hewitt ☎ 252-5149
Renton: 858 Lind S.W. ☎ 255-3162
Hours: Mon-Fri 8-5

To shop here, you must have a business license or represent a non-profit organization. The Renton location is a wholesale-only warehouse servicing grocery stores with a full line of packaged, canned and frozen products representing hundreds of nationally known brands. The Everett branch stocks snack items. Purchases must be made by phone in case or carton lots.

Checks

SYSCO CASH & CARRY/ CONTINENTAL FOOD SERVICE
Seattle: 1242 6th S. ☎ 447-9113 *Southeast of Kingdome*
Hours: Mon-Fri 7:30-5:30, Sat 8-4

Order fresh fruits, vegetables and meats a day in advance. Steaks are sold by the dozen and lettuce, six heads at a time. For parties you can find liquor mixes by the quart and frozen bakery items that appear on the menus of fine restaurants. Distressed and closeout merchandise from the huge Kent warehouse sells for 25% below wholesale in the smaller Seattle outlet.

Checks

Bakery Goods

One of the easiest ways to keep your food bill down is to buy day-old bakery products. Almost all supermarkets with in-store bakeries have a special shelf set aside for day-old products. If you shop at a local bakery, find out when they put their goods on sale. Best buys are on bread, rolls and pastries. Savings start at 20% but, remember, the early shopper gets the best selection. Also look under Eating Out for the Community Colleges that have bakeries.

BADER'S DUTCH BISCUIT COMPANY
Seattle: 1600 14th Ave. ☎ 325-5050 *Capitol Hill*
Hours: Mon-Fri 8-4:30

If you need cookies in large quantities for a school or church function, Bader's is your place! Although they bake and sell in bulk for grocery store chains, you or your organizations can shop here— if you purchase by the case. Cookies run the gamut from traditional favorites like peanut butter, chocolate chip and oatmeal, to fancy assortments and seasonal cut-out styles. Shortbread is the best-seller at around $8 for a case of 22-dozen. Call ahead to order or check what's in stock.

Checks

CASCADE COOKIE COMPANY
Kent: 22755 72nd S., Bldg. E ☎ 872-7773
Hours: Mon-Fri 8-4:30

continued >

Food, Bakery Goods 53

The Cascade Cookie Company supplies cookies to major supermarket chains. A case of 12-dozen peanut butter or chocolate chip cookies sells for around $8. At that price, you can afford to keep your cookie monsters well-supplied. Such fancy blends as double chocolate chip cost more, but prices are lower for seasonal cookies.

Big bags of broken cookies sell for less than $3. Cascade's cookies have a 3-month shelf life despite the fact they have no preservatives.

Checks

THE COOKIE CONSPIRACY
Seattle: 415 N.W. 65th St. ☎ 783-6633 *Ballard*
Hours: Sun-Thurs 8-5, or By appointment

The Cookie Conspiracy has been listed in every edition of the Seattle Super Shopper because the company offers quality products at fantastic savings. You pay $1 each for their cookies when you buy them on espresso carts, the Washington State ferries and at convenience stores, but only 50¢ at the factory. Gourmet varieties like Triple Threat Chocolate Chip and peanut butter dipped in chocolate cost more and must be ordered by the dozen a day in advance. Other temptations include brownies, cheese cake, soft pretzels and jumbo muffins in eight different flavors. Factory seconds, called "oop-ses," may look a little strange, but taste just as good! A great place to stock up for kids' parties or bake sales.

Checks

GAI'S SEATTLE FRENCH BAKING CO., INC.
Bellevue: 13823 N.E. 20th ☎ 641-0293
Bremerton: 2547 Perry Ave. ☎ 377-6377
Everett: 1515 E Marine View Dr. ☎ 252-6260
Kent: 23009 Military Road S. ☎ 878-2242
Lynnwood: 430 164th S. ☎ 743-5799
Seattle: 2006 S. Weller ☎ 726-7535 *International Dist.*
1431 N.E. 49th St. ☎ 782-4992 *Ballard*
5980 1st Ave. S. ☎ 762-2186 *Georgetown*
Tacoma: 8203 Durango S.W. ☎ 584-4200
Hours: Generally, Mon-Sat 9:30-5:30, Sun 10-5

The majority of Seattle's restaurants serve Gai's French bread and rolls. The last time we checked at Gai's thrift shops, a fresh baguette sold for 99¢ and sliced French bread was going for 69¢ a loaf, or three for $2. Breads of every type fill the shelves, and many items are brought in fresh every day except Wed. and Sun., which are markdown days. Look for savings on rolls, croissants, pastries, bread sticks, croutons and muffins as well.

Checks

HOUSE OF PIES THRIFT STORE
Woodinville: 17611 128th Place N.E. ☎ 488-0200
Hours: Mon-Fri 9:30-5:30

continued >

54 Food, Bakery Goods

Pies, cookies, cakes, brownies and muffins are baked daily on the premises for hospitals, restaurants and delis in the Seattle area. You'll find every kind of pie you can name, but apple and banana are still the most popular. Average cost is $5.25 for fresh, $3.75 for day-old pies. Place your order a day in advance to ensure availability of your favorite flavor. Savings on other items may not be as great, but you still pay less than the going rate at bakeries and supermarkets. A standard round cake costs only $5.00 with chocolate, applesauce and banana the best sellers. Organizations get a discount, so inquire the next time your school has a bake sale.

Checks

LANGENDORF BAKERIES
Bremerton: 4800 Arsenal Way ☎ 373-8221
Everett: 3931 Smith St. ☎ 252-6613
Kent: 8621 212th S. ☎ 872-2244
Mountlake Terrace: 4804 212th S.W. ☎ 774-4170
Seattle: 2901 6th Ave. S. ☎ 682-2244 *South of Kingdome*
Tacoma: 11216 Golden Givens Road ☎ 537-0749
Hours: Generally, Mon-Sat 9-5

Almost every Langendorf product you see in grocery stores appears on the shelves of their thrift shops, but selection varies. Sales are based on inventory, and while you can always count on bargains on day-old products, fresh goods also get marked down when the bakery brings in overstock. Prices are particularly good on white bread, which sells for only $1.50 for five loaves. *Country Hearth* was marked down to $2 for three loaves the day we called. You'll find great buys on pastries, as well as cookies for the kids' lunch.

Checks

NEW YORK BAGEL BOYS   NEW LISTING
Seattle: N.E. 45th & 25th Ave N.E. ☎ 523-1340 *University Village*
Bellevue: 156th N.E. & N.E. 8th ☎ 641-5300 *Crossroads Mall*
Hours: Seattle Mon-Fri 7-7, Sat 9-6, Sun 9-5; Bellevue Mon-Fri 7-8, Sat 8-8, Sun 8-4

The best buy in town on freshly made bagels! The regular price is $3.50 for a baker's dozen, and day-old bagels drop down to $1.70. They still taste great. We love the crispy-on-the-outside, crunchy-on-the-inside texture.

Checks

OROWHEAT BAKERS, INC.
Bellevue: 1405 134th N.E. ☎ 641-3116
Everett: 125 S.W. Everett Mall Way ☎ 745-1669

continued >

Food, Bakery Goods 55

Kent: 1510 S. Central ☎ 854-1303
Seattle: 1604 N. 34th ☎ 634-2700 *Fremont*
   7009 Greenwood Ave. N. ☎ 789-7515 *Greenwood*
Tacoma: 104th St. S.W. & Steele St. ☎ 584-4435
Hours: Generally, Mon-Fri 9-6, Sat 9-5

Both fresh and day-old bakery products are sold at these outlets. Inventory varies from store-to-store as stock is geared to the different neighborhoods. Orowheat is best known for whole wheat breads. A fresh loaf of granola bread goes for a little over $1, and day-old is marked down 25%. Also try their pastries, snack items and oat bran. Orowheat does not supply paper bags, so take your own and a few extra to leave. Senior citizens receive a discount.

Checks

ROOS MARKET

Seattle: 1534 Pike Place Market ☎ 624-2945 *Downtown*
Hours: Mon-Sat 10-6

Only day-old bakery products from Brenner Brothers and pocket bread (pita) from Jasmine Bakery are sold here. Everything is priced at 50% or more below retail. Rye bread is their best seller, and it comes in ten varieties. Take advantage of the low prices on pastries, bagels and other bakery goods too.

Cash

RUTH ASHBROOK BAKERY THRIFT SHOP   NEW LISTING

Seattle: 1416 10th Ave. ☎ 325-4900 *Capitol Hill*
Hours: Mon-Fri 8-4:30

Ruth Ashbrook bakes for Western Family, Rainier Farms and Fred Meyer. At the Thrift Shop you'll find a full line of fresh bakery products. Prices vary according to what's in stock that day. Loaves of whole wheat bread can run as low as two for $1. Pastries, hot dog and hamburger buns are always available.

Checks

WONDER BREAD HOSTESS CAKE THRIFT STORES

Bremerton: 3411 11th ☎ 377-4881
Everett: 430 Casino Road ☎ 743-7775
Kent: 310 N. Washington ☎ 852-7050
Seattle: 1924 S. Jackson ☎ 322-4247 *International District*
   14701 15th Ave. N.E. ☎ 364-1991 *North City*
Tacoma: 701 S. Sprague ☎ 627-0137
   10014 Pacific Ave. S. ☎ 536-1435
Hours: Generally, Mon-Fri 9:30-5:30, Sat 9:30-5, Sun 11-4

continued >

Food, Eggs & Dairy Products

All bakery goods at these outlets are fresh except for day-old bread and cakes. Chips, crackers and cookies are made for the thrift shops by different companies. Save by purchasing their Value Pack— a box of 90 cookies for around $2. Wonder Bread gives discount coupons with every purchase featuring two for one specials, and you can ask for their "Thrift Store Dollar Stretcher" card. Each time you shop, they punch the card and when it's full, you get a rebate in merchandise. Senior citizens qualify for a 10% discount on everything in stock on Tuesday. Shop "Bargain Days" on Wednesday and Sunday.

Checks

☑**Consumer Tip:**
☞Put day-old bakery products in the freezer as soon as you get home. Thaw the goodies a couple of hours before serving or pop them in the microwave, and they'll taste almost as good as fresh-baked.

Eggs & Dairy Products

AMBERSON EGG FARM
Everett: 9131 42nd St. N.E. ☎ 334-7272
Hours: Mon-Fri 8-4

Fresh eggs with a small crack or color defect in the outer shell are sold here at savings of 30% or more. Although the membrane on these "chex eggs" must be intact, it's best to use them for baking or hard-boiling. Prices on Grade "B" eggs will be slightly higher. Amberson's also stocks butter and cheeses from the Washington Cheese Co-Op in Mt. Vernon at below-retail prices.

Checks

EASTSIDE CHEESE
Redmond: 2545 152nd Ave. N.E., Bldg. 14 ☎ 883-1568 *Koll Business Park*
Hours: Mon-Fri 9-5, Sat 10-3

Caterers shop here because the selection includes many items rarely found in grocery stores or restaurant supply houses. A big walk-in cooler holds deli meats and imported cheeses at 10% to 30% off the normal bulk price. There's no minimum, but the staff will not cut into 2-lb. bricks. Ruth's Homestyle mixes for soups and baked goods are made here. Specialty items include unusual sauces and spices, sun-dried tomatoes, frozen lasagna sheets, apple dumplings, Devonshire cream and gourmet bakery products. Eastside Cheese sells day-old bread from the Bread Garden Bakery.

Checks

GAFFNEY SUPPLIERS, INC.
Puyallup: 10514 8th St. E. ☎ 927-2800
Hours: Mon-Fri 6-4:30

Visit this egg processing plant for some of the best prices around. They're also a distribution warehouse for dairy products and 30-lb. tins of frozen apples and cherries sold to bakeries for pie fillings.

continued >

Eggs can be purchased by the dozen, but cheese is only sold in 2-lb. or 8-lb. loaves. Margarine and butter are also available. Please note: this working plant does not have a retail counter, so take pains not to disrupt their regular business. Call if you're going to place a large order or simply check prices.

Checks

GREEN RIVER CHEESE AND DAIRY PRODUCTS CO.

Kent: 19029 East Valley Hwy. ☎ 872-7600
Hours: Mon-Fri 8:30-5

This wholesaler specializes in mozzarella and unsalted cheeses for those on a restricted diet, plus special blends for pizza and Mexican dishes. Although most purchases are 5-lb. loaves, smaller sizes are sometimes available. Prices fluctuate with the market. Look for good buys on American and Swiss cheese for hamburgers and sandwiches. You might want to try their pepperoni and salami sticks. Call to find out what's in stock or to request a product list.

Checks

NORTHWEST ICE CREAM NOVELTIES

Federal Way: 35400 Pacific Hwy. S. ☎ 952-5907
Hours: Mon-Sun 9-1, April thru September only

Northwest Novelties sells ice cream treats and frozen novelties just like the ones you buy from the little carts that drive around residential areas in the summer. A case of 72 cool treats will run 10% to 20% above wholesale. Dry ice can be purchased by the pound. The owner will send you a price list. Call ahead to place an order.

Checks

STONEFELT AND COMPANY

Kent: 20241 East Valley Hwy. ☎ 872-7216
Hours: Mon-Thurs 8:30-4:30, Fri 8:30-3

Stonefelt offers excellent buys on imported and domestic cheese. The best bargains are 10-lb. sacks of trims (ends of loaves cut off when cheese is packaged into smaller sizes). Stonefelt is a distributor, so purchases must be made in 5-lb. or 10-lb. loaves. Call in your order four days in advance, and confirm prices at that time. No minimum dollar requirement.

Cash only

VIVIAN'S PRIDE GOURMET ICE CREAM

Redmond: 12248 156th ☎ 885-2339
Hours: Mon-Fri 8-9, Sat 9-9, Sun 11-7

Thirty different flavors of gourmet ice cream are manufactured on the premises and distributed to retail outlets in the Puget Sound. Buy vanilla, strawberry, or chocolate in a 3-gal. tub and pay around $18. (Baskin Robbins charges $28 for the same amount). Call ahead to confirm prices and inquire about other flavors. Sherbets, sorbets and frozen yogurt are also available.

Checks

Fruits & Vegetables

Fresh produce is the most unpredictable cost in your food budget because prices change weekly. If you buy in season when prices are the lowest, and splurge only occasionally during the rest of the year, your savings will add up fast. (Raspberries and asparagus are our downfalls!) Buying in volume is not usually a good idea unless you're planning to freeze the fruits or vegetables since most have a shelf life of only five to seven days. Apples, oranges, onions and potatoes are the exceptions.

CERBONE'S NEW LISTING
Federal Way: 31229 Pacific Hwy. S. ☎ 941-0937
Hours: Mon-Sat 8-7, Sun 8-6

Prices at this huge indoor produce market beat most grocery stores, plus you get personal service. Lettuce is always a good buy, and when we visited we saw outstanding values on tomatoes, mushrooms and Granny Smith apples. Located behind Payless next to Albertson's.

Checks

CITY PRODUCE CO.
Seattle: 710 7th Ave. S. ☎ 682-0320 *International District*
Hours: Mon-Fri 9-5, Sat 9-3

This small wholesale/retail company stocks a large variety of fresh fruits and vegetables. Asian produce includes such exotic items as bitter melons, long beans and lily roots. You can purchase small quantities, but the savings are in the larger amounts. Berries are available in flats by special order. City Produce is not a supermarket, so try to shop without disturbing their more-profitable wholesale business.

Checks

DAVIES PRODUCE CO., INC.
Kent: 8028 S. 200th ☎ 872-0400
Hours: Mon-Fri 6-2:30

Families, co-ops and organizations pay wholesale prices at this warehouse operation. Minimum order is $20, will-call only. All fresh fruits and vegetables are sold by the case, carton, lug or flat. Apples, oranges, or lemons are good investments. Davies also carries dairy products, several different cuts for french fries and a few Oriental items. For your next family picnic, check out the potato or macaroni salad sold by the tub. Selection varies, so it's best to request a price list.

Checks

EVERGREEN FRUIT & PRODUCE
Puyallup: 7812 River Rd. E. ☎ 848-0414
Hours: Mon-Fri 6-3:30

An outstanding selection of fresh produce is shipped year-round to this market from all over the country. Sliced or chopped vegetables and packaged shredded salad mixes are popular items.

continued >

Food, Fruits & Vegetables 59

Apples and a few other fruits can be purchased by the half case. Minimum order is $20, and you should call ahead to place your order. Located in the basement of Your Health, Inc. Enter from the back.

Cash only

GARDEN FRESH FOODS   NEW LISTING
Woodinville: 19600 144th Ave. N.E. ☎ 568-4388
Hours: Mon-Fri 7-5

Garden Fresh Foods prepares vegetables for restaurants and produce houses. Potatoes can be purchased whole or cut up for french fries, hash browns, potato salad, etc. Broccoli, cauliflower, carrots, celery, mushrooms, onions and peppers are also stocked. Minimum order is a 10-lb. bag, and you must call 24 hours in advance.

Cash only

PETERSON FRUIT CO.
Everett: 4720 Chenault Beach Rd. ☎ 355-1050
Hours: Mon-Fri 7:30-4

Case lots of fresh fruit can be ordered from Peterson's, which carries a complete line of apples and citrus fruits, plus any soft fruit you'd find in a grocery store except berries, bananas and exotic items.

Checks

RISING SUN FARMS & PRODUCE
Seattle: 6505 15th Ave. N.E. ☎ 524-9741 *Ravenna*
        1831 E. Madison ☎ 324-4323 *Capitol Hill*
Hours: Mon-Sat 9-8, Sun 10-7

You can't miss this colorful outdoor market with its bright blue exterior and big signs proclaiming everyday low prices on fruits and vegetables. Because they operate on a low overhead and are willing to do a lot of the labor themselves, prices on many items will beat the going rate at grocery stores. The best buys sell out fast, so visit often. Take advantage of volume pricing or the 10% discount on cases. Check out the "Bargain Boxes," where the produce may have lost some of its aesthetic appeal, but is still edible. You'll also find bulk pasta, cereal and legumes, a small dairy department and bakery items, plus friendly service.

Checks

S.T. PRODUCE
Seattle: 426 S. Massachusetts ☎ 622-5492 *South of Kingdome*
Hours: Mon-Fri 6-3

Want to set up a salad bar at your next family picnic or office function? S.T. Produce supplies restaurants and delis with the fixings. You can order prepared salad mixes or separate items—lettuce (chopped or shredded), carrots (shredded or peeled), celery (diced or sliced), onions (peeled, sliced, or diced).

continued >

60 Food, Meat, Poultry & Seafood

All products are packed fresh in 10-lb. bags. Just add the dressing of your choice. The most popular salad is the "ST" (80% iceberg, 15% Romaine and 5% cabbage) at 81¢/lb. in season. Coleslaw is another winner. Ten pounds of salad serves about 60 people!

Checks

TWENTY-FIFTH STREET MARKET
Everett: 2431 Broadway ☎ 252-8773, 252-3111
Hours: Mon-Sat 7-6

For 50 years this corner fruit and vegetable stand has been supplying King and Snohomish County restaurants with fresh produce trucked in daily from local farmers. While the displays may not be as fancy as those found in grocery stores, the prices are hard to beat. Apples, oranges, bananas and tomatoes are dirt cheap in season. You'll also find exotic items like star fruit and blood oranges, as well as prepared salads, coleslaw and garnishes. Dairy products are competitively priced. Home delivery within a designated area costs only $1.

Checks

VALLEY HARVEST
Renton: 458 Hardie Ave. S.W. ☎ 277-0221 *Renton Center*
Hours: Mon-Fri 7-6:30, Sat 7-6, Sun 7-5

Prices at Valley Harvest are downright low, and the owners work hard to keep them that way. They'll often buy produce rejected by grocery chains, use hand labor to cull out the bad items or clean up the merchandise to make it presentable. For the best buys, check the bins in their outdoor market area first. We've seen incredibly low prices on apples, mushrooms and watermelons. Inside, you'll find savings on bulk beans, grains, flours and rice, as well as health food products.

Checks

☑ Consumer Tip:

☞ During the summer, visit one of the many roadside stands and U-pick operations on the outskirts of Seattle. The trip is fun for the whole family and saves money. The Puget Sound Farm Markets Association's yearly guide is available at the Cooperative Extension Service Office in downtown Seattle (3rd floor, Smith Tower), in public libraries, or by mail. Send a self-addressed, stamped envelope to P.S.F.M.A., P.O. Box 1011, Puyallup, WA 98371. If you live in the Snohomish County area, a similar guide to U-picks is available through the Snohomish County Cooperative Extension Service. Call 338-2400 for more information.

Meat, Poultry & Seafood

Meat is the most costly item in a food budget, and many people consume 50% to 100% more protein than they need in a day. Choose your cuts based on cost-per-pound and the number of servings you can get out of a package. A 1-lb. package of hamburger serves four people while the same weight in blade cut pork chops serves only two.

continued >

Food, Meat, Poultry & Seafood

Find out if the store marks down meat after the date on the package has expired. Reduced-price meats may have lost some of their visual appeal, but the stores would not put them out if they weren't edible. For the best selection, shop early in the morning, when dated meat is marked down, and freeze or cook it the same day. If you have a large family, consider investing in a freezer so you can buy in quantity.

AURORA MEATS
Seattle: 17532 Aurora Ave. N. ☎ 542-3755 *Richmond Highlands*
Hours: Mon-Fri 8-6, Sat 9-4

Ninety percent of Aurora Meats' business is wholesale to restaurants. If you're willing to buy meat uncut, you can save on the price of labor. The company specializes in beef, but also stocks poultry and pork. A whole top round was going for $2/lb. the day we called. Round steak was $2.69/lb.

Checks

JONES BROTHERS MEATS   NEW LISTING
Seattle: 5404 22nd Ave. N.W. ☎ 783-1258 *Ballard*
Edmonds: 8220 238th S.W. ☎ 775-5623
Hours: Seattle Mon-Fri 9-6 Edmonds Tues-Sat 10-6

Although this is a retail meat market, low prices on choice New York steak and fresh or frozen ground beef earned them a listing! Lean ground beef goes for $1.19/lb. New York steaks by the strip (10-14 lbs.) sell for $3.49/lb. which includes cutting and wrapping. If you have a freezer, these are good items to stock. Also check out the prices on quantity meat packs.

Checks, Credit cards

LAMPAERT MEATS
Duvall: 1.2 miles North of Duvall on Snoqualmie River Rd. ☎ 467-9841
Hours: Mon & Tues 10-6, Wed 10-5, Thurs & Fri 11-7

This local meat-packer offers a 100% guarantee on their products, which are sold mainly to restaurants. Lean ground beef is always a good buy, and the price goes down 10¢ per pound if you buy more than 25 lbs. The roasts are large, and most are frozen, but you can sometimes buy them fresh. You'll also find top-grade pork, lamb, chicken and veal. Sausage is made fresh on the premises, and whole pigs can be ordered for your next family barbecue. Select organic meats are also available. Call for a price list and place orders a couple of days in advance.

Checks

MJ MEATS   NEW LISTING
Mountlake Terrace: 21706 66th W. ☎ 778-2712
Hours: Mon-Fri 8-4:30

continued >

62 Food, Meat, Poultry & Seafood

Save money on larger cuts, boxes or cases of meats with a $100 minimum order. If you're planning a picnic for a lot of people, check out their prices on lean ground beef or hamburger patties. Poultry, lamb, veal, frozen seafood, cheese and butter are included on a product list, which they'll send on request. Call in your order a day in advance.

Checks

MEAT DISTRIBUTORS INC.
Kirkland: 715 8th ☎ 827-0506
Hours: Mon-Fri 7-3:30

Competitive prices guarantee savings at this wholesale outlet, which services restaurants, hospitals and institutions. Call to inquire about inventory and purchasing policies. Beef, poultry, seafood and lamb, fresh or frozen, must be purchased by the box or in 10-lb. packages. A complete line of kosher meats and food products has been added, along with frozen deserts, quick fry items, cheese and eggs.

Checks

OBERTO FACTORY OUTLET STORE
Kent: 26135 104th Ave S.E. ☎ 852-1219 *Kent Hill Plaza*
Seattle: 1715 Rainier Ave. S. ☎ 322-7524 *East of Kingdome*
Hours: Mon-Fri 8-6, Sat 9-5

Since 1918 Oh Boy! Oberto has been turning out packaged Italian specialty meats, and today their popular products are in grocery stores and delis all over the country. Odd sizes, end pieces, overstock, test products and production overruns end up at these factory outlet stores. Everything is fresh, and you can save as much as 50% on some items. Choose from a terrific assortment of salami, pepperoni and other lunch meats. Purchase the "Sausage du Jour" or buy in quantity for the best deal. A 1-lb. bag of ends and irregular pieces of beef jerky is a super bargain for pizza topping. Even such gourmet items as smoked salmon gift boxes show up at reduced prices.

Checks, Credit cards

TORINO SAUSAGE CO.
Seattle: 700 S. Dearborn ☎ 623-1530 *International District*
Hours: Mon-Fri 7:30-4, Sat 8-12

The bulk of Torino's products appear on the plates of local restaurants. Shop at this small retail outlet for hot, mild and salt-free sausage, large sticks of dry salami, fresh pepperoni and nitrate-free salami. Whole pieces are cheaper than cuts, and end pieces are sold by the bag. Cheeses, hams, sandwiches, olive oil and dried pastas are competitively priced.

Checks

WESTERN FISH AND OYSTER CO., INC.
Tacoma: 1137 Dock Street ☎ 383-1668
Hours: Mon-Fri 8:30-5:45, Sat 8:30-5:30

continued >

Prices at Western Fish and Oyster are great, but you have to purchase a minimum of 25 lbs. Most of the seafood comes from Alaska and is sold to restaurants and retail outlets. Halibut, the most popular item, can be purchased fresh (in season) or frozen. The day we called, fillets were $5.50/lb. and steaks $4.25/lb., but prices fluctuate with the market. Natural smoked kippered salmon is another favorite. Call first to find out what's in stock.

Checks

Beverages

Pop, Fruit Juices & Coffee

To save money on soft beverages, stock up when they go on sale at local supermarkets or drugstores. Refer to Food Service Warehouses and Warehouse Buying Clubs when you're buying in quantity for parties and fund-raising events.

BARGREEN COFFEE

Everett: 2821 Rucker ☎ 252-3161
Hours: Mon-Fri 8-5

The Bargreen family has been in the coffee-making business since 1898. Beans are roasted right on the premises, so you know they're fresh. Restaurants account for the majority of their business, but the public can take advantage of outstanding prices. Best sellers to the industry are Hotel Blend and Mt. Baker. Espresso and gourmet blends are available for more sophisticated tastes. Coffee can be purchased pre-packaged or by the pound (whole or ground).

Checks

CASCADE COFFEE, INC. **NEW LISTING**

Renton: 234 S.W. 16th ☎ 575-1243
Hours: Mon-Fri 8-4:30

Cascade services offices and specializes in ground or roasted gourmet blends. They also carry herbal and decaf teas. Coffee sold in portion packs costs $20 to $40 per case. Tea is sold by the box. Cocoa, soups and juices are also available. Call for a product list.

Cash only

COFFEE BREAK SERVICE CO. **NEW LISTING**

Seattle: 5401 4th Ave. S. ☎ 762-2611 *Georgetown*
Hours: Mon-Fri 8-4:30

Another supplier to businesses, Coffee Break's products are packaged in separate packets and sold by the box or case. Inventory includes all major brands of ground coffee, as well as decaf and gourmet blends. One packet makes 12 six-ounce servings. For tea drinkers, they offer *Lipton, Bigelow and Stash*. *Treetop* apple juice in cases of 48 six-ounce cans costs around $20. They also sell soups, cocoa and paper products.

Cash only

Food, Beverages

THE CIDER SHED
Snohomish: 17902 Interurban ☎ 668-5888
Hours: Mon-Sun 8-6

Look for this popular label in grocery and health food stores. If you're in Snohomish, take time to visit their "backyard factory" and stock up on freshly made cider at prices below retail. During the warm months, the Cider Shed conducts tours for schools and organizations.

Checks

COLD MOUNTAIN JUICE CO.
Seattle: 2311 N. 45th St. ☎ 632-0446 *Wallingford*
Hours: Mon-Fri 8:30-7, weekends during summer months

Cold Mountain fruit and vegetable juices show up on the shelves of Larry's Market and Puget Sound Consumer's Co-op. Buy factory-direct and save 20% or more. Orange and carrot juice are their best sellers, but they also stock apple, strawberry, papaya and grapefruit juices, plus tropical mixtures. Sizes vary from one-half pint to one gallon. For health food practitioners, fresh wheat grass juice is available by the glass. In summertime, the cooler is stocked with fresh-squeezed lemonade. Since fresh juice only lasts 3 to 5 days, buy no more than you can consume or share with friends.

Cash only

WAX ORCHARDS
Vashon Island: 131st S.W. & S.W. 232nd ☎ 463-9735
Hours: Mon-Fri 8-4:30, Sat 10-4

Visit the farm where Wax Orchard's products are made and pay less than retail stores prices. A half-gallon of thirst-quenching apple cider goes for $2.25. Blends like apple-raspberry cost a bit more. Other products you might like to sample include syrups, fancy preserves, butter and chutney. Their conserves make great toppings for ice cream or waffles. Products contain no sugar or additives, and they taste "just like Grandma used to make."

Checks, Credit cards

Wine, Beer & Spirits

Grocery stores and specialty beverage houses offer the best selections of beer and wine, and the Washington State Liquor Stores, Costco and Price Savers offer the best prices. Most merchants give a 10% to 15% discount on cases. Look for coupons at the Liquor Store and in the beer or wine departments of supermarkets.

BEVERAGE HOUSE **NEW LISTING**
Des Moines: 21411 Pacific Highway S. ☎ 824-6031
Hours: Mon-Thurs 10-10, Fri & Sat 10-11, Sun 10-9

Prices are lower on beer, wine and pop because the owner takes advantage of sales offered by distributors and passes the savings on to his customers. Although *Budweiser* is the #1 selling beer, the selection of imports is impressive. Discounted 6-packs can be mixed or matched.

continued >

Food, Beverages

Buying by the half case saves you money, and full cases are even cheaper. Washington State wines are featured in a special section, but you'll also find a limited selection of California and premium wines. Watch for monthly specials.

Checks

THE BEVERAGE HOUSE, LAKESHORE MINUTE MART & PETE'S SUPERMARKET
NEW LISTING

Bothell: The Beverage House, 22627 Hwy. 527 ☎ 481-3319 *Canyon Park Shopping Ctr.*
Seattle: Lakeshore Minute Mart, 4036 E. Madison ☎ 325-2150 *Madison Park*
Seattle: Pete's Supermarket, 58 E. Lynn ☎ 322-2660 *Lake Union*
Hours: Daily 7-9:30

These three stores are owned by George Kingen, who has carved out a niche in the beverage market by consistently beating supermarket prices. All beer, soft drinks and wines are discounted 15%, and the large selection keeps customers coming back. Sparkling wines and champagnes average $7 to $10 a bottle.

Checks, Credit cards

McCARTHY & SCHIERING WINE MERCHANTS

Seattle: 6500 Ravenna Ave. N.E. ☎ 524-0999 *Ravenna*
Hours: Mon-Fri 10-7, Sat 10-6

McCarthy & Schiering has a reputation for being progressive in their selection of wines and aggressive in their marketing. Beer and wine are competitively priced, but the big savings come when you join their Vintage Select program for $50 per year, which allows you to purchase any bottle or case of wine at 17% off retail. Other benefits include a monthly newsletter, special dinners and wine tasting parties. For $100 you can become a life-time member. The shop will special-order rare wines, deliver large orders free and quote prices over the phone.

Checks, Credit cards

MONDO'S WORLD

Seattle: 4223 Rainier Ave. S. ☎ 725-5433 *Rainier Valley*
Hours: Tues-Sat 12-6

For $20/year you can join The Academy of Wines and receive a monthly hot-sheet listing exceptional wine bargains, wine tasting events and dinners featuring specialty wines. In addition, you may order any of the 10,000 wines sold in the State of Washington at 10-15% off retail. Close-outs may run below wholesale.

Checks, Credit cards

QFC
NEW LISTING

Seattle: N.E. 45th St. & 25th Ave. N.E. ☎ 523-5160 *University Village*
Hours: Daily, 24 hours

continued >

Food, Beverages

Although most QFC's have a wine and beer department, the staff at this store works hard to compete with the nearby Safeway. A wine expert is on hand daily from 8-5, and you can find something for every budget and taste. Best buys are in the $5 to $7 price range for dry wines and Northwest labels. Check out posted specials and read QFC's weekly newspaper ads to keep up with the ever-changing array of sale items.

Checks

SAFEWAY — NEW LISTING
Seattle: 3020 N.E. 45th St. ☎ 522-7821 *U-District*
Hours: Daily, 24 hours

Out of the 3,000 wines they normally stock, you'll always find 100 to 200 labels on sale. (Only Costco, Price Savers and the Liquor Store beat their prices.) By purchasing close-outs from distributors and buying in volume, they pick up sensational values that save you 30 to 40% off retail. If you have a large order that needs to be chilled before an event, Safeway will store it for you in their walk-in cooler. A wine specialist is on duty seven days a week from 8 a.m. to midnight.

Checks

WASHINGTON STATE LIQUOR STORES

Wine prices are lower at the Liquor Stores than at most retail outlets because the state buys in volume and has a lower overhead. Something different goes on sale each month and stays on sale until the end of the month or the inventory sells out. Sometimes you can find exceptional buys on award-winning labels. Every fall the Washington State Liquor Board sponsors "Washington Wine Month", a rare opportunity to stock up on your favorites or sample new labels at bargain prices. At any one time, a variety of name-brand liquors will be on sale and, less frequently, a selection of beer. Because it's illegal for the liquor stores to advertise, you have to shop regularly to catch the lowest prices. If you're buying hard liquor, be sure to check for in-store coupons.

Checks

THE WINE WAREHOUSE
Kirkland: 128 Park Lane ☎ 827-0859
Hours: Thurs-Sat, 11-6

The owner calls his business a "wine paradise" because inventory is mostly close-outs and slow-movers priced between $1 and $5. With over 10,000 bottles of foreign and domestic wines in stock, the emphasis is on California and Washington labels from well-known vineyards.

Checks

See area locator index for this section on page 222

Sweets & Treats

We can guarantee you'll save money at the outlets listed in this category, but we can't guarantee you'll keep your waistline! If you're contemplating a large purchase of your favorite candy, inquire about its shelf-life. Chocolate requires a cool and constant temperature, and the flavor will deteriorate after about two months. Wrapped hard candies are good for months, maybe even years. Soft caramels and taffy should be eaten sooner, but their shelf-life is longer than chocolate. Watch for candy sales in supermarkets and drugstores before and after Easter, Halloween, Valentines Day and Christmas. You know it's fresh, so why not treat yourself.

BAKER'S CANDY COMPANY
Seattle: 12534 Lake City Way ☎ 365-1888 *Lake City*
Hours: Daily 8-10

This family-owned business has been around since 1929. Their old-fashioned candies can be found in stores throughout the Northwest and at their Buddy Squirrel retail outlets. Boxed European truffles sell for about $18/lb., dipped chocolate goes for $6/lb., and all outlets stock "Buddy's Boo Boo's" (broken chocolates) for under $4/lb. The factory is located on the lower level of Baker's, a popular restaurant that the family operates in conjunction with the candy counter. Inquire about a volume discount.

Checks

BOEHM'S
Burien: 15207 6th S.W. ☎ 243-2027
Issaquah: 255 N.E. Gilman Blvd. ☎ 392-6652
Lynnwood: 18411-C Alderwood Mall Blvd. ☎ 774-5455
Seattle: 559 E. Ravenna Blvd. ☎ 523-9380 *Ravenna*
Hours: Burien, Mon-Sat 10-6; Issaquah, Daily 9-6; Lynnwood, Mon-Sat 10-9, Sun 12-6; Seattle, Mon-Fri 7-7, Sat 7-8

Boehm's opened its first candy kitchen in 1942 and has since become nationally known for quality European chocolates. All stores sell imperfect and broken chocolates, but the best selection and lowest prices can be found at the factory in Issaquah. You can't miss the picturesque grounds as you drive past on I-90. Visitors can peek through the window at the factory and watch the candy being made. All candies are fresh and hand dipped. Nine flavors of fruit and liqueur truffles, which sell for $25 to $35/lb. in most stores, are a real bargain at $20/lb. Filled chocolates that didn't pass inspection and chunks of broken chocolate (white, dark and light) sell for $5.75/lb.

Checks, Credit cards

Food, Sweets & Treats

BROWN AND HALEY
Tacoma: 110 E. 26th A St. (Seconds outlet) ☎ 593-3067
1940 E. 11th St. (Factory) ☎ 593-3000
Hours: Mon-Fri 9:30-6, Sat & Sun 10-6

Visit the seconds outlet to buy *Almond Roca, Mountain Bars* and filled chocolates. Who cares if the shape isn't quite right? You'll even find first-quality products when the factory makes too much of a good thing. The day we visited, a 3-lb. box of chocolates was only $6.99. Stop in the summer for raspberry yogurt bars. The factory is open three weeks before Easter and Christmas to sell overstock on novelty items, basics, and seconds. What a great resource for organizations that sponsor holiday events! There's a mailing list for preferred customers.

Checks, Credit cards

DILETTANTE CHOCOLATE, INC.
Seattle: 2300 E. Cherry ☎ 328-1530 *Capitol Hill*
Hours: Mon-Thurs 8-4, Fri 8-6

Satisfy that craving for gourmet chocolate by visiting the seconds counter at one of the country's leading candy factories. Everything is 50% off retail due to slight imperfections in color or shape. Purchase chocolates filled with nuts or cream by the piece, pound, or box. Novelty items are sometimes available. Yummy chocolate sauces show up frequently— a real treat on ice cream or for fondue dipping. No gift boxes.

Checks, Credit cards

HARLAN-FAIRBANKS CO.
Lynnwood: 12420 Evergreen Dr. ☎ 355-3143
Hours: Mon-Fri 8:30-5

Theaters and concessions shop here for all those goodies you know you shouldn't eat and can't resist. No minimum purchase, but you must buy in specified amounts. Pretzels come by the case, popcorn by the pound, slush puppies and sno-cone syrups by the gallon. Carmel Corn, hot dogs and cotton candy supplies are other favorites on their product list, which they'll send upon request.

Checks

HYDE'S NORTHWEST CANDY, INC.
Seattle: 1916 E. Mercer ☎ 322-5743 *Capitol Hill*
Hours: Mon-Fri 9-4

This factory outlet gives you a good deal on "mistakes" as well as regular merchandise. A 1-lb. bag of imperfect chocolates goes for $3. Prices on divinity, fudge, cashew or peanut clusters, and hard candy (malt, barley, honey and molasses) run slightly above wholesale. Hyde's is the only candy company in the area that makes candy canes; a case of 144 sells for around $15.

continued >

Food, Sweets & Treats

For health food stores, they make candy canes and mints with honey and molasses instead of white sugar, plus carob, caffeine-free chocolate and yogurt bars, which must be purchased by the box. Enter through the warehouse office on the north side of Mercer off 19th.

Checks

JOHNSON CANDY CO.

Tacoma: 924 S. K ☎ 272-8504
Hours: Mon-Sat 10-6

For over a half-century Johnson Candy Company has specialized in ice mints, which are popular treats at weddings, showers, and anniversaries. One of their newest products is an ice cream bar similar to a *Dove Bar* at half the price. You can always pick up a 1-lb. bag of imperfect chocolates or creams for around $4.50. Watch for advertised specials on peanut clusters and fudge.

Checks, Credit cards

NORTHWEST VENDING SUPPLY

Seattle: 5609 Rainier S. ☎ 725-4361 *Rainier Valley*
Hours: Mon-Fri 9-5

Northwest supplies gumballs, roasted nuts and candies for those vending machines that kids love. You can even buy capsules with toys inside. Pay about $2/lb. or buy a 5-lb. bag and save even more. Call first so they can to pack your order.

Checks

ROGER'S CANDY COMPANY

Tukwila: 14040 Interurban S. ☎ 433-0133
Hours: Mon-Fri 9-5, Sat 11-4

Satisfy your sweet tooth by shopping at this factory outlet. Seconds sell for about half the price of perfect filled chocolates, and you can buy them by the piece. Peanut brittle, taffy, almond bark, fudge and divinity are always available. Sometimes you'll find overstock in perfect condition. Prices and selection will vary, but savings are guaranteed. Since 1906 Roger's has been making fine candies sold in Hazel's Candy stores and under private labels.

Checks, Credit cards

SUTLIFF'S CANDY COMPANY

Seattle: 353 N.W. 41st St. ☎ 784-5212 *Freemont*
Hours: Mon-Fri 6:30-4:30

Sutliff's makes personalized after-dinner mints for hotels and restaurants. One-inch chocolate squares layered with a creamy filling are wrapped in gold foil. When the name or logo printed on the foil doesn't come out quite right or the wrapping doesn't pass inspection, the end results are sold as "miswraps" or "misprints." A 1-lb. bag can be yours for around $4; broken mints are reduced even more. Customized mints can be ordered for weddings or anniversaries.

Checks

Food, Ethnic

TOTEM FOOD PRODUCTS, INC.
Kent: 6203 S. 194th ☎ 872-9200
By appointment only

Totem is a wholesale distributor of snack foods and sandwiches sold in schools, bars and convenience stores. Minimum order is $25, which must be placed at least one day ahead. If you need sandwiches for a crowd, purchasing them here saves time, as well as about 40% off the deli price. Selection includes burritos and submarines. Most sandwiches will keep 10-14 days in the refrigerator. Totem also sells nuts and chips in 5 to 20-lb. bags. Savings on snack items vary, but check out these products for school lunches.

Checks

Ethnic Foods

ABCO PIZZA SUPPLY CO.
Lynnwood: 17830 Hwy. 99 ☎ 743-6880
Hours: Mon-Fri 7-4:30

If you're addicted to pizza, this is the place! ABCO sells the makings for Italian goodies to pizza parlors, stores and restaurants. There is no minimum, but cheeses and meats must be purchased in bags or boxes. Pizza sauce, sliced olives, mushrooms, green peppers and tomatoes are sold by the can or case. Ready-made crusts, pizza cooking equipment and paper goods are also in stock. If you are buying for a fundraiser or a party, ABCO will give you a breakdown on amounts and ingredients for various types of pizza, plus the approximate cost. Other products include fresh or frozen pasta dishes, cookies in 2-gal. tins and 22 flavors of frozen yogurt by the case or tub. Call for a price list.

Checks

GOLDEN PHEASANT NOODLE CO.
Seattle: 206 5th S. ☎ 623-3296 *International District*
Hours: Mon-Fri 8:30-5

This tiny factory is not geared for walk-in trade, so we suggest you call first and place as large an order as possible to make it worth their while. Wonton skins and steamed noodles sell in up to 10-lb. packages for about $1.50/lb. Fortune cookies go for the same price. "Unfortunates" (factory rejects) are even less.

Cash only

See area locator index for this section on page 222

HOVEN FOOD CO.

Seattle: 512 S. King ☎ 340-0774 *International District*
Hours: Mon-Sat 10-6, Sun 11-5

In most grocery stores, tofu sells for approximately 75¢/packet. Ten or more pieces cost 65¢ apiece at Hoven or buy 20 pieces for $11. They make it fresh four days a week. Call a day in advance. Hoven gives away by-products from the soybean manufacturing process, which you can use for fertilizer.

Checks

IKEDA AND COMPANY

Seattle: 6749 E. Marginal Way ☎ 762-4100 *International District*
Hours: Mon-Fri 9-6

This is where grocery stores and restaurants stock up on Oriental staples, so you'll be taking home sugar, flour and cornstarch in 25-lb. sacks, soy sauce in 5-gallon containers, and packaged dry goods by the carton. Savings will vary. An 80-lb. sack of California long grain white rice costs about $18, which is a terrific bargain if you have a hand truck or strong back to pack it in the house. Phone in orders ahead of time.

Checks

LA MEXICANA

Seattle: 10020 14th Ave. S.W. ☎ 763-1488 *White Center*
Hours: Mon-Fri 9-5

Believe it or not, Seattle has its own tortilla factory! Choose from a dozen varieties of flour or corn tortillas. Pay only $1 for 3 dozen corn tortillas, a price that has remained constant for 18 years. Buy by the case and save even more. Freeze the excess for future consumption. Masa dough for making tamales should be ordered a day in advance. La Mexicana also carries a complete line of Mexican food products which can be purchased by the can or case. If you're planning a fiesta, you can buy piñatas, Mexican cookies and candy. Call ahead to find out what's in stock or have them send you a product list.

Checks

MERLINO'S FINE FOODS

Seattle: 5605 Martin Luther King Way S. ☎ 723-4700 *Rainier Valley*
Hours: Mon-Fri 10-4

Restaurants and delicatessens buy imported Italian cheeses, pastas, meats, tomato products and olive oil from this wholesaler. *Paradiso* is one of the well-known brands they carry. Products must be purchased by the case or in large cans. Pastas are sold in 5 to 20-lb. cartons and cheeses and salamis by the loaf. Try their frozen pasta entrees, for a quick and easy meal. At Christmas time, they even stock Italian candy!

Checks

72 Food, Ethnic

THE MEXICAN GROCERY
Seattle: 1914 Pike Place Market ☎ 441-1147 *Downtown*
Hours: Mon-Sat 9-5

Visit the retail outlet for the La Mexicana tortilla factory and buy Mexican food products for less than supermarket prices. Tortillas are delivered fresh three times a week, and prices are still a bargain at $2/lb. The store stocks a good selection of bottled and canned products and makes their own salsa. Cheese and tamales are shipped up from California.

Checks

PACIFIC FOOD IMPORTERS
Seattle: 1001 6th Ave. S. ☎ 682-2022 *South of Kingdome*
Hours: Tues-Fri 9-5:30, Sat. 10-2

Asian, Middle Eastern, and Mediterranean foods are the specialty at this small outlet for a wholesale restaurant supply warehouse. Customers come from ethnic communities all over the state to buy staples, as well as such exotic items as dried eggplant or Malaysian squid in milk. A dozen varieties of olive oil are sold by the gallon, tomato paste comes in 28 oz. cans, and spices and grains are sold by the pound out of cardboard drums. Beans come in 20 different varieties from Egyptian foul to Italian fava. Salami, cheeses and pastas are best selling items. Frozen prepared pasta dishes are a real treat. Volume packaging keeps prices way below retail.

Checks

PAMBIHIRA ORIENTAL FOOD MART
Seattle: 6026 Martin Luther King Way ☎ 722-2354 *Ranier Valley*
Hours: Mon-Sat 10-8, Sun 11-6

Pambihira offers good prices and a great selection of Chinese, Filipino and Asian food products. If you buy in quantity, inquire about wholesale prices.

Checks

TSUE CHONG CO.
Seattle: 801 S. King ☎ 623-0801 *International District*
Hours: Mon-Fri 9-5:30

Visit the largest Chinese noodle and fortune cookie factory in the Northwest to buy products manufactured under the *Rose Brand label*. Won ton pi (flat square dough wrappers), egg roll wrappers and rice noodles are made fresh daily. A 2-lb. package of noodles costs $2 and makes an incredible amount! Luckily, noodles and wrappers freeze well. A 1-lb. bag of fortune cookies sells for $2. Pay $5 for a 5-pound bag of unfortunates. Customized fortune cookies can be special-ordered with your own message inside. There's a 5-lb. minimum per message, but what a great idea for a business promotion!

Checks

Natural Foods & Health Products

Special growing and handling processes make natural foods more expensive than food produced the conventional way. Be sure to comparison shop the bulk items sold by the gram, ounce, or pound from bins and barrels. One outlet may have especially good grain prices while another beats everyone else's price on seeds. Don't forget to check out the health food products in local supermarkets. Fred Meyer stores with grocery departments have become very aggressive in this market.

Joining Central Co-op or Puget Consumers Co-op is another way to ensure savings, and you can participate in the running of the store. Each store will gladly explain its policies over the phone or send you a brochure. Non-members are welcome to shop but must pay 13% to 15% above the posted price. If you are visiting for the first time, the store will waive the non-member markup. In a spirit of cooperation, the two co-ops offer members a coupon book that lists over 100 businesses and services that offer patrons a discount.

CENTRAL CO-OP

Seattle: 1835 12th Ave. ☎ 329-1545 *Capitol Hill*
Hours: Daily 9-9

The focus at this natural foods grocery store is on organically grown fresh produce. Members have voted to eliminate wine, meat and products containing white sugar from the shelves. You'll find a full range of health foods, including soy, macrobiotics and fresh dairy products, plus a good selection of herbs and spices. Vitamins and body care products round out the inventory. Senior citizens can join for a one-time $5 fee.

Checks

ENER-G FOODS

Seattle: 5960 1st Ave. S. ☎ 767-6660 *Georgetown*
Hours: Mon-Fri 8:30-5

Ener-G is a manufacturer of foods made especially for people who cannot eat wheat, gluten, eggs or milk products due to food allergies, celia-sprue disease or renal failure. Most products are packaged baking mixes made from rice, corn, potatoes, tapioca flour, barley or oats. They also offer ready-made pastas, cereals, pizza shells, bakery goods, soup mixes and seven varieties of bread. Many of their products are sold in health food stores nationwide. Buying direct from the warehouse will save you anywhere from 20% to 30%, and there is no minimum. Call for a product list and place your order in advance. Shipping is available for a minimal fee. As a special service, the company will compile a list of recipes to meet individual dietary requirements. Enter through the Sam Wylde office.

Checks, Credit cards

74 Food, Natural Foods & Health Products

THE FOOD CUPBOARD
Seattle: 9414 Roosevelt Way N.E. ☎ 524-6800 *Northgate*
Hours: Tues-Fri 2-6, Sat 9-3 or by appointment

The Food Cupboard carries a wide assortment of bulk and dehydrated food products, which are not always easy to find in their natural state. Bulk wheat is a big seller for those who grind their own flour. Dry milk can be purchased in 50-lb. bags.

Backpackers, campers and boaters shop here because the store has one of the largest selections of dehydrated foods in the state. They also stock a variety of kitchen equipment— food processors, juicers, dehydrators and flour milling apparatus.

Checks

GREEN EARTH NUTRITION   NEW LISTING
Renton: 125 Airport Way ☎ 226-7757
Hours: Mon-Fri 9:45-6:30, Sat. 9:45-6:00

This spacious store offers discounted prices, a huge selection of health food items, and a knowledgeable service-oriented staff. Vitamin supplements average 5% to 15% below retail, and you'll find everyday low prices on vegetables, oils, soups and juices, plus lots of bulk items. Raw milk and acidophilus are always available. Green Earth makes a habit of passing good buys on to customers, but since their low overhead limits advertising, it's best to visit or call frequently to find out about the latest specials.

Checks, Credit cards

MANNA MILLS, INC.
Mountlake Terrace: 21705 66th W. ☎ 775-3479
Hours: Mon-Fri 10-8, Sat & Sun 10-5

Savings at this large natural food warehouse start at 20% below high-end retail outlets. And if you're willing to buy $100 worth of merchandise, you qualify for wholesale prices, which means another 25% discount. Look for terrific buys on bulk grain products because they purchase by the truckload. Wholewheat flour was 29¢/lb. the last time we checked, and oat bran was cheaper here than anywhere else. Bakeries use Manna Mills's freshly ground flour, which is milled on the premises. Dried fruits are unsulfered. Small produce and organic meat departments service basic needs. You'll also find a full line of natural beauty products.

Checks

See area locator index for this section on page 223

Food, Natural Foods & Health Products

MARKET SPICE
Federal Way: 32040 23rd S. ☎ 839-0922
Seattle: 85-A Pike Place Market ☎ 622-6340 *Downtown*
I-5 & N.E. Northgate Way ☎ 364-5665 *Northgate Mall*
Tacoma: 616 Tacoma Mall ☎ 474-7524
Hours: Generally, Mon-Sat 10-6, Sun 12-5

Large glass jars filled with herbs and spices line the shelves of these establishments. Everything is sold in bulk, so prices are 20% to 30% below what you would pay in a grocery store. Selection varies from familiar cooking condiments to exotic spices. Over 25 salt-free seasonings to flavor soups, beef or fish are available, along with 45 varieties of coffee, ranging from inexpensive to gourmet blends.

Checks, Credit cards

NATURAL FOOD SUPPLEMENTS
Kirkland: 10790 N.E. 68th ☎ 822-2086
Lynnwood: 3815 196th St. S.W. ☎ 775-5924 *Alderwood Village*
Seattle: 4336 Roosevelt Way N.E. ☎ 547-0316 *U-District*
West Seattle: 5633 California Ave. S.W. ☎ 938-4222
Hours: Generally, Mon-Fri 10-9, Sat 10-6, Sun 12-5

Body builders and athletes shop here because vitamins and food supplements are priced 15% to 20% below retail every day. They carry over 70 product lines, including such nationally known brands as *Schiff, Twinlab, Kal. Richlife. Nature's Plus and American Health.* Simple-cell foods like brewer's yeast, lecithin and protein powder are also stocked. Credit cards are accepted on mail orders only. There's no shipping charge if you buy 10 or more items.

Checks

NUTRA SOURCE — NEW LISTING
Seattle: 4005 6th Ave S. ☎ 467-7190 *South of Kingdome*
Hours: Mon-Fri 8:30-5

If you are willing to spend $100 or more, you can buy natural food and health products direct from this warehouse distributor at 15% above wholesale. Call and they'll send you a 1" thick catalog that outlines their ordering policies and lists a huge selection of name-brand products sold in health food stores all over the country. Prices go down even more with larger orders. Free delivery if you purchase $350 worth of merchandise. Just remember, most items are sold by the case or carton.

Business checks, Cashiers checks, or Money orders only

76 Food, Natural Foods & Health Products

PUGET CONSUMERS CO-OP
Kirkland: 10718 N.E. 68th ☎ 828-4621
Seattle: 6504 20th Ave. N.E. ☎ 525-1450 *Ravenna*
6522 Fremont Ave. N. ☎ 789-7144 *Greenwood*
5041 Wilson Ave. S. ☎ 723-2720 *Seward Park*
6514 40th Ave. N.E. ☎ 526-7661 *Ravenna*
Hours: Seattle Mon-Sat 9-9, Sun 10-7, Kirkland Daily 8-10

Started in 1960 as a buying club, the co-op now boasts 25,000 members, making it the largest food co-op in the country. Special services include cooking demonstrations, classes and a monthly newspaper. You can even grind your own peanut butter on the premises.

Savings add up fast on the terrific selection of bulk items. Watch for markdowns on locally grown fruits and vegetables, many of which are organic. Meat products contain no antibiotics, additives or hormones. Fish is delivered fresh daily. Natural dairy products and baked goods are also available, along with cosmetics, kitchen wares, gift items and lots of literature on how to stay healthy. Senior citizens (65 and older) pay a $2 one-time-only membership fee.

Checks, Credit cards

SILVER BOW HONEY COMPANY
Snohomish: 1220 13th ☎ 568-2191
Hours: Mon-Fri 8-5, Sat (April thru August) 9-3

A trip to this fascinating honey "factory" will net you savings on products sold all over the Northwest in grocery stores and health food outlets. Purchase honey by the quart, gallon or barrel. Bring your own container and save even more. (A gallon bucket holds 12-lbs.) Buy five gallons and the price hits rock bottom. Their sample table is an added attraction: you can taste exotic floral honeys and discover special discounts on close-out items.

Checks, Credit cards

Personal Care

Drugs & Sundries

It's easy to save 30% to 50% on sundries because so many name-brand products go on sale on a regular basis, and big chains offer private-label goods that are cheaper than name-brands. Diligent shoppers compare prices by reading the colorful Sunday sale supplements and using coupon books put out by drugstore chains and mass merchandisers. Something different gets marked down every week, so it's best to stock up when you see a bargain rather than wait until you run out. Maximize your savings by combining a coupon clipped off a box or out of a magazine with a store coupon or in-store sale.

On name-brand prescription drugs, a 15% savings is the most you can expect, even at discount pharmacies. Generic prescription drugs and over-the-counter medicines can undercut name-brands 30% to 50% because you're not paying for the high cost of research, development and advertising. FDA guidelines require that ingredients must be identical if a generic is to be substituted for a name-brand prescription drug. To keep costs down, insurance companies, government agencies and welfare programs now require generics whenever possible.

Some doctors, out of habit, prescribe name-brands instead of generics, so it pays to ask if there is a substitute, keeping in mind that generics are not available or feasible for all prescriptions. Don't be afraid to ask your pharmacist if there is a less expensive drug on the market that could replace the one prescribed. He or she will call your doctor to get the change approved. Our survey revealed that prices on generic prescription drugs can vary as much as 30% from one pharmacy to another.

It's easy to comparison shop prescription drugs because state law requires that pharmacies quote prices over the phone. Have the name, dosage and quantity available. While one store may offer a rock-bottom price on a name-brand, another store may beat their price on a generic. It pays to shop around! If you're on maintenance drugs, purchase as large a quantity as possible since the fee you pay the pharmacists for preparing your prescription is the same whether you buy 30 pills or 100. Most chains and independent drug stores give a 10% discount to seniors.

Over-the-counter generics are usually stocked next to name-brands, so it's easy to compare prices and ingredients on aspirin, cough syrups, cold remedies, etc.

78 Personal Care, Drugs & Sundries

APEX WHOLESALE
Seattle: 521-A 1st Ave N. ☎ 285-2639 *Queen Anne*
Hours: Mon-Fri 8-3

If you have a tax number, you can buy in volume and save 30% to 40% on sundries, toiletries and non-prescription drugs. This wholesaler's $100 minimum may sound steep, but by the time you add up the cost of a year's supply of shampoo, toothpaste, film and batteries, the savings mount.

Use in-store catalogs to familiarize yourself with the inventory and pricing structure. Some items must be purchased in the carton or by the dozen. Located in an alley behind Dick's Drive-In, parallel to Queen Anne Blvd.

Checks

DRUG EMPORIUM
Everett: 7725 Evergreen Way ☎ 348-0900
Federal Way: 2030 S. 314th ☎ 946-3777
Kent: 25406 104th Ave. S.E. ☎ 850-0696
Kirkland: 12515 116th N.E. ☎ 820-0440 *Totem Lake W.*
Lynnwood: 3815 196th S.W. ☎ 771-5944
Seattle: 818 N.E. Northgate Way ☎ 771-5944 *Northgate Village*
Silverdale: 2779 N.W. Myhre Rd. ☎ 692-1120
Tacoma: 5401 6th Ave. ☎ 752-1400
           7901 S. Hosmer ☎ 472-7485
Tukwila: 17348 Southcenter Pkwy. ☎ 575-3103 *Parkway Plaza*
Hours: Mon-Fri 9:30-10, Sat 9:30-8, Sun 9:30-6

The family budget got a break when this big national discount chain came to town. Prices on prescription drugs are competitive with other area discounters. They offer low prices every day on name-brands, and you'll be amazed at the selection of hair care products, vitamins, cleaning supplies, skin creams, baby needs and over-the-counter drugs. You'll find a big inventory of trial sizes, which are great for travel or testing a product. Prices start at 35% off on every popular line of cosmetics and men's fragrances. Gift wrap, greeting cards, ribbon and stationary are discounted 40%. Savings will vary week-to-week on the same item, so it pays to shop often and compare competitors' advertised sales.

Checks, Credit cards

THE MEDICINE MAN
Seattle: 1752 N.W. Market ☎ 789-6804 *Ballard*
           323 N.W. 85th ☎ 789-0800 *Greenwood*
Hours: Mon-Fri 9:30-6, Sat 9:30-2

These small drugstores advertise that they'll undersell the biggies on prescription and over-the-counter medications. We're happy to say that their price quotes on generic and name-brand prescriptions did indeed beat the big chains we called. Other aggressive marketing tactics include a $5 discount on all prescriptions transferred from another pharmacy with the first refill and free mailing anywhere in the world for AARP members.

continued >

Personal Care, Drugs & Sundries 79

Diet pet food is a specialty. Over-the-counter drugs and vitamins are sold at everyday low prices, and they have a large selection of reading glasses and eye products.

Checks, Credit cards

THE RUBBER TREE
Seattle: 4426 Burke Ave. N. ☎ 633-4750 *Wallingford*
Hours: Mon-Fri 11-8, Sat 11-7

Set up by the local chapter of Zero Population Growth, this store sells non-prescription contraceptives at 10% to 40% less than retail. Call or write for one of their brochures. At the store, you'll find free information on all forms of contraception, sexually transmitted diseases, optional parenthood and population issues. The Rubber Tree is the only store of its kind in the country. They've been advocating safe sex since 1975.

Checks

Here is a list of pharmacies that quoted us the lowest prices on prescription drugs:

COSTCO WHOLESALE PHARMACY
Federal Way: 35100 Enchanted Pkwy. S. ☎ 874-4431
Kirkland: 6829 120th Ave. N.E. ☎ 822-0414
Lynnwood: 19105 Hwy. 99 ☎ 774-4210
Seattle: 4401 4th Ave. S. ☎ 682-6244 *South of Kingdome*
Silverdale: 1000 Mickelberry Rd. ☎ 698-1155
Hours: Mon-Fri 11-7, Sat 10-6

COST LESS
Tacoma: 5431 Pacific Ave. ☎ 474-9493
Hours: Mon-Fri 9-6, Sat 9:30-5

COST PLUS RX
Statewide toll-free ☎ 800/ 444-5079
Burien: 17644 1st Ave. S. ☎ 244-4106
Tacoma: 204 N. I St. ☎ 572-6473
　　　　　7304 Lakewood Dr. W. ☎ 473-7246
Hours: Generally, Mon-Fri 9-6, Sat 9-3

Prescriptions mailed statewide for 50¢; no shipping charge for seniors.

KEY DISCOUNT DRUGS
Kent: 23422 Pacific Hwy. S. ☎ 878-3900
Hours: Mon-Fri 9-7, Sat 10-4

LINCOLN SAVE-RITE PHARMACY
Tacoma: 701 S. 38th ☎ 475-6212
Hours: Mon-Fri 9:30-6:30, Sat 9:30-4

SAV-ON DRUGS
Tacoma: 1811 S. K St. ☎ 383-1765
Hours: Mon-Fri 9-6, Sat 9-4

Cosmetics & Grooming Products

Beauty supply stores are excellent places to shop if you want to realize the best value for your money on hair care supplies and equipment, nail and skin products and cosmetics. While the public is welcome at most of these outlets, some items can only be sold to licensed beauticians because they require special salon procedures that are not fully explained on the package. Do not buy anything unless you know how to use it or the staff is willing to provide detailed instructions. Consider visiting a beauty school for a professional application before trying a new product yourself.

Prices aren't necessarily lower on beauty supply merchandise, but the quality is often better because products manufactured especially for professional salons are subject to industry standards. More time and money is spent on ingredients than on expensive advertising. Salon formula shampoos, conditioners, permanents, hair dyes, rinses, mousses and sprays are more concentrated, PH balanced and better for your hair. Although you won't recognize the labels, some of the best buys are on generic knock-offs of famous brands and large-size containers not usually available in retail stores. Brushes, combs, scissors, rollers, curling irons and blow dryers are made for professional use, so you know they're going to last. Try the makeup and skin care products if you aren't satisfied with what's available in drugstores.

All beauty supply shops will stock certain best-selling lines, but inventory varies from store to store. Some will have a wider variety of makeup or nail supplies, while others may focus on implements. Fancy hair ornaments are always good buys at these stores. Also look for items not normally available at cosmetic counters, like lash and brow tint, ethnic products and formulas made especially for men. Don't be afraid to ask questions since the stores are staffed by trained professionals.

EVERETT BEAUTY SUPPLY
Everett: 7207 Evergreen Way, Suite H ☎ 347-5866
Hours: Mon-Fri 9-5, Thurs 9-9, Sat 10-5

Professional beauticians buy their nail, skin and hair products at this outlet. The general public is welcome to shop in a special area that has been set aside for non-professionals and contains products not requiring a license to purchase.

Checks, Credit cards

HAIR PERFORMERS
Tukwila: 16949 Southcenter Pkwy. ☎ 575-6446
Hours: Mon-Fri 10-9, Sat 10-6

Save 15% to 50% on major name-brand hair products used only in beauty salons. Save time by calling for a catalog, ordering by phone, and having the products shipped to your home.

Checks, Credit cards

Personal Care, Cosmetics & Grooming Products 81

K'S BEAUTY SUPPLY & SALON
Everett: 1001 N. Broadway, Suite A-7 ☎ 258-2866
Hours: Mon-Fri 10-6, Sat 10-6

This small shop carries makeup, hair care products and small equipment. Over-the-counter prices to the public are good, especially on *Nexus* products.

Checks, Credit cards

KARIN'S BEAUTY SUPPLY
15 Locations. Check yellow pages
Hours: Generally, Mon-Sat 10-6, Sun 12-5

Since most of the business at Karin's is wholesale to the trade, you can purchase anything here you'd find in a full service beauty salon, including equipment and fixtures. Best selling products are shampoos, perms and conditioners by *Nexus, Paul Mitchell, KMs, Focus 21 and Joico*, plus makeup by *Janelle, La Femme and CiCi*. Prices are competitive with other beauty supply outlets and once a month "something old and something new" goes on sale. The selection is amazing, and the newest products on the market pop up here first.

Checks, Credit cards

LIPPS BEAUTY SUPPLY
Bellevue: 1645 140th N.E. ☎ 747-0994 *Evergreen Village*
Hours: Mon-Fri 10-6, Thurs until 7:30, Sat 10-4:30

This store carries an outstanding selection of professional hair care products, cosmetics and nail supplies. Save by purchasing in quantities— half-dozen allotments or gallon jugs, which must be specially ordered. Samples are available for many of the cosmetic lines. You might want to test a popular brand called *La Femme*, which comes in myriad colors, or the store's exclusive label. *Redken* products are big sellers in the hair care department, and a multitude of fancy hair ornaments add the finishing touch.

Checks, Credit cards

MARQUIS BEAUTY PRODUCTS & SALON
Federal Way: 1706 S. 320th ☎ 839-5881 *Sea-Tac Village*
Hours: Mon-Fri 10-6, Sat 10-5

The most popular items at this beauty supply outlet are shampoos, hair color and permanents by *Paul Mitchell, Focus 21, Nexus*. *Anita of Denmark* is the top-selling cosmetic line. A complete selection of small equipment is also available.

Checks, Credit cards

NEW ATTITUDE BEAUTY SUPPLY & SALON   NEW LISTING
Kirkland: 12548 120th Ave. N.E. ☎ 821-4488
Hours: Mon-Fri 9-8, Sat 10-6, Sun 12-5

continued >

Personal Care, Cosmetics & Grooming Products

Prices on hair care products will be cheaper here than at beauty salons, and they carry twelve major lines. Shampoos and conditioners are best-sellers. Stock up on hair ornaments, makeup, and products for cutting and styling hair.

Checks, Credit cards

P.J.'S BEAUTY SUPPLY

Lynnwood: 18700 33rd Ave. W. ☎ 774-1999 *Alderwood Terrace*
Hours: Mon-Sat 9-9, Sun 12-6

P.J.'s stocks a little of everything in professional beauty supply lines for hair and nails. A set of 20 nail tips averages $20; $3 extra for the glue. Permanents, shampoos, tints, dryers, curling irons and brushes are plentiful.

Checks, Credit cards

PRESTIGE FRAGRANCE & COSMETICS   NEW LISTING

Tukwila: 17900 Southcenter Parkway ☎ 575-3991 *Pavilion Mall*
Hours: Mon-Fri 9:30-9:15, Sat 9-8, Sun 9-6

Prestige, one of the fastest growing off-price chains in the country, sells internationally known cosmetics, perfumes and skin care products at 25% to 60% off the normal retail price. Expensive lines such as *Charles of the Ritz, Christian Dior, Anne Klein, Lancome and Halston* are purchased from department store surpluses and stores going out of business, so the stock is always changing. Best buys are on the cosmetic kits, which give you a chance to sample a variety of products. Less expensive lines like *Revlon, Almay and Maybelline* are also carried. Beautifully packaged soap and perfume collections make wonderful gifts.

Checks, Credit Cards

VAAR-M BEAUTY SUPPLY & SALON

Redmond: 17212 Redmond Way N.E. ☎ 883-8889 *Bear Creek Village*
Hours: Mon-Fri 9-7, Sat 9-6, Sun 12-5

Prices are good on an array of beauty supplies here. Shop their weekly and monthly sales for the best buys or purchase *Volume Ex*, an economy line of hair care products. A 16-oz. bottle of shampoo costs only $4.95. Permanents are available for every type of hair. Hair cutting scissors range in price from $10 to $60. The store promotes a special line of conditioners and shampoos for swimmers and Redmond residents who build up minerals in their hair from drinking the local well water.

Checks, Credit cards

See area locator index for this section on page 223

Grooming Services

We've ferreted out several good sources to help you keep costs down on personal grooming services. In the past few years a number of local and national hair salon chains have entered the market, catering to the whole family and offering fast service and low prices. Their extended hours make it easier to get a hair cut, but if you're in a hurry, you should avoid weekends or make an appointment.

Instead of listing the addresses of the chains with multiple locations, we're going to give you an overview of their prices and services. Hours may vary, so we suggest you check the phone book for one near you and call for information. Higher-priced haircuts include a shampoo and blow dry. Permanents increase in price with the length of the hair and procedure used.

EEJAYS HAIRCUTTER & BEAUTY SUPPLY — NEW LISTING
Four locations. Check yellow pages
Hours: Generally, Mon-Fri 9-6, Sat 9-6, Sun 12-5

Eejay's bills itself as a budget salon for the entire family, and comparing prices, you'll find that they're definitely competitive with the big discount chains. Plus, they offer a complete line of professional hair, nail, and skin care products by leading manufacturers.

Checks, Credit cards

FANTASTIC SAM'S
Six locations. Check yellow pages
Hours: Generally, Mon-Fri 9-8, Sat 9-5, Sun 11-4

Adult haircut, $7.95 to $9.95; kid's haircut, $4.95 to $5.95; perms, $24.95 and up. Walk-in trade only.

Checks, Credit cards

GREAT HAIRCUTS — NEW LISTING
Redmond: 16795 Redmond Way ☎ 883-2970
Hours: Mon-Fri 10-7, Sat 9-5

Hair cuts here are competetively priced with the family-oriented discount chains. Adult haircuts are $10, while kids under 10 pay only $8. Make an appointment for a perm, which starts at $35.

Checks, Credit cards

HAIRCRAFTERS
Twenty locations. Check yellow pages
Hours: Generally, Mon, Wed, Fri 9-7, Tues & Thurs 9-9, Sat 8:30-5

Adult and kids haircut, $7.95 to $11.95; perms, $24.95 to $49.98. Walk-in trade only.

Checks

84 Personal Care, Grooming Services

HAIRMASTERS
Twenty-six locations. Check yellow pages
Hours: Generally, Mon-Fri 9-9, Sat 9-6, Sun 11-5

Adult haircut, $9.95 to $12.00; kid's haircut, $7.75 to $10; perms: $30 and up. Walk-in and appointments.

Checks, Credit cards

PRECISION HAIR CUTTERS, KING'S DEN & PRO-BEAUTY
Seven locations. Check yellow pages
Hours: Generally, Mon-Fri 9:30-9, Sat 9-6

Adult haircut, $8 to $10; kid's haircut, $6 (if under 6 years of age); perms, $35 to $45. Appointments preferred, will take walk-ins.

Checks, Credit cards

SUPER CUTS
Fifteen locations. Check yellow pages
Hours: Generally, Mon-Fri 9-9, Sat 9-7, Sun 11-5

Adult haircut, $9 to $13; kid's haircut, $6 (if under 12 years of age). No perms. Walk-in trade only.

Checks, Credit cards

Beauty Schools and Community Colleges are great resources for low-cost basic hair care and beauty services. Prices average about half what you would pay a licensed cosmetologist. All procedures are supervised by an instructor, and costs will vary depending on the level of the student. There are over a dozen beauty schools in the area. We've listed only a few. Check the yellow pages for a school near you, and when you visit, remember you're not only saving money, but also giving the students a chance to practice their craft. Here's the range of services and costs you may expect: haircuts, $4.50 to $8.50; perms, $15 to $27.50; manicures, $2.50 to $5; pedicures, $5.50 to 7.50; facials, $2.50 to $12.50; and nails: $15 to $20 per set.

ABC NAIL & SKIN COLLEGE — NEW LISTING
Bellevue: 14508 N.E. 20th ☎ 643-4283
Hours: Tues-Fri 10-8, Sat 10-6

This is your chance to try out beauty services normally beyond the family budget. While advanced students hone their skills, you can get a set of artificial nails for $25.95. Facials cost only $18, and European electrolysis is $10.95 for a 15 minute treatment. Investigate such luxuries as waxing, make-up applications, manicures and pedicures.

Checks, Credit cards

GENE JUAREZ ADVANCED TRAINING CENTER — NEW LISTING
Seattle: 1514 6th Ave. ☎ 622-6611 *Downtown*
Hours: Tues-Sat 10-4:45

continued >

Personal Care, Grooming Services

Treat yourself to a day of pampering at one of Seattle's leading beauty salons. Prices are going to be higher here than at Gene Juarez's Beauty School located near Northgate, but not as expensive as at one of his regular salons, which are among the top-rated in the country. All services at the training center are performed by licensed cosmetologists, many of whom are already employed in Gene Juarez salons. A haircut and styling runs $9 to $14. Permanents start at $35, which is half the regular price. Manicures are $8.50, pedicures (including a foot massage) are $18, and a full set of nails cost only $35.

Checks, Credit cards

Cosmetology departments at the following community colleges are open to the public:

EVERETT COMMUNITY COLLEGE
Everett: 1110 N. Broadway Ave. ☎ 259-7151
Hours: Mon-Fri 8:30-4

SEATTLE CENTRAL COMMUNITY COLLEGE
Seattle: 1500 Harvard ☎ 587-5477
Hours: Mon & Tues 11-4, Wed 12-7:30, Thurs & Fri 8-4

SHORELINE COMMUNITY COLLEGE
Seattle: 16010 Greenwood Ave. N. ☎ 546-4631
Hours: Mon-Fri 9:30-3

SOUTH SEATTLE COMMUNITY COLLEGE
Seattle: 6000 16th Ave. S.W. ☎ 764-5814
Hours: Mon-Fri 8:30-3

Home Building and Remodeling

Whether you're planning a large or small remodeling project, indoors or out, the best places to start comparison shopping are Ernst, Pay 'N Pak and Henry Bacon. You won't find them listed in our pages because they are so well-known and their advertisements keep you informed about prices and list the locations. Henry Bacon is geared to the trade since contractors make up a large part of their business. Lumber is stocked in quantity, as well as cedar packages for fencing or decking. Take advantage of free "do-it-yourself" demos. You'll also find plumbing fixtures, tools and kitchen cabinets made exclusively for the company.

Prices are low at Pay 'N Pak because they buy close-outs and imports, and they buy in volume. Visit any one of their 15 stores for good buys on water heaters, kitchen cabinets, housewares, tools, electrical supplies, and lighting and plumbing fixtures. Watch for big sales three or four times a year.

Building Materials, Tools & Hardware

In addition to the sources listed below, refer to our Mass Merchandisers section for liquidators and dealers who stock building supplies and tools. Fred Meyer superstores sometimes offer outstanding values. Pawn shops are another good source of tools.

Building Materials

BOEING SURPLUS

Kent: 20651 84th Ave. S. ☎ 773-9684
Hours: Tues-Fri 11-6, Sat 9-4

Customers come from out of state just to spend the day browsing through this incredible surplus outlet. A huge warehouse contains thousands of new and used items left over from the construction of airplanes and the running of Boeing's corporate offices. The outside yard overflows with cast-off building materials and scrap iron. A semi-truck unloads goods weekly, so inventory changes constantly.

Businesses shop for office furnishings, supplies and technical equipment. Manufacturers pick up steel drums, electrical equipment, motors, fasteners, cutting tools, sheet metal, aluminum, plastic and rubber components. Many of these products can be adapted to use for remodeling and shop projects. Free wood can be picked up 24 hours a day at the corner of 206th St. and 84th Avenue South. Lumber goes fast, so get there early. Even company vehicles are sold on the grounds. We're still trying to decide how to recycle airline seats!

Checks

Home Building and Remodeling, Building Materials

CAPTAIN SAM'S

Seattle: 410 2nd Ave. S. ☎ 624-1478 *Pioneer Square*
Hours: Mon-Fri 8-5, some Saturdays

Captain Sam's buys the salvage rights to businesses and private residences in Seattle. As long as you don't mind the mess, a thorough search will turn up old doors, windows, and hardware, plus plumbing and lighting fixtures, many of which are vintage. Nothing is marked—prices are negotiable.

Checks, Credit cards

CHINOOK DOOR

Tacoma: 1515 S. Tacoma Way ☎ 472-9614, 241-1832
Hours: Mon-Fri 8-4:30

Buy a prehung door direct from the factory and cut out the cost of a middleman. Scrap wood goes in a dumpster where people pick it up for kindling and gardening stakes.

Checks

THE DOOR STORE

Tacoma: 3110 Fuston Way ☎ 752-1900
Hours: Mon-Fri 8-5, Sat 9-4

Save on interior or exterior doors at this factory outlet, which boasts the largest selection of solid wood doors in the state. Seconds, which have cosmetic flaws, are the best value. Buy five or more first-quality doors and get a break on price. Pre-hanging service available.

Checks, Credit cards

GROW & SONS LUMBER   NEW LISTING

Everett: 11409 Hwy. 99 ☎ 355-9829
Hours: Mon-Fri 8-6, Sat 9-4:30

Used materials salvaged from warehouses, barns and large buildings are often available at this lumber yard. Give them a ring to find out what they've demolished recently. New lumber will often be cheaper here than in Seattle.

Checks

HOME CLUB

Kent: 18230 E. Valley Hwy. ☎ 251-9400
Lynnwood: 17300 Hwy. 99 ☎ 742-7900
Tacoma: 1913 S. 72nd St. ☎ 472-6767
Hours: Mon-Fri 7-9, Sat 7-6, Sun 8-6

Home Club is the first place many people visit when they start a remodeling or building project. (Contractors and builders included.) The huge warehouses stock an incredible selection of lumber, hardware, tools, electrical supplies and plumbing fixtures. Other large sections offer windows, doors, paint, flooring, wallpaper and decorative items, plus garden supplies and patio accessories.

continued >

Home Building and Remodeling, Building Materials

Although similar in appearance and marketing strategy to Costco and Price Savers, Home Club has staff available to answer questions, the inventory is mainly building supplies, and you don't have to be a member to buy. Non-members pay 5% above the posted price. Anyone can join for $15, and the fee is only $10 for those with a business license or an affiliation with a credit union or government agency.

Checks, Credit cards

KISKI CABINETS — NEW LISTING
Seattle: ☎ 782-8227
By appointment only

Buying from Bill Kiski, a wholesale broker who sells kitchen cabinets made in Germany and shipped out of Canada, saves you money on the exchange rate, plus it eliminates the retail markup. Although his wood and laminate cabinets can be found at Sears and Pay 'N Pak stores, most of his business is with contractors, interior designers and apartment owners. Call to look at samples. Allow four weeks for delivery.

Checks

LIGHTING SUPPLY, INC. — NEW LISTING
Seattle: 2729 2nd Ave. ☎ 441-5075 *Downtown*
Hours: Mon-Fri 8-5

Here's a great place to save money on lighting fixtures and light bulbs, especially if purchased by the case. Don't expect a big fancy showroom since this is a low overhead operation that deals mainly with contractors. If they don't have what you want in stock, order out of their catalogs.

Checks, Credit cards

McLENDON HARDWARE, INC.
Renton: 710 S. 2nd ☎ 235-3555
Sumner: 1111 Fryar Ave. ☎ 863-2264
Woodinville: 17705 130th N.E. ☎ 485-1363
Hours: Mon-Sat 8-6, Sun 9-5. Renton open until 7:30 weeknights

These huge stores (combination lumber yard, hardware store, home center and nursery) are packed with an incredible variety of merchandise. You'll find ten models of any given item, and every one of the more than 100,000 items in stock is discounted. They'll do anything to keep prices down, including buying overstock, surplus and manufacturers' specials. Green and orange tags help you compute savings, which start at 10%. Every month the store sends out a bulk-rate sales catalog advertising hundreds of bargains. If you don't live in the area, call and get on their mailing list. A family-owned local business since 1926, McLendon's prides itself on friendly service and expert advice in every department.

Checks, Credit cards

See area locator index for this section on page 223

MUTUAL MATERIALS
Bellevue: 605 119th N.E. ☎ 455-2869
Hours: Mon-Fri 7-5

Bricks, tile and clay products manufactured by *Mutual and Interpace* are used to build skyscrapers, houses, fireplaces, chimneys and patios. Price is the same for one brick or 1,000. Although the majority of customers are contractors and masons, do-it-yourselfers stop in for small projects. Tools and mortar mixes are also stocked, and the helpful staff will answer questions. This is the main office and largest yard for Mutual, which has other retail locations in Auburn, Everett, Kenmore and Tacoma.

Checks

NATIONAL KITCHEN SALES
Auburn: 233 D Street N.W. ☎ 924-0220
Hours: Mon-Fri 8-5, Sat 10-4

National Kitchen Sales is a factory-owned showroom offering one-stop shopping for constructing new kitchens or remodeling old ones. Everything is quoted at 50% or more off list price. There's a huge display of kitchen cabinets by *DeWils* in dozens of wood and laminate styles. Some inventory is stocked in a nearby warehouse for immediate delivery. Plan on 3-1/2 weeks if the Vancouver factory has to custom-build your cabinets. Compare prices on *Armstrong* vinyls, floor coverings, *Frigidaire*, *Whirlpool* and *Dacor* appliances.

Checks, Credit cards

THE OLD HOBBY SHOP
Lynnwood: 17707 Hwy. 99 ☎ 743-1003
Hours: Tues-Sat 9:30-5:30

For years this second hand shop has been the clearing house for overstock and unclaimed merchandise from the largest aluminum window manufacturer in the state. Over 7,000 windows are in stock, and prices depend on size and condition, but savings average 20% to 50%. All windows qualify for government subsidized weatherization programs. Purchase new or used glass— there's no charge for custom cutting. A small selection of leaded glass and old wood windows is scattered about.

Checks

PACIFIC INDUSTRIAL SUPPLY
Seattle: 2960 4th Ave S. ☎ 682-2100 *South of Kingdome*
Hours: Mon-Fri 8-5, Sat 9-3

continued >

Home Building and Remodeling, Building Materials

Loggers, boat owners, commercial fisherman and contractors shop here for new and used equipment of all kinds— salvaged metal and fittings, hydraulic hoses, cylinders, pumps and valves, plus motors, wood and metal-working tools, and industrial machines. A big warehouse in back contains chains, cable, pulleys and hoists in every size imaginable. New merchandise is surplus, often sold at below list price. Used merchandise comes from liquidations.

Checks, Credit cards

PACIFIC IRON'S BUILDING MATERIALS
Seattle: 2230 4th Ave. S. ☎ 628-6256 *South of Kingdome*
Hours: Mon-Fri 8-5:30, Sat 9-5:30, Sun 10-3

You'll find tools, windows, hardware, moldings, laminates, particle board, fiberglass roofing, metal sheeting, pipe and chain, plus a huge selection of doors. Lumber, metal and acrylic glass is cut-to-order, free of charge. Floating hot tub covers are a specialty. An odd assortment of household items passes in and out of this warehouse. We've seen sinks, shutters, furniture and kitchen cabinets. Factory close-outs, overstock, or freight-damaged goods are priced below wholesale and limited to stock-on-hand.

Checks, Credit cards

READ PRODUCTS, INC.
Seattle: 3615 15th Ave. W. ☎ 283-2510 *West Queen Anne*
Hours: Mon-Fri 8-5

If you're interested in buying major kitchen appliances like *Dacor and Sub-Zero*, counter tops, and floor and window coverings at 10%-20% above wholesale, visit this contractors' showroom. All merchandise must be special-ordered, but Read has lots of catalogs and samples.

Checks

SEATTLE BUILDING SALVAGE, INC.
Seattle: 202 Bell St. ☎ 448-3453 *Downtown*
Hours: Tues-Sat 10:30-5:30

Looking for a claw foot bathtub, leaded glass windows, or antique faucet to add a little character to your home? Seattle Building Salvage restores old doors, windows, hardware, plumbing and lighting fixtures to their former glory. Some merchandise goes for half what you would normally pay. Put your name on the mailing list to find out about sales. The owner, who is an electrician, offers cut rates on repairing old light fixtures.

Checks, Credit cards

SEATTLE MASTER BUILDERS ASSOCIATION — NEW LISTING
Seattle: ☎ 451-7920
Annual sale

Call to get on the mailing list for this fall sale. Surplus or slightly damaged building supplies are donated by area contractors and retail stores, and proceeds benefit the Affordable Housing Council, an organization dedicated to researching and lobbying for low-cost housing. Bargain hunters show up at the crack of dawn to pick up appliances, kitchen cabinets, plumbing and lighting supplies, plus just about everything else that goes into building or remodeling a house.

SHERMAN SUPPLY
Seattle: 2456 1st Ave. S. ☎ 624-0061 *South of Kingdome*
Hours: Mon-Sat 8-5

Sherman sells plumbing, irrigation and industrial supplies, most of which come from salvage operations: rope, hoses, pipes and fittings of all sizes, motors, compressors, blocks, winches, etc. Florescent lighting fixtures are always in stock. Bath tubs were cheap the last time we visited.

Checks, Credit cards

TIMBER WINDOWS
Everett: 3333 111th Pl. S.W., South Complex #101 ☎ 745-9665
Hours: Mon-Fri 8-4:30, sometimes Sat

"Boneyard glass" is what this window factory calls its odd sizes and unclaimed stock. Sometimes wood frame windows end up in the sale pile. Savings can amount to 60%, and all glass carries a guarantee. Call ahead to find out what's in stock.

Checks

WILL-WOOD PREFIT, INC.
Tacoma: 4720 S. Tacoma Way ☎ 473-6673
Hours: Mon-Fri 8-5, Sat 9-3

Don't expect a fancy showroom, but count on savings when you buy doors, locks and millwork direct from the factory. Select A or B grade, prefinished or unfinished styles. Odd-sized doors machined to fit. Best prices are on factory rejects and unclaimed stock. Visit in July and August during the big inventory close-out sale.

Checks

Tools & Hardware

AIRCRAFT PARTS EXCHANGE
Kent: 13812 8th S. ☎ 242-4059
By appointment only

A.P.E. buys and sells surplus and salvaged equipment. The owner says he carries or can get "anything under the sun mechanical." If you're in the market for hydraulics, machinery, hardware or tools, give him a call.

Checks

ARONSON-CAMPBELL INDUSTRIAL SUPPLY, INC.

Seattle: 5300 Denver S. ☎ 762-0700 *Georgetown*
Hours: Mon-Fri 8-5

Tools here are sold mainly to contractors, carpenters and tradespeople, so the quality is better than commercial brands found in hardware stores. Prices, however, may be a little higher. Drill presses, band saws, miter boxes, sanders and grinders by *Bosch, Delta and Porter Cable* carry long-term warranties. The large showroom features a lot of in-store specials on tools, machinery, abrasives and shop supplies. Attend their big sale in November. Call for a comprehensive product catalog.

Checks, Credit cards

COAST TOOLS, INC.

Seattle: 8926 Roosevelt Way N.E. 527-4474 *Northgate*
Hours: Mon-Fri 8:30-5:30, Sat 9-2

This company sells industrial-quality power and electrical tools below list price. *Makita and Bosch* are their major lines, with fine woodworking tools and supplies a specialty. Prices are quoted by phone.

Checks, Credit cards

GREENSHIELD'S INDUSTRIAL SUPPLY

Everett: 710 N. Broadway ☎ 259-0111
Hours: Mon-Fri 8-5, Sat 8-12

Small portable electrical tools by *Proto and Milwaukee* are always discounted 25% to 30% at this distributor. *Proto* is manufactured by *Stanley* and comparable to *Craftsman*, a line put out by Sears. Savings will vary on other lines in stock or items that must be special-ordered. Greenshield's also carries automotive tools.

Checks, Credit cards

HARDWICK'S SWAP SHOP

Seattle: 4214 Roosevelt Way N.E. ☎ 632-1203 *U-District*
Hours: Tues-Sat 9-6

In business since 1932, Hardwick's looks like your basic second-hand store. However, it specialty is used tools for machinists, carpenters, plumbers, mechanics and gardeners. Trade-ins accepted on electrical tools. New tools are priced 25% to 30% below retail. When we called, this popular place had a lot of mechanical, carving and masonry tools on hand. It's also a good resource for lawnmowers.

Checks, Credit cards

TACOMA SCREW PRODUCTS ANNEX

Tacoma: 2001 Center ☎ 572-3444
Hours: Mon-Fri 8-5, Sat 9-1

continued >

Home Building and Remodeling, Tools & Hardware

The building industry shops at Tacoma Screw's five stores for hardware, tools, fasteners and equipment. Everything sold at the Annex is discounted because it's left-over sale merchandise or surplus purchased from Los Angeles importers. Best buys are on the specials, which change frequently.

Checks, Credit cards

TACOMA TOOL

Tacoma: 1513 S. Tacoma Way ☎ 473-7800
Hours: Mon-Fri 8-5, Sat 9-3

Take advantage of Tacoma Tool's discounted prices on hand and portable electrical tools and workshop supplies. They sell mainly to the building industry, so well-known brand names include *Bosch and Milwaukee*. Basic shop items are stocked in depth. Choose from hundreds of socket sets, dozens of tarp sizes. Watch for red tag specials.

Checks, Credit cards

TOOL TOWN

Everett: 4811 Evergreen Way ☎ 259-2590
Des Moines: 23639 Pacific Hwy. S. ☎ 878-1148
Kirkland: 12700 N.E. 124th St. ☎ 821-3007
Seattle: 11522 Lake City Way N.E. ☎ 367-5151 *Lake City*
  652 Elliott Ave. W. ☎ 281-1166 *West of Seattle Center*
  19811 Aurora Ave. N. ☎ 542-0910 *Richmond Highlands*
Tacoma: 9440 Pacific ☎ 535-1166
Hours: Mon-Fri 9-6, Sat 9-4

These small stores rely on volume buying, large stock and low overhead so they can offer everyday low prices on all kinds of tools and shop equipment. Industrial lines by *Milwaukee and Mikita* are carried along with such well-known brands as *Skil and Black and Decker*. Because some of the inventory is imported, it's hard to compare prices. Everything is discounted 20% to 40% off the list price. Tool Town also carries a large selection of specialty automotive tools.

Checks, Credit cards

WESTERN TOOL SUPPLY   NEW LISTING

Kent: 8613 S. 212th St. ☎ 395-3102
Hours: Mon-Fri 7-5, Sat 9-2

If you plan on investing in name-brand industrial-grade tools, this is a good place to comparison shop since Western claims to have the lowest prices and best selection around. Inventory is geared to contractors and cabinet makers, so you'll always find good buys on portable power tools, fasteners, abrasives and shop supplies. Promotional catalogs are sent out every four to six weeks. Annual sales held in August and March. Call to get on the mailing list.

Checks, Credit cards

YOUR TOOL HOUSE, INC.
Renton: 155 Rainier Ave. S. ☎ 255-1216
Hours: Mon-Fri 8:30-5:30, Sat 9-5

If you like to repair cars or motors, this wholesale/retail distributor cuts prices on industrial-grade hand tools used by mechanics and machinists. Everything is discounted, including leading brands.

Checks, Credit cards

Here's a list of factory service centers where you can purchase rebuilt tools at substantial savings:

BLACK AND DECKER
Seattle: 701 3rd. Ave N. ☎ 282-6432 *North of Seattle Center*
Tacoma: 2602 S. 38th ☎ 473-6040

Also stocks small household appliances.

PACIFIC AIR TOOL
Seattle: 7400 2nd Ave. S. ☎ 762-3550 *South Park*

PORTER-CABLE
Renton: 268 S.W. 43rd St. ☎ 251-6680

SKIL CORP.
Seattle: 101 S. Branden ☎ 762-1127 *Georgetown*
Tacoma: 1610 Center ☎ 572-7107

Floor Coverings

Competition is the name of the game in the Puget Sound area. Many floor covering stores advertise discount prices, especially on carpeting, so we strongly advise you to shop around before making a final decision. To save time, visit a locale with a high concentration of stores like Bellevue's famous Carpet Row on 130th & Bellevue-Redmond Road or Lake City Way at 125th.

BAYSIDE SUPPLY CO.
Everett: 2919 Rucker Ave. ☎ 259-4994
Hours: Mon-Fri 8-5:30, Sat 8-5

Builders and contractors shop for budget-priced floor coverings at this large warehouse where hundreds of carpets are packed floor to ceiling. Discontinued styles, off colors, seconds, special purchases and remnants are all priced way below retail. Some rolls have never been opened, and you get a discount if you buy the full roll. Their best seller is commercial-grade carpet for apartments. If you're interested in higher quality carpet, visit Bayside's upscale division, Broadloom

continued >

Home Building and Remodeling, Floor Coverings

Northwest, located nearby. Bayside also carries name-brand sheet vinyl, Formica countertops, *Olympic and Lucite* paints, plus installers' tools.

Checks, Credit cards

BENOY'S CARPET WAREHOUSE
Tacoma: 5235 S. Washington ☎ 475-3434
Hours: Mon-Fri 10-5:30, Sat 10-5

Benoy's specializes in roll ends and remnants from such nationally known companies as *Philadelphia, Salem and Armstrong.* Sizes range up to 30'lengths, so there's plenty of leeway for carpeting a hall or a living room. Most prices run 30% to 50% off retail. We spotted a 24-yd. roll of Berber wool priced at only $200. Area rugs made in Belgium, vinyl floor covering remnants and tile are also discounted.

Checks, Credit cards

BROADLOOM NORTHWEST — NEW LISTING
Everett: 2601 Colby ☎ 259-6088
Hours: Mon-Fri 9-5:30, Sat 10-5

Although its name implies only carpeting, this company sells a number of products to the building industry, all factory-direct. The showroom is filled with samples of tile, carpet, paint, wallpaper and window coverings. Some items are in stock; many must be special ordered. Off-brand refrigerators, dishwashers and ranges are available for immediate delivery at super low prices. Call for price quotes.

Checks, Credit cards

CARPETERIA — NEW LISTING
Bellevue: 12001 N.E. 12th St. ☎ 453-4408
Seattle: 9861 Aurora Ave. N. ☎ 524-0826 *Greenwood*
Tukwila: 17220 Southcenter Pkwy. ☎ 575-1687 *Parkway Plaza*
Hours: Mon-Fri 9-9, Sat 9-6, Sun 10-6

With 65 stores on the West Coast, Carpeteria has the buying power to purchase directly from the mills. Their low-end carpet starts at $10.99/sq. yd., including pad and installation. They carry most major brands, including commercial-grade carpet for offices. A large selection of area rugs, vinyl and wood floor coverings completes the inventory.

Checks, Credit cards

THE CARPET EXCHANGE
Bellevue: 12802 Bel-Red Rd. ☎ 455-8332
Federal Way: 30820 Pacific Hwy. S. ☎ 839-2142
Lynnwood: 5501 196th S.W. ☎ 771-1477
Seattle: 1251 1st Ave. S. ☎ 624-7800 *South of Kingdome*
Silverdale: 3200 N.W. Randall Way ☎ 692-7732
Tacoma: 6818 Tacoma Mall Blvd. ☎ 474-9034
Hours: Generally, Mon-Fri 9-9, Sat 9-6, Sun 11-5

continued >

These stores stock more carpet than any other dealer in the state. You'll find a wide range of brands for every budget. Management claims they can beat anyone's prices. The Seattle warehouse carries the largest selection of discontinued styles and colors, plus hundreds of roll ends.

Checks, Credit cards

CARPET REMNANT OUTLET   NEW LISTING
Issaquah: 1875 N.W. Poplar Way ☎ 391-7383
Kirkland: 524 Central Way ☎ 822-4290
Redmond: 7805 Leary Way ☎ 885-3734
Seattle: 12505 Lake City Way N.E. ☎ 364-0865 *Lake City*
Hours: Mon-Fri 9:30-6:30, Sat 9:30-5:00

Remnants of every size line the walls of this no frills operation and good deals abound. Large rolls up to 30' can be special-ordered for you. Samples are piled all over the place, and at $1 to $2 each, they make great door mats or places for pets to sleep. Name-brand vinyl floor covering can be purchased as remnants or by the foot at below-retail prices.

Checks, Credit cards

COLOR TILE   NEW LISTING
Bellevue: 121 106th N.E. ☎ 455-5135
Bremerton: 3324 Wheaton Way ☎ 373-1458
Burien: 105 S. 152nd St. ☎ 243-3766
Federal Way: 31007 Pacific Hwy. S. ☎ 941-3316
Lynnwood: 4232-A 196th S.W. ☎ 775-5477
Renton: 134 Rainier Ave. S. ☎ 271-4550
Seattle: 809 N.E. Northgate Way ☎ 365-2950 *Northgate*
Tacoma: 2602 S. 38th St. ☎ 473-2611
Hours: Mon-Fri 8-8, Sat 9-6, Sun 10-5

An extensive selection of ceramic, vinyl and wood floor coverings, Formica, carpeting and wallpaper made exclusively for Color Tile's 850 stores is often priced extraordinarily low. You can also purchase the materials necessary to install any of their products. Color Tile even rents a ceramic tile cutter. First-timers can get expert advice on any project, or the company will supply professional installation. Refunds are given on unused tile or uncut rolls of wallpaper.

Checks, Credit cards

CONSOLIDATED CARPET WAREHOUSE
Bellevue: 14150 N.E. 20th ☎ 641-4552
Kent: 310 N. Washington ☎ 852-7100
Seattle: 5235 4th Ave. S. ☎ 762-6270 *Georgetown*
          200 N. 85th St. ☎ 789-7737 *Greenwood*
Hours: Mon-Fri 9-8, Sat 9-6, Sun 11-5

continued >

Home Building and Remodeling, Floor Coverings

Prices on carpets and vinyl floor coverings are low here because much of their 2,000 roll inventory consists of mill close-outs purchased below wholesale. Remnants are cut from the carpet stock to ensure a fast turnover. New items arrive regularly. The main warehouse on 4th Ave. S. has the largest selection.

Checks, Credit cards

DIRECT CARPET SALES

Bellevue: 13000 Bellevue-Redmond Rd. ☎ 453-2050
Lynnwood: 18503 Hwy. 99 ☎ 778-5057
Seattle: 11724 Lake City Way N.E. ☎ 364-9061 *Lake City*
Hours: Mon-Fri 9-9, Sat 9-6, Sun 11-5; Seattle, Mon-Fri 9-7

Direct Carpet Sales buys in large quantities directly from the mills and passes the savings on to customers. Some of the carpeting has been specially made and private-labeled. Prices are in the medium range, and the selection is large. Roll ends sell for up to 25% off regular prices, remnants are 40% off.

Checks, Credit cards

EMMANUEL RUG & UPHOLSTERY CLEANERS   NEW LISTING

Seattle: 1105 Rainier S. ☎ 322-2200
Hours: Mon-Fri 8-5, Sat 10-2

Although Emmanuel's is best-known for its rug cleaning expertise, the company stocks a selection of factory remnants, plus used oriental rugs on consignment.

Checks, Credit cards

FLOOR DESIGN WEST   NEW LISTING

Federal Way: 32411-C Pacific Hwy S. ☎ 838-2266 927-2030
Hours: Mon-Fri 10-8, Sat 10-6, Sun 12-5

With low markups and low overhead, this small shop purports to offer the best prices in the area on tile and excellent prices on name-brand vinyl floor coverings. They try to meet or beat competitors' prices on everything in stock.

Checks

FLOORS TO GO

Renton: 336 Burnett Ave. S ☎ 271-7133
Hours: Mon-Fri 10-6, Sat 10-5, Sun 12-5

This low-budget operation offers some of the best prices in town on name-brand carpet and vinyl floor coverings. Hundreds of manufacturers are represented in their warehouse. You'll find lots of remnants and roll ends. No terms are available, and cash will probably get you a better deal.

Checks, Credit cards

Home Building and Remodeling, Floor Coverings

MIDLAKE'S FLOOR COVERINGS
Bellevue: 306 105th N.E. ☎ 454-3941
Hours: Mon-Fri 9-5, Sat 10-4

Visit Midlake's remnant store located next door to their showroom if you're looking for a bargain on such better-quality carpeting as *Galaxy and Woodcraft*. Sizes vary, but some rolls are quite large for remnants. Vinyl floor coverings and tile are also discounted.

Checks, Credit cards

MILLER'S INTERIORS, INC.
Bellevue: 1811 130th Ave. N.E. ☎ 883-9755
Kent: 18439 E. Valley Hwy. ☎ 251-0674
Lynnwood: 15615 Hwy. 99 ☎ 743-3213
Seattle: 7726 15th Ave. N.W. ☎ 783-4888 *Ballard*
Hours: Mon-Fri 8:30-5:30, Sat 11-5

Millers advises you to "buy where the builders buy". Their carpet is custom-made at the mill under their own label and purchased in carload lots, which makes their prices competitive with other "discount" floor covering outlets in the area. Behind the main store in Lynnwood is a large warehouse where roll ends are sold at 50% off.

Checks, Credit cards

THE REMNANT KING   NEW LISTING
Everett: 4117 Rucker Ave. ☎ 259-4922
Seattle: 800 N.W. 65th ☎ 789-7553 *Ballard*
Hours: Tues-Thurs 10-7, Fri & Sat 10-5; Seattle open Sun 1-4

You don't have to guess at this outfit's specialty! Remnants here are larger than at other stores— some measure 35' long. Most of the inventory is discontinued styles and colors. Prices vary from $5.50 to $10/sq. yd. on name-brand carpets that would normally run $20 to $30/sq. yd. The best buys are on short-looped or cut-pile carpets frequently used in areas where heavy traffic is a problem.

Checks

THE RUG BARN   NEW LISTING
Spanaway: 14621 Pacific Ave. ☎ 537-1473
Hours: Mon-Fri 10-6, Sat 10-5

Not only does this outlet specialize in discontinued styles and seconds, but also it sells "thirds" (carpet that has been installed and pulled up right away due to some problem) and used carpet from offices, apartments, condos and private residences. You can find fine-quality carpeting for $10/sq. ft. that would normally go for three times as much. The factory seal is still intact on some of the rolls. Carpet can be exchanged if you change your mind after unrolling it at home. Pay cash and get a discount.

Checks

Home Building and Remodeling, Paint & Wallpaper Products

SOUND VIEW FLOORS

Des Moines: 22247 Pacific Hwy. S. ☎ 784-2822
Hours: Mon-Fri 9-5; Sat, by appointment

Having been in the floor covering business for three generations, this company's prices are very competitive. (A *Mohawk* carpet that Sears was selling for $10.95/sq. yd. was priced at $8.95 here.) Their biggest seller to building contractors is a short plush at $9.95/sq. yd. Better-quality, heavy-duty carpet averages $11 to $15/sq. yd.

Checks, Credit cards

SUN WEST CARPETS

Seattle: 501 Dexter Ave. N. ☎ 625-1536 *Downtown*
Hours: Mon-Fri 8:30-4:30

A brokerage business. Sun West sells floor coverings to interior decorators, builders and the public at 10% above cost. Choose from hundreds of samples representing top-quality nationally known manufacturers of carpet, ceramic tile, sheet vinyl and wood floor coverings. Orders come directly from the factory to a nearby trucking terminal where you pick them up. For an extra fee, they'll arrange installation.

Checks

☑ Consumer Tip:

☞ When you're buying mill ends, close-outs and remnants, low prices do not necessarily mean low quality. The best way to judge a carpet is by the density of the yarn and the feel.

☞ If a retailer advertises free pad and installation, the cost probably has been added into the price of the carpet. A good pad runs approximately $3/yard and installation about the same, so subtract $6 from the per yard cost to figure the amount you're really paying for the carpet.

Paint & Wallpaper

The first place you want to check for bargains on paint is the "boneyard"— a special section set aside in retail stores, where mismatched colors, overages on special orders, and unclaimed custom tints are sold. The chemical content determines the price of paint, so be sure to compare prices based on ingredients. Latex is cheaper than acrylic and works fine for interior paint jobs, but if used in large proportions in exterior paint, will eventually cause the paint to fade and chalk. Exterior paint should have a high acrylic base to do the best job, especially in our area where its water shedding properties are so important.

Home decorating stores almost always carry discontinued patterns and close-outs on wallpaper. Watch the newspapers for seasonal sales, which can sometimes net you 50% off the retail price.

See area locator index for this section on page 224

100 Home Building and Remodeling, Paint & Wallpaper Products

FARWEST PAINT — NEW LISTING
Kirkland: 12545 116th N.E. ☎ 821-1334
Tukwila: 4522 S. 133rd ☎ 244-8844
Hours: Mon-Fri 7:30-5, Sat 9-1

Although paint manufacturers abound in the Puget Sound area, this is the only one we could find that keeps its prices at least $1/gallon less than national brands on all merchandise. Choose from a complete line of industrial and commercial products, or have your paint custom-tinted. Far West has been in business since 1925, which indicates customer satisfaction.

Checks

MAJOR BRANDS
Seattle: 2418 1st Ave. S. ☎ 623-3550 *South of Kingdome*
Hours: Mon-Fri 9-6, Sat 10-5

Major Brands is a good place to comparison shop for name-brand paints, tile, wallpaper, Formica, vinyl floor coverings, plus an assortment of general hardware items. Everything is discounted 25% or more because most of the stock comes from suppliers' close-outs, dealers going out of business, and goods damaged in shipping. We saw outstanding buys on *Armstrong* linoleum, *Fuller* paint and counter top Formica.

Checks, Credit cards

RODDA DECOR CENTER — NEW LISTING
Bellevue: 1034 116th N.E. ☎ 451-1666
Federal Way: 310th & Pacific Hwy. S. ☎ 941-9717
Kent: 25615 104th S.E. ☎ 859-5115
Lynnwood: 18811 28th Ave. W. ☎ 672-0231
Puyallup: 11907 Meridian S.E. ☎ 840-2111
Redmond: 16717 Cleveland St. ☎ 881-5583
Seattle: 5055 4th Ave. S. ☎ 767-6043 *South of Kingdome*
   3633 Stoneway N. ☎ 547-7405 *Wallingford*
Tacoma: 6249 Tacoma Mall Blvd. ☎ 472-7286
Hours: Mon-Fri 7:30-6, Sat 8-6, Sun 12-5

This Portland-based paint manufacturer has opened eight "affordable home decorating" stores in the Puget Sound area since 1987. They offer one-stop shopping for interior and exterior paint, wallpaper and window coverings. Volume buying and cutting out the middle man keep prices competitive. Decorating consultants will come to your home or office to show samples, take measurements, and arrange for installation.

Checks, Credit cards

Home Building and Remodeling, Paint & Wallpaper Products

STANDARD BRANDS

Bellevue: 14625 N.E. 24th ☎ 747-5555
Burien: 636 S.W. 152nd ☎ 246-8800
Everett: 7825 Evergreen Way ☎ 353-0606
Federal Way: 30919 Pacific Hwy S. ☎ 941-8222
Lynnwood: 21558 Hwy. 99 ☎ 774-8861
Seattle: 1702 4th Ave. S. ☎ 682-7887 *South of Kingdome*
  9701 Aurora Ave. N. ☎ 522-6666 *Greenwood*
Tacoma: 4824 S. Tacoma Way ☎ 475-8444
Hours: Mon-Fri 9-9, Sat & Sun 9-5:30

Nationally advertised products are discounted 20% to 30% everyday. Paint manufactured especially for these stores sells for $9 to $11/gallon vs. $15 elsewhere. Check out the terrific selections of sheet and tile vinyl floor coverings and specialty items like indoor/outdoor carpet, artificial turf and genuine marble tiles. Carpets vary in price from high-end to bargain basement remnants. Blinds can be custom-made or purchased from stock. The store will arrange installation for any of these products. A large art supply department attracts artists and a free weekly "How to Wallpaper" class appeals to do-it-yourselfers. Sales are promoted via frequent bulk rate mailings.

Checks, Credit cards

WALLPAPERS TO GO

Bellevue: 2245 148th N.E. ☎ 747-0150
Lynnwood: 19417 36th Ave. W. ☎ 774-9646
Tacoma: 2901 S. 38th ☎ 472-9679
Tukwila: 17456 Southcenter Parkway ☎ 575-4035 *Parkway Plaza*
Hours: Mon-Fri 10-9, Sat 10-6, Sun 12-5

Beautiful rooms begin at this national chain, where you'll find a large selection of in-stock vinyl, pre-pasted, texturized and foil patterns—750 to be exact. They cater to do-it-yourselfers. Instructional videos and books can be "checked out" with a refundable deposit, or you may sign up for free wallpapering clinics. Close-outs and discontinued styles are usually available at 50% to 75% off the original price. Window coverings can also be custom-ordered at reasonable prices. Watch for big spring and fall sales.

Checks, Credit cards

Mail-order Wallpaper Suppliers

You can save 25% or more by ordering wallpapers, matching fabric and borders from nationwide discounters. The drawbacks are that delivery takes seven to ten days and do-it-yourselfers have no one to answer their questions.

Here's how to order: When you call, have the name of the book, pattern number and name, and amount of paper you need. Pre-pay by check or credit card; delivery will take longer if you send a check since they will not ship until the check clears. Post Wall Covering Distributors will send an order C.O.D. or accept money orders.

continued >

Return policies will vary with each company and the manufacturers, so be sure to inquire before you buy. Usually uncut double rolls may be returned within a prescribed period of time but are subject to a 25% to 33-1/2% restocking fee, except on defective merchandise. Post is the only company that will not take returns on unused wallpaper. Borders and fabrics cannot be returned.

Shipping fees will vary. Post offers free shipping. Yorktowne Wallpapers charges $3 for shipping if you order fewer than seven rolls.

Feel free to ask questions. All the operators we talked to were friendly and well-informed.

ACTION DISCOUNT WALLCOVERINGS
Tulsa, OK ☎ 800/972-7691
Hours: Mon-Fri 9:30-5 (Central Time)

AMERICAN DISCOUNT WALLCOVERINGS
Pittsburgh, PA ☎ 800/245-1768
Hours: Mon-Fri 9-5, Sat 9-1 (Eastern Time)
Window coverings by major manufacturers are also available.

POST WALLCOVERING DISTRIBUTORS
Bloomfield Hills, MI ☎ 800/521-0650
Hours: Mon-Sat 9-5:30 (Eastern Time)

YORKTOWNE WALLPAPERS
York, PA ☎ 800/847-6142
Hours: Mon-Fri 9-9, Sat 9-4 (Eastern Time)

☑ **Consumer Tip:**
☞ Because so many of the wall surfaces in houses here are routinely "texturized" as a quick, inexpensive means of finishing wallboard, vinyls and texturized wallpaper (which hide uneven surfaces) are the most popular wallcoverings in our area. Vinyls, which are usually fabric-backed, work great in kitchens, bathrooms and kids' rooms because they're durable and washable.

Window Coverings

Because they're both fashionable and inexpensive, blinds are the most popular form of window covering today. Comparison shopping is easy because you can get quotes over the phone— a real time saver for the dedicated bargain hunter. Visit a nearby showroom and decide exactly what you want. When you call to compare prices, stick with one window size.

Home Building and Remodeling, Window Coverings

ALLIED CUSTOM DRAPERY STORES, INC. & WINDOW WARES

Kent: Allied Custom Drapery; 21620 84th Ave. S. ☎ 872-5710
Mill Creek: Window Wares; 15712 Mill Creek Blvd. ☎ 771-4900
Hours: Mon-Fri 9:30-6, Sat 10:30-5

These jointly owned companies can order blinds, shades or verticals from any name-brand manufacturer and give you a big discount to boot! Save time and even more money by calling with your window measurements, and they'll look through the unclaimed stock to see if they have anything that will work. Their workroom also turns out custom draperies, bedspreads, swags, cornices and balloon shades.

Checks, Credit cards

AMARANT BLINDS   NEW LISTING

Bellevue: 2560 152nd Ave. N.E. ☎ 867-5365
Federal Way: 31840 Pacific Hwy. S. ☎ 941-9482
Lynnwood: 19725 40th Ave. W. ☎ 778-4693
Tukwila: 7681 S. 180th St ☎ 251-0989
Hours: Mon-Fri 10-6, Sat 10-5, Sun 12-5

Have your mini-blinds and verticals custom made in Amarant's Southcenter factory and get delivery in five to ten days instead of the usual three weeks. Quality-wise, Amarant's blinds are made with a slightly heavier gauge aluminum slat than *Levolor's*, but don't close as tightly. Price-wise, you'll pay about $20 less per blind. You can also order draperies, which are custom-made by a local workroom, and many other types of window coverings from nationally known manufacturers.

Checks, Credit cards

AMERICAN DRAPERY & BLINDS

Renton: 700 S. 3rd St. ☎ 226-5920
Hours: Mon-Fri 9-7, Sat 9-5

Need window coverings fast? This company makes draperies and blinds, mainly for apartments, and promises three day delivery. Loaner draperies are even available if you need something sooner. We found everyday prices on their 1" mini-blinds to be far below the name-brands, and they use top quality slats. Custom-made draperies are an exceptional buy. You should have no problem finding just the right fabric since they stock over 30,000 yards. The offshoot of this busy workroom is a huge selection of unclaimed first-quality blinds, pleated shades and custom-made draperies which are sold at close to cost. Ready-to-hang draperies and accessories are also discounted. Do-it-yourselfers will love the selection of low-priced fabrics and plentiful remnants.

Checks, Credit cards

DISCOUNT WINDOW COVERINGS   NEW LISTING

Seattle: P.O. Box 81191 (98108) ☎ 762-8206
Hours: Mon-Fri 9-5

continued >

Home Building and Remodeling, Window Coverings

Discount Window Coverings sells mainly to commercial accounts, but if you call for an appointment, a representative will come to your home with samples and will measure your windows free-of-charge. They carry a variety of name-brand window coverings, including *Levolor, Hunter Douglas, LouverDrape, Kirsch, Del Mar and Verosol*. Their quote was one of the lowest in town on *Levolors*. Shipping charges are included in the price, and they'll arrange installation.

Checks, Credit cards

FACTORY DIRECT DRAPERIES
Seattle: 8300 Aurora Ave. N. ☎ 525-7932 *Green Lake*
Hours: Mon-Sat 9:30-5:30

Visit this showroom to get decorating ideas and compare prices on their extensive display of window treatments. Be sure to check out the bargains on custom-made draperies that were not picked up or didn't quite meet specifications. Sometimes blinds and shades are available at drastically reduced prices. If you want to try your hand at making draperies, you'll find an excellent selection of fabrics.

Checks, Credit cards

WESSCO
Seattle: 3208 15th W. ☎ 285-5455 *West Queen Anne*
Hours: Mon-Fri 9-6, Sat 10-5

Call Wessco for the lowest bid in town on blinds. They'll mail free samples and worksheets, so you can do your own measuring. Pay in full upon ordering, and the blinds will be sent by UPS from the factory to your home. If you prefer to visit the showroom, helpful staff will show you their outstanding selection, which includes top-of-the-line manufacturers. *Levolor's* 1" Riviera blinds are their biggest seller. For a fee, Wessco will send someone out to measure your windows and/or arrange for installation.

Checks, Credit cards

☑Consumer Tip:
☞ Blinds vary in quality, just like everything else. A metal blind should not bend easily. Pleated shades, while somewhat more expensive than metal, are a good choice if you are seeking energy efficiency.

See area locator index for this section on page 224

Home Furnishings

Furnishing a home is expensive, especially if you're starting from scratch. But, with a little creativity and time, diligent shoppers can create their own "House Beautiful" without paying full retail price! Visit stores in your area to get an idea of quality, styles, and price ranges. Then start calling around for price quotes from brokers, discounters and factory outlets. For the best prices, buy factory-direct whenever possible.

Tukwila is the center for the wholesale and retail home furnishings market in the Pacific Northwest. Visit the many warehouses that sell direct and the off-price retailers in Parkway Plaza on Southcenter Parkway.

When purchasing major appliances or furniture, don't be afraid to negotiate a lower price. Some stores offer a cash discount. Shop in January when furniture stores traditionally have their biggest sales; floor samples and one-of-a-kind merchandise are usually the best buys. Keep your eyes open year-round for great bargains on furniture and appliances that have been scratched or dented during shipping. Minor flaws may not be a problem— especially if the piece is to be shoved into a corner or against a wall.

Furniture

If you're on a limited budget, used furniture is a good option. Rental furniture sales make up a large part of this market. By law, all rental furniture returned to stores must be cleaned and sanitized before the pieces are rented again or sold. Adventuresome shoppers also find hidden treasures by scrounging through the eclectic inventories at secondhand stores and liquidators. Refer to Mass Merchandisers and Office Furniture, where you'll also find big-ticket items for the home at discount prices.

A-AMERICA WHOLESALE OAK FURNITURE & THE OAK BARN

Federal Way: A-America; 322 Pacific Hwy. ☎ 874-8243 *Larkspur Center*
Lynnwood: The Oak Barn; 19701 37th Ave. W. ☎ 775-3334
Tukwila: The Oak Barn; 17600 W. Valley Hwy. ☎ 251-9345
Hours: Mon-Fri 10-9, Sat 10-6, Sun 11-5

Look no further than these three outlets if you love Victorian-style furniture. A-America is a huge wholesale warehouse that specializes in antique replicas, some of which they make themselves. Contemporary styles are also available, especially in office furniture, entertainment centers and upholstered pieces. Prices are definitely below retail and the selection is overwhelming. When they have a sale, you can snap up some great buys on roll-top desks, oak tables and traditional country-style chairs. Prices are even lower at The Oak Barn where you'll find close-outs, overstock and slightly damaged goods marked below wholesale.

Checks, Credit cards

Home Furnishings, Furniture

ABODIO CLEARANCE CENTER
Seattle: 2203 Airport Way S. ☎ 621-1903 *South of Kingdome*
Hours: Mon-Sat 10-6, Sun 12-5

If you're a frequent shopper at the Abodio retail stores, be aware that their distinctive contemporary designs can be purchased for 30% to 70% less at the warehouse where discontinued, slightly damaged and returned merchandise is sent. Stock changes all the time and selection ranges from housewares and kitchen accessories to furniture for the bedroom, living room or office. Put your name on the mailing list for advance notice of big sales held in September and March.

Checks, Credit cards

ANTIQUE LIQUIDATORS
Seattle: 503 Westlake N. ☎ 623-2740 *East of Seattle Center*
Hours: Mon-Sat 9:30-5:30

Although we chose to exclude antiques as a separate category because determining what is a "bargain" is such a subjective task, we couldn't pass up mentioning this favorite haunt of professional dealers and amateur collectors. Browse 'til your heart's content through three floors of furniture dating from 1890 to 1930. Stately wardrobes, ornate hall trees, Victorian sideboards and country hutches are packed into every nook and cranny of this no-frills warehouse. New shipments arrive continually. The high turnover and owner's willingness to negotiate keep prices low.

Checks

BOB STAFFORD
Kent: ☎ 854-7300
By appointment only

When you find a piece of furniture you like, call this broker, give him the particulars, and he'll order it factory-direct at 20% to 30% below retail. You'll have no showroom or samples to peruse, but be assured that with over 30-years experience in the home furnishing market, Bob can track down just about anything you want.

Checks

BON MARCHE HOME FURNISHINGS AND ELECTRONICS   NEW LISTING
Tukwila: 17000 Southcenter Pkwy. ☎ 575-2164
Hours: Mon-Fri 10-9, Sat 10-6, Sun 12-5

If you're more comfortable shopping established retailers, stop by The Bon's clearance center where there's a big selection of furniture and accessories, all tastefully displayed. Prices will usually be below Bon sale prices except on floor stock. TV's, stereos and VCR's come with full warranties. Most everything is a floor model, returned merchandise, overstock or "as is" goods, so when you see something you like, you had better snap it up. Occasionally they'll have a "mate" in the backroom— ask if you want a pair.

Checks, Credit cards

Home Furnishings, Furniture

CORT FURNITURE RENTALS CLEARANCE CENTER
Tukwila: 1230 Andover Park East ☎ 575-4119
Hours: Mon-Fri 10-7, Sat 10-6, Sun 12-6

Check out this clearance center for outstanding savings on rental returns from model homes, apartments and offices. Their motto is, "You save more because we rented it before".

Checks, Credit cards

DESIGN CENTER NORTHWEST — NEW LISTING
Seattle: 5701 6th Ave. S. ☎ 762-1700 *Georgetown*
Periodic sales

Ever dream of giving your home that "Architectural Digest" look? Here's your chance. Two or three times a year, for one day only, the Design Center, which houses the Northwest's premier showrooms, opens its doors to the public. Samples of the finest quality American and European furniture for the home and office and decorative accessories are sold at dealer cost. Be prepared to make your own delivery arrangements the day of the sale. Call to get on the mailing list or watch the newspapers for ads. Please, don't bring children under 16.

Checks, Credit cards

THE FOAM SHOP
Seattle: 5312 Roosevelt Way N.E. ☎ 525-2301 *U-District*
Hours: Mon-Sat 10-6, Sun 12-3

Need replacement cushions for chairs or sofas? How about a mattress for a van, camper or an odd-size bed? The staff here will cut any shape or size of foam from 12 different densities and 18 levels of firmness, and they won't charge for the service. Bring covers in, and The Foam Shop will install the foam of your choice while you wait. They'll also made cushions from your fabric or theirs. Shredded foam for making pillows runs $1/lb.

Check, Credit cards

FOR YU FURNISHINGS — NEW LISTING
Bellevue: 156 N.E. & N.E. 8th ☎ 865-9886 *Crossroads Ctr.*
Hours: Mon-Fri 10-7, Sat 10-6, Sun 10-5

Here's a consignment shop that stocks only furniture, accessories and decorative items. Styles range from contemporary to antique, and the owner prefers name-brand or unique pieces. The inventory, which is all in good condition, comes mainly from furniture showrooms and private individuals. Consignees get 40%-50% of the selling price.

Checks, Credit cards

GRANTREE FURNITURE RENTAL CLEARANCE CENTER
Tukwila: 13400 Interurban S. ☎ 246-6882
Hours: Mon-Fri 10-7, Sat 10-6, Sun 11-6

continued >

Home Furnishings, Furniture

Rental returns from Grantree's four stores are sold here, along with close-outs and discontinued stock. All used furniture has been cleaned and repaired; much of it is in showroom condition and priced accordingly. We found a 3-cushion, multi-colored sofa priced at $150, a recliner at $100, a walnut coffee table at $64 and bargains on office furniture as well.

Checks, Credit cards

GREENBAUM'S CLEARANCE CENTER
Bellevue: 905 Bellevue Way N.E. ☎ 455-1707
Hours: Mon, Fri 10-9; Tues, Wed, Sat 10-6; Sun 12-5

Browse through two floors of quality clearance merchandise from Greenbaum's home furnishings stores. Savings often amount to 50% or more. New shipments arrive every week, and the best buys go fast. This is a good place to start if you're in the market for decorative accessories. Located behind Pier One Imports.

Checks, Credit cards

HUNTER'S FURNITURE OUTLET — NEW LISTING
Tacoma: ☎ 588-8897
By Appointment Only

After owning a furniture store for ten years, Hunter decided to eliminate the high cost of a retail operation by arranging for customers to visit a 5-story wholesale warehouse normally open only to dealers. Select from a huge inventory of furniture just like you'd see at department stores and pay 25% off retail. Save another 5% by picking up your order instead of having it delivered.

Cash, Credit cards

J.C. PENNEY'S FURNITURE WAREHOUSE — NEW LISTING
Tukwila: 17200 Southcenter Pkwy. ☎ 575-4792
Hours: Mon-Sat 9-5, Sun 12-5

This clearance warehouse where overstock, discontinued goods and unclaimed special-orders are sold is located on the north side of Penney's Distribution Center. Damaged goods should be clearly marked. Instead of waiting for retail sales, shop here for guaranteed savings of 35% to 50% on sofas, chairs, bedding and a limited selection of decorative items.

Checks, Credit cards

JOHN'S FURNITURE FACTORY — NEW LISTING
Everett: 716 S.E. Everett Mall Way ☎ 353-8097
Kirkland: 8427 122nd Ave. N.E. ☎ 827-7799
Tukwila: 512 Strander Blvd. ☎ 241-6263
Hours: Generally, Mon-Fri 10-7, Sat 10-7, Sun 11-6

continued >

Home Furnishings, Furniture

Oak bookcases, entertainment centers and roll-top desks are big sellers here, often at 40% off suggested retail prices. You'll also find bedroom sets, sofas, love seats and solid wood dining room furniture. Some products are made on the premises in their factory, others are purchased from local or national manufacturers. Watch for sales on floor models, discontinued items and freight-damaged goods.

Checks, Credit cards

LENORA SQUARE SHOWROOM — NEW LISTING
Seattle: 100 Lenora Street ☎ 621-7500 *Downtown*
Hours: Mon-Fri 9-5

You don't have to go into debt to buy designer furniture. Samples are sold-year round on the 1st and 5th floors of this huge furniture mart. Inventory varies from vintage to large contemporary pieces. When we shopped, there was a lot of office furniture in stock. Once or twice a year the showroom throws a big sale to make room for new styles. Call to get on their mailing list.

Checks

MOBILI LTD.
Issaquah: 317 N.W. Gilman Blvd. ☎ 391-1849 *Gilman Village*
West Seattle: 2611 California Ave. S.W. ☎ 932-8688
Hours: Mon-Sat 10-6, Thurs 10-8, Sun 12-5

One of the owners of these elite home furnishings stores is an interior designer. Inventory is an eclectic collection of showroom samples, avant garde styles, vintage pieces and imported objects d'art from local factories, Northwest craftsmen and the Design Center. Local artists supply one-of-a-kind paintings and jewelry. Used furniture is carefully screened and treasures show up frequently. Consignees get 60% of the selling price. The Issaquah store carries more traditional styles.

Checks, Credit cards

NATIONAL FURNITURE RENTALS AND SALES, INC.
Seattle: 2440 1st Ave. S. ☎ 682-8680 *South of Kingdome*
Hours: Mon-Fri 9-7, Sat 9-5

The Seattle store stocks 75% of the rental return furniture sold by National even though their stores in Everett, Tacoma, Kent and Bremerton always have a small selection on hand. Check the telephone book for the one nearest you. Everything is sold "as is", and there are no returns or warranties.

Checks

OFF CENTER FURNITURE WAREHOUSE
Tacoma: 2926 S Steele St. ☎ 627-2862
Hours: Mon-Sat 10-6, Sun 10-5

continued >

110 Home Furnishings, Furniture

A lot of stores advertise discount prices, but few can compete with the quality and prices we found here. Furniture and accessories for the whole house, from bunk beds to grandfather clocks, come from well-known manufacturers like *Dixie, Stanley and Goodman*. These are current styles, not close-outs or seconds, so you can compare prices elsewhere. A bona fide warehouse setting and word-of-mouth advertising keep overhead and prices low. The owners guarantee the best deal around on oak furniture.

Checks, Credit cards

ORIENTAL FURNITURE WAREHOUSE — NEW LISTING
Bellevue: 322 Bellevue Way N.E. ☎ 646-9553
Seattle: 1111 Elliott Ave. W. ☎ 286-3139 *Northwest of Seattle Center*
Hours: Seattle, Mon-Sat 11-6, Sun 12-5; Bellevue, Tues-Sat 10:30-6

East meets West. Decorate your home with imported oriental furnishings in contemporary, traditional and antique styles. You'll find one-of-a-kind pieces in teak, rosewood and black lacquer. Decorative accessories include panel screens, nesting tables, porcelains and fish bowls— the latest rage—in a variety of sizes.

Checks, Credit cards

PEOPLE'S FURNITURE RENTAL
Tacoma: 6818 Tacoma Mall Blvd. ☎ 474-5501, 800/922-1231
Hours: Mon-Fri 10-7, Sat 10-5

Bargain hunters head for People's back room, where returned rental furniture is sold. Sofas start as low as $90. Add a matching chair and pay around $150. Dinette sets run $100-$150. We saw a dinette set still in the original box and good buys on coffee tables, lamps and mattresses. The best time to shop is the beginning of the month since that's when most rental furniture comes back.

Checks

PIKE PLACE FURNITURE CLEARANCE CENTER
Seattle: 2200 Western Ave. ☎ 441-0531 *Downtown*
Hours: Mon-Sat 9-5:30, Sun 12-4:30

Continental Furniture uses this warehouse to clear out new and used inventory from their retail stores and rental businesses. Choose from complete room groupings, individual pieces, accessories and office furniture, all priced according to their condition. You'll always find a big selection of sofas.

Checks, Credit cards

SCHOENFELD'S
Tacoma: 1423 Pacific Ave. ☎ 272-4171
Hours: Mon, Fri 9:30-9, Tues-Thurs, Sat 9:30-6, Sun 12-5

continued >

Home Furnishings, Household Appliances

The fourth floor of this old downtown establishment houses all the store's close-out, damaged and discontinued merchandise. You'll spot something for every room in the house from large pieces of furniture to decorator items. Check out the inventory on the other three floors where bright orange tags denote sale merchandise. This store has been in business since 1864 and is not related to the Schoenfeld's furniture store in Seattle.

Checks, Credit cards

SEATTLE FURNITURE FACTORY
Tukwila: 17500 W. Valley Hwy. ☎ 872-8989
Hours: Generally, Mon-Thurs 9-7, Fri 9-3:30, closed Sat, Sun 11-5

This factory started out as an upholstery shop and their motto is, "It's less because we make it". Sofas that run $300 to $500 can be converted to queen-size sleepers for about $200. Love seats, sectionals, chairs and children's furniture sell for 30% to 50% less than comparable items in retail stores. Purchase what's in stock for immediate delivery or have your furniture made-to-order from a variety of fabrics and styles. The showroom also has end tables, coffee tables, bookcases, lamps and accessories at remarkably low prices.

Checks, Credit cards

Household Appliances

Look in Food Service Warehouses and Kitchen Equipment for commercial-grade appliances, and refer to Audio-Video listings for TV's, VCR's, stereos, etc.

ACTION SMALL APPLIANCE SERVICE
Bellevue: 11818 N.E. 8th ☎ 455-3578
Seattle: 2125 2nd Ave. ☎ 448-2020 *Downtown*
Hours: Mon-Fri 9-5

Action buys such well-known brands as *Braun, Hamilton Beach, Toastmaster and Kitchen Aid* directly from the factory and passes on the savings. You'll always find a selection of coffee makers and men's shavers, which are good buys because many are seconds.

Checks, Credit cards

AJAX ELECTRIC, INC.
Seattle: 2911 1st Ave. S. ☎ 622-9945 *South of Kingdome*
Tacoma: 747 Fawcett Ave. ☎ 383-3446
Hours: Mon-Fri 8-5:30, Sat 9-2

Ajax is the factory-authorized parts and service shop for over 80 small appliance manufacturers. Top selling lines are *Black and Decker, Hamilton Beach, Kitchen Aid and West Bend*. Save by buying reconditioned items. Occasionally, Ajax offers the consumer exceptional bargains on discontinued styles and factory overstock.

Checks, Credit cards

Home Furnishings, Household Appliances

ALBERT LEE APPLIANCE — NEW LISTING
Seattle: 1476 Elliott Ave. W. ☎ 282-2110 *Queen Anne*
Hours: Mon-Fri 9-6, Sat 9-4

You'll find a variety of name-brand major kitchen and laundry appliances, but prices are lowest on *General Electric*, which they buy by the truckload. Fifty years ago the company opened as a furniture store, and while the emphasis has shifted, look for bargains on *Spring Aire* mattresses and box springs.

Checks, Credit cards

AMERICAN APPLIANCES — NEW LISTING
Seattle: 1001 Westlake N. ☎ 282-4488 *Northeast of Seattle Center*
Hours: Mon-Fri 9-6, Sat 9-5

Used appliances are always available at American, but the selection is catch-as-catch-can. If price is your #1 objective, take a look at the used coin-operated washers and dryers, which look utilitarian, but were built to last.

Checks, Credit cards

BOTHELL APPLIANCE AND TV
Bothell: 10042 Main St. ☎ 485-0551
Hours: Mon-Sat 9-5:30

A week or two after school is out, Bothell Appliance and TV has a terrific sale on *GE* ranges, washers, dryers, refrigerators and freezers used the previous nine months for instructional purposes in local schools. They look and operate like new. All factory warranties are included, and savings start at 30%. Occasionally the company liquidates floor samples and "scratch 'n' dent" inventory for major suppliers. Full warranties apply, and you save 40%.

Checks, Credit cards

COHO SUPPLY INC. — NEW LISTING
Kent: 8504 S. 228th ☎ 623-5480
Hours: Mon-Fri 8-6, Sat 10-5

Coho sells major appliances, cabinets and lighting fixtures to builders, but their showroom is open to the public. They'll quote prices over the phone on specific brand and model numbers. We hear this is a good place to stock up on light bulbs.

Checks, Credit cards

DAVE'S APPLIANCE REBUILD — NEW LISTING
Seattle: 1601 15th Ave. ☎ 324-3270 *Capitol Hill*
Hours: Mon-Fri 9-5:30, Sat 10-2

For 15 years Dave has been buying, selling and trading used appliances. Landlords and property managers are his best customers and suppliers, so there's a constant turnover. Prices are negotiable. Refrigerators average $129 to $299, and cookstoves go for about $150.

Checks, Credit cards

Home Furnishings, Household Appliances

J & S SEWING AND HOUSEWARES — NEW LISTING
Renton: 2836 N.E. Sunset Blvd. ☎ 255-8900
Hours: Mon-Fri 9-6, Sat 10-5

Most of the used sewing machines at J & S come from the 60 local schools they supply every year. Prices are lowest at the beginning and end of the school year. Call to let them know you're interested. Look for a big selection of *Singer*, along with *Viking, Elna and White*. Prices are competitive on new and used vacuum cleaners and small kitchen appliances. Watch for special sales on store demonstrators and overstock.

Checks, Credit cards

KING & BUNNY'S DISCOUNT APPLIANCE & TV — NEW LISTING
Renton: 4608 N.E. Sunset Blvd. ☎ 277-0600
Hours: Mon-Fri 10-7, Sat 10-6, Sun 12-5

This small family-operated business maintains low prices with low overhead. You'll find excellent buys on name-brand major appliances, especially *Whirlpool*, which they stock at a nearby warehouse. If you buy more than one appliance, you get an even bigger discount.

Checks, Credit cards

MAJOR BRAND APPLIANCES — NEW LISTING
Federal Way: 34419 Pacific Hwy. S. ☎ 838-7056
Hours: Mon-Fri 9-6, Sat 9-5

One of the largest inventories of quality used appliances and parts in the area awaits you at this large warehouse. Choose from dozens of ranges, refrigerators, washers and dryers, freezers, water heaters, dishwashers, disposers and microwave ovens, most of which are fairly old. Swap your machine for one of theirs, and they'll give you $50 credit toward the trade-in. Senior citizens and property managers get a discount.

Checks, Credit cards

PICKERING APPLIANCE & TV — NEW LISTING
Renton: 909 S. 3rd ☎ 226-3232
Hours: Mon-Fri 8:30-6, Sat 8:30-5

Pickering handles a lot of discounted appliances. Some come from model homes or incorrect orders, so they're practically new. You can realize big savings if you don't mind minor flaws. *General Electric and Hotpoint* are their primary lines.

Checks, Credit cards

REMINGTON SHAVER FACTORY SERVICE
Seattle: 1909 4th Ave. ☎ 682-1522 *Downtown*
Hours: Mon-Fri 9-5, Sat 10-2

continued >

114 Home Furnishings, Household Appliances

Prices at Remington are competitive with most discount stores. If your old shaver is in good condition, they'll give you $10 on a trade-in. They also sell name-brand cutlery, sporting goods, knives and sewing scissors. Chefs and cooking school students get a discount if they purchase three or more knives.

Checks, Credit cards

SARCO (Seattle Appliance Repair Company)
Kirkland: 220 Kirkland Ave. ☎ 827-5739
Seattle: 2416 2nd Ave. ☎ 441-5977 *Downtown*
Hours: Seattle, Mon-Fri 8-5, Sat 9-1; Kirkland, Mon-Fri 10-6, Sat 9-2

When it comes to buying a name-brand electric shaver, you can always find a good deal at SARCO. The company repairs small household appliances like irons, heaters and lamps. Their motto is "we'll do anything to make customers happy, so long as we don't go broke doing it." They have a good selection of new and factory rebuilt appliances by such manufacturers as *Braun, Hamilton Beach, GE, Black & Decker, Toastmaster, Panasonic and Sunbeam.*

Checks, Credit cards

SEWING MACHINE SERVICE CO. INC.   NEW LISTING
Renton: 315 Main Ave. S. ☎ 255-8673
Hours: Mon-Fri 8:30-5:30, Sat 8:30-4:30

SMS carries one of the largest inventories of industrial and household sewing machines in the Northwest. The day we visited there were 30 used machines, ranging in price from $100 to $600. If you are a serious seamstress who wants the same specialized equipment used by garment manufacturers, check out the used overlock, hemming and blind-stitching machines.

Checks, Credit cards

SILO
Bellevue: 14315 N.E. 20th St. ☎ 746-6080 *Ross Plaza*
Everett: 811 S.E. Everett Mall Way ☎ 355-7390
Federal Way: 31621 23rd Ave. S. ☎ 941-6810
Lynnwood: 18833 28th Ave. W. ☎ 771-2282
Seattle: 10409 Aurora Ave. N. ☎ 527-5000 *North Park*
     809 N.E. 45th St. ☎ 545-3506 *U-District*
Silverdale: 10796 Myhre Place N.W. ☎ 692-0775
Tacoma: 2951 S. 38th St. ☎ 475-7001
Tukwila: 17550 Southcenter Pkwy. ☎ 575-1012 *Parkway Plaza*
Woodinville: 17638 140th Ave. N.E. ☎ 481-5885
Hours: Mon-Fri 9-9, Sat 10-9, Sun 12-6

continued >

The most visible and aggressive off-price retailer on the West Coast selling name-brand appliances, electronic and audio/video equipment, Silo buys in huge quantities and sells at incredibly low markups. Prices tend to fluctuate since they're constantly having sales, so we recommend you use the frequent bulk-mailing sale brochures for comparison shopping. The company won't quote prices over the phone. If you find somebody selling the same item for less (floor models don't count), Silo will reimburse you the difference plus 10%. Costco and Price Savers are Silo's chief competitors on small electronics, but neither has as wide a selection. Every once in a while a discount chain will have a special promotion that beats Silo's prices.

Checks, Credit cards

SINGER REGIONAL FACTORY SERVICE CENTER
Bellevue: 1519 130th Ave. N.E. ☎ 462-1274
Hours: Mon-Sat 8-4:30

The only sewing machines sold here are trade-ins or factory-reconditioned, which come with the same warranty as new machines, but are 35% to 50% off the suggested retail price. Two models are always in stock: a basic open arm straight stitch for $109.99 and a solid state that sells for $299.99.

Checks, Credit cards

Kitchen Equipment

Restaurant supply emporiums offer everything used in the food service industry from furniture, appliances, dishes and paper products to cleaning supplies. Large families will be interested in the huge refrigerators, dishwashers and ranges. Serious chefs will love the quality of professional-grade cookware as well as the selection of gadgets. Oversize pots, pans and utensils are both decorative and practical. Restaurant china, glassware and silverware can be surprisingly handsome and sturdy. Prices are not necessarily lower than those of a department store or kitchen shop, so you have to weigh performance against cost. It stands to reason that products built to withstand heavy daily use will be a better long-term investment than those designed for the consumer market. Used items may be your best buy.

Also see Food Service Warehouses for many of the same items sold by restaurant supply houses. Refer to Household Appliances for name-brand kitchen equipment and small electrical appliances.

AAA NEW & USED RESTAURANT EQUIPMENT
Kent: 7835 S. 212th ☎ 872-7474, 622-2525
Hours: Mon-Fri 9-5:30

continued >

Home Furnishings, Kitchen Equipment

If you want to outfit your kitchen with a commercial-grade, six-burner stove or buy stainless steel cookware similar to *Cuisinart*, but less expensive, this 15,000 sq. ft. showroom is a good place to start. It's crammed with appliances, sinks, tables and chairs, and cooking and serving items. In the used department, you'll find everything from walk-in freezers to silverware at 25% to 85% savings. The friendly staff probably won't let you leave without purchasing one of their best selling items— a $4.10 rubber scraper that never comes apart.

Checks

BARGREEN-ELLINGSON, INC.
Seattle: 1275 Mercer St. ☎ 682-1472 *East of Seattle Center*
Tacoma: Tacoma Mall Blvd. at S. 38th ☎ 475-9201, 838-3515 Tacoma Mall
Hours: Mon-Fri 8-5, Sat 9-1

Bargreen's caters to the needs of fine restaurants, taverns and institutional kitchens. It would take pages to describe the 8,000 items in their huge showrooms, so plan on taking your time to look around. We were impressed with the glassware, cutlery, china and furniture.

You can purchase everything from bar stools to drink mixes and cocktail napkins for social occasions. Commercial-grade ranges and refrigerators are available, plus cookware of every description.

Checks, Credit cards

DICK'S RESTAURANT SUPPLY
Seattle: 2963 1st Ave. S. ☎ 382-0160 *South of Kingdome*
Hours: Mon-Fri 8:30-5

New and used equipment for bakeries, delis and restaurants fill Dick's 20,000 sq. ft. warehouse. Best sellers are gas ranges and commercial appliances. You can expect a good selection of utensils, cutlery and commercial-grade pots and pans. Slightly-flawed, brand-new china is one of the best buys. Used equipment turns over fast and is guaranteed.

Checks, Credit cards

THE DISHRACK   NEW LISTING
Tukwila: 17900 Southcenter Pkwy. ☎ 575-1153 *Pavilion Mall*
Hours: Mon-Fri 9:30-9:30, Sat 9:30-7, Sun 11-6

Save up to 40% on name-brand housewares at this off-price outlet. Inventory consists mainly of dinnerware, glassware, cookware, cutlery and kitchen accessories. Some items are closeouts and discontinued styles, but even regular stock is discounted. Lines can be special-ordered.

Checks, Credit cards

RESTAURANT MART
Seattle: 2851 Eastlake E. ☎ 322-4900 *East Lake Union*
Hours: Mon-Fri 8:30-5, Sat 10:30-3

continued >

Home Furnishings, Bedding & Linens

Restaurant Mart supplies the food and beverage industry with new and used fixtures, equipment and kitchenwares at competitive prices. Commercial-grade coffee makers, mixers, slicers and cheese melters add new dimensions to the home kitchen. Items such as glassware, silverware and dishes must be purchased by the case or dozen, but you're guaranteed 25% off. Cookware is sold by the piece.

Checks, Credit cards

Bedding & Linens

Futons are the fastest growing segment of the bedding industry, and Seattle boasts more suppliers than any other city in the country. Many people buy futons as guest beds because they don't take up much room and are easy to move and less expensive than sleeper sofas. The market is very competitive.

BEDS, BUNKS & MATTRESSES
Tacoma: 9530 Bridgeport Way S.W. ☎ 582-3483
Hours: Tues-Sat. 10-5:30

Bring the kids when you shop this off-price outlet, where there's the largest selection of bunk beds in the state. Name-brand mattresses and bedroom furniture make up the rest of their inventory. Everything in stock is current-style and their motto, "80% off all items all the time", appeals to serious bargain hunters.

Checks, Credit cards

BEDS NORTHWEST   NEW LISTING
Puyallup: 15317 S. Meridian ☎ 841-4836
Woodinville: 13644 N.E. 175th Street ☎ 481-7835
Hours: Mon-Sat 10-6, Sun 12-5

Store policy is to "sell more beds for less", and since this is a wholesale liquidator for local manufacturers as well as two Canadian firms, you know prices are going to be low. Last time we checked, mattress and boxsprings for a single bed started at a little over $100, king-size $250. You'll also discover frames and pillows in stock.

Checks, Credit cards

BEDSPREAD & LINEN WAREHOUSE
Factoria: I-90 & I-405 ☎ 747-1115 *Loehmann's Plaza*
Lynnwood: 3333 184th St. S.W. ☎ 362-5602 *Mervyn's Plaza*
Hours: Mon-Fri 10-9, Sat 10-6, Sun 12-6

There's something so comforting about plump pillows, fluffy bedspreads and frilly curtains when you know you don't have to pay full price! Everything here is first-quality, current-style merchandise by well-known manufacturers, as well as designer lines. Also find bathroom accessories and gift wares. Anything not in stock can be special-ordered. Discount coupons are sometimes given out with purchases and included in Value Pack mailers. Sidewalk sales go on all summer long.

Checks, Credit cards

118 Home Furnishings, Bedding & Linens

BUR-BANK DOMESTICS, INC.
Seattle: 2213 15th Ave. W. ☎ 282-1551 *Ballard*
Hours: Mon-Fri 8:30-5

If you need a large supply of linen, visit this wholesale distributor. They sell basic stock from *JP Stevens, Cannon and Fieldcrest* to institutions and department stores. Everything comes in packaged lots. Purchases that amount to less than $100 are subject to a 10% service charge, but you're still paying far below list price. The warehouse also represents *Health Tex and Carter's*, so you can save money on your children's wardrobe at the same time.

Checks

CASCADE CO.
Seattle: 1243 6th Ave. S. ☎ 467-9651 *South of Kingdome*
Hours: Mon-Fri 8-5

Cascade supplies motels, hotels and institutions with basic white linens. Towels, pillowcases, sheets and bedspreads by *Cannon and China* can be purchased by the dozen or half-dozen at prices below retail. Pillows cost $19.50/dozen, oversized flat sheets are $115/dozen and fitted sheets cost $106/dozen.

Checks, Credit cards

DISCOUNT WATERBEDS, INC.
Bellevue: 11010 N.E. 3rd Place ☎ 455-4314
Hours: Mon-Fri 11-8, Sat 11-6, Sun 12-5

You'll notice this is the only waterbed store listed because we're convinced they offer the best prices and friendliest service in town. They've been in business for 14 years, so they must be doing something right. Although the store appears to be a small house, you'll be impressed when you see the large inventory of conventional and flotation beds inside. Quality oak furniture is made especially for the company, as well as waterbed sheets that really fit and stay put. Discount Waterbeds is the only place we know that offers a 30-day in-home trial for a nominal fee, gives credit on account for customers you refer to them, and encourages visitors to scribble messages on the walls.

Checks, Credit cards

FUTON FACTORY OUTLET   NEW LISTING
Bellevue: 320 Bellevue Way N.E. ☎ 453-5575
Seattle: 13555 Aurora Ave. N. ☎ 367-5575 *Haller Lake*
Tukwila: 17358 Southcenter Pkwy. ☎ 575-9342 *Parkway Plaza*
Hours: Generally, Mon-Fri 10-7, Sat 10-6, Sun 10-5

continued >

Home Furnishings, Bedding & Linens

Inventory changes constantly, but you can count on big discounts because they sell overstock, imperfect, damaged and liquidation goods mainly from their own and other local factories. Basic to deluxe frames and futons in many different styles are always in stock. Covers are often priced at 50% off. Nomads, pillows, bean bag chairs and related accessories show up frequently.

Checks, Credit cards

FUTON OF NORTH AMERICA WAREHOUSE — NEW LISTING
Seattle: 810 Dexter ☎ 286-8557 *Northeast of Seattle Center*
Hours: Daily 11-6

This futon manufacturer is the oldest and largest in the Puget Sound area. Visit the warehouse to pick up good buys on discontinued styles and irregular futons, frames, covers and pillows. They offer the most extensive warranty around. If your futon looses its "oomph" after three or four years, they'll rejuvenate it for the cost of materials. Shop for a down comforter in the spring when they clear out their inventory at 50% off the marked price.

Checks, Credit cards

JEN-CEL-LITE CORP.
Seattle: 954 E. Union ☎ 322-3030 *Capitol Hill*
   6951 Martin Luther King Way S. (no phone) *Holly Park*
Hours: Capitol Hill Mon-Fri 7-3:30, closed for lunch 11:30-12; Holly Park, first and third Sat of each month, 9:30-4

The factory on Union Street makes outerwear, bedding and sleeping bags for local and nationally known retailers including Roffe, REI and L.L. Bean. The outlet in the old Wigwam store in Holly Park sells the factory's overstock, seconds and irregulars. Comforters start at $22, sleeping bags at $16. Look for bargains on pillows, baby bags, nylon fabrics and notions. Call the factory to find out what will be offered at the next outlet sale. You can pick up quilt scraps for under $1/yd. and 30-yd. rolls of batting for 50¢ to $3/yd. at the factory. Place your order ahead.

Checks

LUXURY LINENS / BURLINGTON COAT FACTORY — NEW LISTING
Edmonds: 2411 Aurora ☎ 776-2221
Tukwila: 17900 Southcenter Pkwy. ☎ 575-3995 Pavilion Mall
Hours: Mon-Fri 10-9, Sat 10-6, Sun 11-6

Famous-brand linens and accessories sell for 20% to 50% below retail. Seasonal sales and special promotions lower prices even more on a big selection of merchandise that includes basic as well as specialty and designer lines such as *Laura Ashley* linens and Battenburg tablecloths.

Checks, Credit cards

120 Home Furnishings, Bedding & Linens

MATTREST — NEW LISTING
Lynnwood: 20101 44th Ave. W. ☎ 776-0999
Tukwila: 17310 Southcenter Pkwy. ☎ 575-8560 *Parkway Plaza*
Hours: Mon-Fri 11-8, Sat 10-6, Sun 12-5

Mattresses by *Serta, Sealy and Spring Aire* are sold at these low-overhead outlets for much less than the same brands are priced in department stores. Anything not in stock can be ordered. Mattrest advertises free delivery and a free frame with the purchase of each set.

Checks, Credit cards

MATTRESS OUTLET — NEW LISTING
Tacoma: 2602 Bridgeport Way ☎ 383-4333
2410 84th St. S. ☎ 584-2025
Hours: Mon-Sat 9-6, Sun 12-5

Folks in Tacoma find name-brand mattresses at reduced prices here. Among the fifty models on display are such names as *Serta, Sealy and Therapedic*. Factory close-outs, when they're in stock, are your best buy. Low overhead keeps this company competitive with department store sale prices. Mattress Outlet also stocks name-brand appliances at discount prices.

Checks, Credit cards

PACIFIC LINEN OUTLET
Bellevue: N.E. 8th & 156th ☎ 562-9801 *Crossroads*
Everett: 7815 Evergreen Way ☎ 355-9745
Federal Way: 2130 S. 314th Street ☎ 941-8085
Kent: 26102 104th Ave. S.E. ☎ 852-8900 *Kent Hill Plaza*
Lake Forest Park: 17130 Bothell Way N.E. ☎ 365-1413
Lynnwood: 19509 Hwy. 99 ☎ 774-7700
Puyallup: 3500 S. Meridian ☎ 841-4220
Seattle: 13510 Aurora Ave. N. ☎ 364-5350 *Haller Lake*
Silverdale: 10876 Myhr Place N.W. ☎ 692-7007
Tacoma: 5401 6th Ave ☎ 756-2141
Hwy. 16 & Union Ave. ☎ 572-4445
10401 Gravelly Lake Dr. S.W. ☎ 584-1122
Tukwila: 17900 Southcenter Pkwy. ☎ 575-3999 *Pavilion Mall*
Hours: Generally, Mon-Fri-10-9, Sat 10-6, Sun 11-6

Everything you need from basic necessities to fashionable decorator items for the bed, bath, or kitchen can be found on the shelves of this successful local chain. Visit their super store in Bellevue for the best selection. Because Pacific Linen buys nationally known brands direct from the mill, prices average 30% less than you would normally pay for the same item in department stores. Watch for outstanding values during month-long sales or try to attend their huge clearance events in July and August when an incredible quantity of premium goods sells at rock bottom prices. Some items are discontinued styles, close-outs or irregulars. The stores also stock a limited selection of day beds and futons, along with assorted housewares and gift items.

Checks, Credit cards

Home Furnishings, Bedding & Linens

SIT 'N' SLEEP
Bellevue: 13310 Bel-Red Road ☎ 643-7378
Woodinville: 14130 N.E. Woodinville-Duvall Rd. ☎ 485-7378
Hours: Generally, Mon-Fri 10-8, Sat 10-6, Sun 12-5

Sit 'N' Sleep offers every kind of sleeping apparatus available— recliners, futons, electric beds, flotation systems. Choose from a huge selection of name-brand mattresses and sleeper sofas. We liked all the colors available in the tubular steel loft bed set for kids. Call for store hours at the Bellevue warehouse/clearance center.

Checks, Credit cards

THE WELL-MADE BED — NEW LISTING
Bellevue: 990 102nd Blvd. ☎ 455-3508 *University Bookstore Complex*
Seattle: 1427 Western Ave. ☎ 343-5066 *Downtown*
Hours: Mon-Fri 10-6, Sat 10-5, Sun 12-5

White sale prices are in effect year round at these small shops, but don't be fooled by their size. Even though they only stock king and queen-size sheets in 50 or 60 patterns, almost any pattern put out by a leading manufacturer can be special-ordered, including twin and standard bed sizes. Matching comforters, dust ruffles and shams are also available, as well as custom-made comforters, bedspreads and blankets.

Checks, Credit cards

Here's a list of mattress manufacturers in the area that sell directly to the public: (Many of these companies will renovate or rebuild mattresses, and some specialize in odd-size bedding for boats, RV's and trucks.)

ARTY'S CUSTOM-BILT MATTRESS AND UPHOLSTERY
Tacoma: 5415 S. Puget Sound ☎ 474-4800
Hours: Mon-Fri 8-5, Sat by appointment

CASE LITTELL
Seattle: 8214 Greenwood Ave. N. ☎ 782-3131 *Greenwood*
Hours: Mon-Sat 9-5, Mon & Wed 9-8

EASTSIDE MATTRESS CO.
Redmond: 7858 Leary Way ☎ 885-2156
Hours: Mon-Fri 10-6, Sat 10-4

EVERREST MATTRESS
Seattle: 1907 15th Ave. W. ☎ 284-9531 *Ballard*
Hours: Mon-Fri 8-5, Sat 9-4

See area locator index for this section on page 225

122 Home Furnishings, China, Crystal & Silver

IMPERIAL MATTRESS CO.
Seattle: 462 N. 34th St. ☎ 632-2240 *Fremont*
Hours: Mon-Fri 8:30-5, Sat 10-1

RESTMORE MATTRESS AND FURNITURE FACTORY
Tacoma: 1541 Market ☎ 272-2429
Hours: Mon-Fri 8-6, Sat 9-1

SLEEP-AIRE MATTRESS CO.
Bellevue: 13120 Bel-Red Road ☎ 454-0310
Kent: 25447 Pacific Hwy. S. ☎ 839-6003 *Midway*
Seattle: 19022 Aurora Ave. Ave. N. ☎ 546-4195 *Richmond Highlands*
6110 Roosevelt Way N.E. ☎ 523-3702 *U-District*
2444 1st Ave. S. ☎ 682-4063 *South of Kingdome*
Tacoma: 4816 S. Tacoma Way ☎ 473-3220
Hours: Generally, Mon-Wed 9-6, Thurs, Fri 9-8

China, Crystal & Silver

CARROLL AND ASSOCIATES
Seattle: 3rd & Stewart, Securities Bldg. ☎ 621-8341 *Downtown*
Hours: Mon-Fri 9-3, Closed July and August

Three generations of the Carroll family have been buying and selling gold, silver, gemstones and fine jewelry, establishing a reputation for legitimate savings, quality service, and one-of-a-kind items. Inventory is purchased mainly from estates and private parties and then skillfully renovated to look brand-new. Sterling silver candlesticks, tea services and flatware sell at 50% or more below retail prices. Their collection of stainless patterns rivals Frederick & Nelson's. They also custom-design jewelry and appraise objects d'art.

Checks

CHINA, SILVER & CRYSTAL SHOP
Seattle: 2809 2nd Ave. ☎ 441-8906 *Downtown*
Hours: Mon-Fri 9-5:30, Sat 10-3

What a find for wedding and anniversary gifts! The selection of china patterns includes such world-famous names as *Lenox, Royal Doulton, Minton, Noritake, Ainsley, Gorham, Dansk, Royal Copenhagen and Villeroy and Boch.* Choose from sterling and stainless flatware by *Reed and Barton, Oneida, Lunt and Buccellati.*

Waterford collectors will be delighted when they compare prices. During sales in January and July, prices plummet to cost on some items. Everything is first-quality. The helpful staff will quote prices, take phone orders, and arrange shipping.

Checks, Credit cards

Home Furnishings, Decorative Accessories

KOKESH CUT GLASS CO.

Seattle: 301 N.E. 65th ☎ 527-4848 *Ravenna*
Hours: Tues-Fri 11-5, Sat 10-1

This is a great place to purchase customized gifts in the $15 to $35 range for weddings or anniversaries. Choose from a big selection of crystal stemware, bowls, pitchers, vases, salt and pepper shakers or sugar and creamers. Monogrammed champagne glasses for the bride and groom are popular. Business logos can be engraved on corporate gifts and trophies.

Checks, Credit cards

KUSAK CUT GLASS WORKS

Seattle: 1911 22nd Ave. S. ☎ 324-2931 *Mt. Baker*
Hours: Mon-Fri 9-4:30

Visit the magnificent showroom of this cut glass factory and you'll understand why department stores and better gift shops all over the country sell Kusak's exquisite handmade crystal ware. All glass is imported from Europe and cut or engraved on the premises in a tradition established 75 years ago by the founder of this family-owned business. Although prices in the showroom are retail, the company hosts two annual sales to clear out overstock and irregulars at 20% to 50% below retail. The spring event features stemware and chandeliers, dripping with Austrian faceted crystals. The fall sale, usually the last ten days of October, offers a dazzling array of glassware from $5 to $500. The pitchers, bowls, glass sculpture and paper weights make wonderful Christmas gifts. Just before the sales, Kusak's repairs chipped and broken crystal for a nominal fee. Call for exact dates. Kusak's own crystal is accepted for repair year-round. Fill out a postcard at the factory to be notified of the next sale. Custom-engraving and guided tours are available.

Checks, Credit cards

Decorative Accessories

CLAY ART CENTER

Tacoma: 2636 Pioneer Way E. ☎ 922-5342
Hours: Mon-Fri 9-5:30, Sat 10-2

Artists make glazed porcelain, high-fire stoneware, pottery and sinks at this studio and sell the pieces at art fairs, mall shows and in the Clay Art Center's gallery. Prices are going to be less at this "factory outlet" than you would pay in Seattle gift shops for merchandise of the same quality. There's always a shelf full of seconds, and many are excellent buys. Pottery and ceramic supplies and equipment are less expensive here too.

Checks, Credit cards

Home Furnishings, Decorative Accessories

CUT-THE-CORNER FRAME SHOP
Tukwila: 17900 Southcenter Parkway ☎ 575-8272 *Pavilion Mall*
Hours: Mon-Fri 9:30-9:00, Sat 9:30-9, Sun 11-6

Cut-the-Corner offers creative custom picture framing at do-it-yourself prices. Average cost is $60 to frame a 24-in. by 36-in. picture using quality materials, which the owner guarantees will last for 150 years. A large collection of framed and unframed original works, limited-edition prints, posters and graphics sell for at least 20% below retail.

Checks, Credit cards

GENESIS FINE ARTS   NEW LISTING
Normandy Park: 853 S.W. 174th St. ☎ 248-1016
Hours: Mon-Fri 9-5, Weekends by appointment

Want to give your bare walls a new look? Genesis publishes and sells original art and prints by American and Northwest artists. Purchase the artwork at their showroom and pay 25% less than you would at local galleries.

Checks

INTERIOR ART AND FRAME   NEW LISTING
Kirkland: 123 Lake St. S. ☎ 827-5324
Hours: Mon-Thurs 10-7, Fri, Sat 10-9, Sun 12-5

Volume discounts are available on custom framing, but what appealed to us was "Art Wrap", the latest innovation in inexpensive mounting. For half the cost of framing, you can have posters and prints mounted and shrink-wrapped with a heat-set process that prevents warping.

We also liked their easy pricing system for framing: multiply the width by the length and multiply that figure by 50¢. Artists get a 25% discount.

Checks, Credit cards

K AND K COMPANY
Seattle: ☎ 282-6198
Periodic sales

This home-based business makes napkins, placemats, coasters, table runners and scarves from decorator fabrics. They sell at local craft fairs, bazaars and consignment shops, but irregulars and close-outs are sold at their periodic sales. Christmas designs are a specialty. Appointments can be made year-round to look at wares in the evenings and on weekends, or add your name to the mailing list.

Checks, Credit cards

L.A. FRAMES
Renton: 309 S. 3rd ☎ 228-1693
Hours: Mon-Fri 9:30-6, Sat 10-5

With the largest selection of ready-made frames in the Northwest, you're sure to find just the right setting for your work of art or family photo. Don't forget to check out the half-price rack. Custom-framing takes about a week, but rush orders can be done in 48 hours at no extra charge.

continued >

Home Furnishings Decorative Accessories

Save 25% by having a staffperson cut the frame, mat, and glass so you can do-it-yourself. Art students get a 10% discount on drawing and painting supplies. Posters and limited edition prints are also available.

Checks, Credit cards

LAKE CITY PICTURE FRAMING

Seattle: 14028 Lake City Way N.E. ☎ 363-2100 *Lake City*
Hours: Mon-Sat 9-6

The prices here on custom framing and ready-made materials may be the lowest in town! The trained staff will help you pick out just the right mat and molding from hundreds of samples, cut the glass, mat, and frame and send you home with instructions on how to assemble it. Or, pay the unbelievably low price of $4 to $18 for labor and pick up the finished product a week later. You'll also find racks of completed frames. Buy ten of the same item and get 10% off; buy more, and get a bigger discount.

Checks, Credit cards

SILK AND FLORAL EXCHANGE

Seattle: 5957 4th Ave. S. ☎ 763-8334 *Georgetown*
Hours: Mon-Fri 9-6, Sat 9-4

This floral warehouse sells artificial trees, plants, and flower arrangements to hotels and offices. They offer a complete selection of silk flowers, baskets, vases, floral and wedding supplies. Prices may not be competitive on every item. Designers at the Silk and Floral Exchange will custom-make anything you need.

Checks, Credit cards

SPECIALTY CANDLES BY LUNDS

Auburn: 131 30th N.E. ☎ 939-5385
Hours: Tues-Fri 9-5, Sat 10-2

Lunds is a nationwide mail-order company that makes and distributes unique candles and gift items. Best-sellers are their customized wedding, anniversary and birth candles. Call or write for their free catalog or visit the factory where seconds and overstock sell for up to 50% off. Seasonal items dominate, so this is a great place to shop for Christmas gifts.

Checks, Credit cards

TRU-ART PICTURE FRAME CO.

Tacoma: 2609 6th Ave. ☎ 572-7972
Hours: Mon-Fri 10-6, Sat 10-3

The owner says he's framed everything from pistols to pigtails. Tru-Art buys molding from all over the world and manufactures frames, which keeps prices low. Solid oak is the favored material, but you'll find a few metal frames among the hundreds of ready-made frames and molding samples Custom framing averages $35 to $48. Artists receive a 20% discount. Anyone who buys five or more of the same item qualifies for a discount.

Checks, Credit cards

Plants, Flowers & Greenery

With its multitude of nurseries, greenhouses and plant shops, the Puget Sound area is a mecca for plant lovers. Most of these businesses rely on quality, service and selection to generate sales rather than discount prices. Quality is the key issue here, because plants require tender loving care. It is possible to pick up good buys, but a "bargain plant" is not a good buy at all if it harbors insects or disease, is severely root-bound from being too long in its container, or is poorly adapted to this region. The more you know about plants, the more likely you'll be able to "rescue" a sickly sale item or know a terrific buy when you see it.

Nurseries

In general, large garden centers that buy in volume directly from the growers can offer lower prices than smaller specialty nurseries. You may be able to save money by visiting some of the nurseries and garden centers that dot the outlying rural communities where land costs are lower. Here are some helpful aids you might want to take along:

"Retail Nursery Locator Map", published by the Washington State Nursery and Landscaping Association lists over 70 nurseries. Call 800-672-7711 for a free copy.

"Specialty Nursery Guide", a detailed map and listing of 37 little nurseries located between Stanwood and Puyallup that feature rare and unusual plants. Copies are available through libraries or send a stamped, self-addressed #10 envelope to Specialty Nursery Association, 11907 Nevers Rd., Snohomish, WA 98290.

If you have a green thumb, you may find some great buys on "used" tropical plants at shops that lease them. There are no guarantees or returns on these purchases. Fred Meyer, K-Mart and Chubby & Tubby have some of the lowest prices in town on house plants and bedding plants. However, quality will vary considerably.

BAKER & CHANTRY ORCHIDS
Woodinville: 18611 132nd N.E. ☎ 483-0345
Hours: Mon-Sun 10-5

"Growing orchids is not a hobby," says the owner, " it's an incurable disease!" If you're fascinated by the royalty of the flower world, get on the mailing list for this specialty nursery's quarterly sales. You can pick up a price list, and the knowledgeable staff will answer any questions.

Checks

EDMONDS COMMUNITY COLLEGE
Lynnwood: 20000 68th Ave. W. ☎ 771-1500
Annual sale

continued >

During the third week of May, the Horticulture department hosts a fundraiser in the greenhouse. Specialty nurseries throughout the area contribute unusual perennials, bedding plants and flowering baskets. Prices are usually below retail. Lectures and workshops held each quarter are open to the public and often free of charge.

Checks

GROWING GREEN INTERIORS

Des Moines: 14420 Des Moines Memorial Dr. ☎ 248-0320
Hours: Mon-Fri 8-5

Growing Green sells, leases and maintains indoor foliage. In May and September, the company turns over its stock at wholesale prices. Call at the beginning of the month to get the exact date.

Checks

INTERIOR PLANT DESIGN / KIMURA NURSERY

Redmond: 3860 N.E. Bellevue-Redmond Rd. ☎ 883-4455
Hours: Mon-Fri 7-5, Sat & Sun 9-5

These commonly-owned businesses collaborate on big sales every April and October. Prices start at 15% off, and the inventory is drawn from recycled rental plants and nursery overstock. Call to receive an announcement and use the coupon that accompanies it to save another 15%. Staff takes special care to rejuvenate plants before the sale. They always have a good selection of ficus trees, dracaena, bamboo and kentia palms.

Checks, Credit cards

PLANTS & PLANTING GREENHOUSES

Puyallup: 7722 48th St. E. ☎ 922-6994, 838-0254
Hours: Mon-Sat 8-4:30

Plan on spending the day so you can stroll leisurely through five greenhouses and an equal number of acres brimming with greenery. The best bargains are on overruns, which must be cleared out to make room for new seedlings. Call for information on their November indoor plant sale. If you're doing major landscaping, you'll get a discount on purchases of $200 or more.

Checks

SQUAK MOUNTAIN GREENHOUSE

Issaquah: 7600 Renton-Issaquah Rd. S.E. ☎ 392-1025
Hours: Mon-Sat 9-6

Squak Mountain's specialty is colorful seasonal plants. In spring, buy geraniums, petunias, fuchsias, begonias and impatiens to bring joy to your garden and buy vegetable bedding plants to get a head start on the growing season. Landscape trees, shrubs and ground covers are in stock year-round. In December, the greenhouse is filled with poinsettias and Christmas trees. Put your name on their mailing list for sales.

Checks, Credit cards

TROPICAL FOLIAGE

Renton: 210 Wells Ave. S. ☎ 277-0922
Hours: Mon-Fri 10-5, Sat 10-3

Visit the "plant orphanage" at this interior landscaping warehouse and "adopt" a plant at close to cost. Most of the inhabitants have been leased to commercial accounts and are in need of tender loving care. Tropical Foliage carries a good selection of plants brought in from Hawaii, Florida and Southern California.

Checks, Credit cards

Annual sales sponsored by various community organizations offer seasoned shoppers more great opportunities to pick up good plants at good prices. And even if some of the plants aren't sold at rock-bottom prices, all proceeds go to worthy causes. We've listed several of the most established annual sales. You'll need to watch the newspapers or contact the organizations for specific information:

ARBORETUM FOUNDATION

Seattle: ☎ 325-4510
Spring, Fall and Holiday Sales

CHILDREN'S ORTHOPEDIC HOSPITAL

Seattle: ☎ 526-2153
Spring Sale

MASTER GARDENERS

Seattle: ☎ 296-3440
Spring Sale

NORTHWEST HORTICULTURAL SOCIETY

Seattle: ☎ 527-1794
Summer Fern Festival and Fall Sale

SEATTLE TILTH ASSOCIATION

Seattle: ☎ 633-0451
Spring Sale

VOLUNTEER PARK CONSERVATORY

Seattle: ☎ 684-4743
Fall Sale

☑**Consumer Tip:**
Amateur landscape gardeners and houseplant lovers should take advantage of the many free services and publications available:
☞ The Center For Urban Horticulture / Washington Park Arboretum /University of Washington. Call 543-8616 to receive "Urban Horticulture Presents", a newsletter that includes a calendar of events for plant sales, public lectures and garden tours.

Plants, Flowers & Greenery, Garden Ornaments & Florists

☞ The Co-operative Extension, a partnership between Washington State University, U.S. Department of Agriculture, and King and Snohomish Counties, offers over 500 bulletins and fact sheets on all aspects of gardening, farming, food preservation and pest management. Call 296-3986 (King) or 338-2400 (Snohomish).

☞ Master Gardeners offer classes in gardening and pest management, gardening advice at plant clinics, special events, and over the telephone. Call 296-3440 (King), 338-2400 (Snohomish), Mon-Fri 10-2.

☞ King County Dial Extension provides 400 taped telephone messages on gardening, pest management and food preservation. Call 296-DIAL or call 1-800-325-6165 from outlying areas. Gardening information is available in Snohomish County from 10 am until 2 p.m. by calling 338-2400.

Garden Ornaments

POTTERY SALES NORTHWEST
Seattle: 1950 1st Ave. S. ☎ 682-1404 *South of Kingdome*
Hours: Mon-Fri 9-5, Sat 11-3

You'll see more flower pots in this rustic old brick warehouse than most people see in a lifetime. The inventory is imported from all over the world. The bargains are on terra cotta discontinued items, seconds and damaged goods, which sometimes walk out of the store for under $1. First-quality merchandise sells at the normal retail price.

Checks

WASHINGTON POTTERY CO.
Tukwila: 13001 48th Ave. S. ☎ 243-1191
Hours: Mon-Fri 8-4:30

Washington Pottery Co. makes and sells flower pots, cement statuary, bird baths and fountains to nurseries, garden shops and mass merchandisers. Drive out to their factory store and pay up to 50% off retail for the same items. Seconds are terrific buys, and sometimes the defects are hardly noticeable. Pottery shards sold by the cubic yard can be used not only to promote drainage in the bottom of pots, but also to pave entire driveways!

Checks

Florists

FLOWERS PLUS
Tacoma: 5600 6th Ave. ☎ 756-0909
Hours: Mon-Fri 9-9, Sat 9-7, Sun 9-5

If you want to save money, buy your flowers loose and put together your own arrangements. Flowers Plus has a huge selection and great prices on cut flowers because they buy in bulk. Enter their walk-in cooler and be surrounded by a profusion of colors. Roses are $1.49 a stem, carnations run $7.95/dozen, and they both come in lots of hues.

continued >

130 Plants, Flowers & Greenery, Florists

Daisies, iris, and alstromeria bloom year-round here. You can buy a container here or bring in your own. The staff will help you create a floral arrangement from fresh, dried, or silk flowers to suit any occasion.

Checks, Credit cards

ROSE HEARTS
Lynnwood: 6925 216th S.W. ☎ 774-7673 *Goodwin Business Park*
Hours: Mon-Thurs 6:30-4, make an appointment for pick-up

Need a lot of roses for a special occasion? Buy them in bulk from Rose Hearts, a wholesaler that has dozens of roses air-freighted in daily from California to sell at grocery and convenience stores. Although walk-in trade is not a big part of their business, they will sell a bundle of 25 roses for around $10. Prices go up in the fall and winter, but even then no one will be able to beat their prices.

Checks

SOUTH SEATTLE COMMUNITY COLLEGE
West Seattle: 6000 16th Ave. S.W. ☎ 764-5325 (Flower Shop),
764-5323 (Garden Center)
Hours: Mon-Fri 9:30-3:30

Students interested in floristry practice their art in the Florist Shop on the east side of the campus (visitors enter through the north lot). The shop carries loose flowers as well as arrangements. They'll take special orders for big events like weddings. Nearby, horticulture students grow house plants in the winter and bedding plants in the spring, which are sold through the Garden Center every year in May. Call for specifics.

Checks

These three florists quoted us the lowest prices in town for rose arrangements or bouquets:

PACIFIC FLOWER MARKET
Federal Way: 33600 Pacific Hwy. S. ☎ 927-8289

PACIFIC ROSE HOUSE
Tacoma: 9313 S. Tacoma Way ☎ 584-1995

UNIVERSITY ROSE GARDENS
Seattle: 5220 University Way N.E. ☎ 527-3227 *U-District*

A select group of grocery stores have added floral departments, which offer not only the convenience of 24-hour-a-day, one-stop shopping, but also low prices and excellent selections. Inventory usually includes fresh cut flowers (sold in bouquets or singly) and flowering potted plants. The stores take special orders and put together arrangements with 24-hrs. notice. Roses (single, in bouquets or arrangements) cost less than you pay at florists. Baby's breath, greenery, and vases are available to put together your own arrangement.

LARRY'S MARKET

As an upscale grocery store with the latest in food products, Larry's four markets have set aside space for a floral department. Cut flowers are the big seller here with carnations going for 69¢ each and a "bunch" (more than a dozen) of daisies priced at $1.99.

SAFEWAY

While most Safeways have a floral department, the best selections are at the superstores located in Burien, North City, West Seattle, White Center, University Village, and at 153rd and Aurora. They also stock a terrific inventory of helium balloons for every occasion.

QFC

The University Village, Bellevue, Mercer Island, and Issaquah stores have outstanding floral departments that live up to QFC's reputation for quality, service and good prices. Customers can choose from an array of bouquets and unusual flowers like ginger lilies, liatris, anthuriums and orchids. Chrysanthemums and cyclamens are their best selling potted plants.

QUEEN ANNE THRIFTWAY

Seattle: 1908 Queen Anne Ave. ☎ 285-3474 *North of Seattle Center*

It seems only appropriate that Seattle's favorite meeting place for singles should have the largest selection of fresh flowers and be the only grocery store that delivers. Tropical flowers and unusual blooms imported from around the world give their floral department an edge. Custom arrangements, gift baskets and balloons can be special-ordered for weddings, parties, and business functions.

Holiday Greenery

For years, the Chubby & Tubby stores in Seattle have sold Christmas trees at unbelievably low prices. The best trees go fast, so try to be there when the truck unloads.

Many people enjoy the tradition of cutting their own tree at Christmas time. Not only is it fresher and less expensive than one purchased in city lots, but the whole family can participate in a fun outing. Each farm sets its own prices, which will vary with the quality of the tree. A 6-ft. Douglas fir will normally cost $30 to $35 pre-cut, while a U-cut farm may charge about half that. Most farms supply saws and twine.

Early in the holiday season, watch for articles and advertisements in the local newspapers on U-cut Christmas tree farms. If you can't find information and maps at local libraries or businesses, call the Snohomish County Extension (296-3900) or the King County Extension (344-2686). A "Choose and Cut Christmas Tree Map" put out by the Puget Sound Christmas Tree Association, Inc. can be obtained by writing 15703 22nd Ave.E., Tacoma, Wa 98445. For those interested in a more rugged outing, the National Forest Service issues a limited number of Christmas Tree permits yearly. (Call 442-0170 for more information.)

Office Needs

Many items listed in this category can also be used in the home. Office furniture is often of better quality and less expensive than name-brand household furniture. Attractive desks, chairs and bookcases are easy to find. Office supply warehouses that cater to big companies will sell to individuals as well, and you don't have to own a business to buy.

Home-based businesses and small offices on a budget improve their profit margin by renting furniture, buying used furniture and equipment, and buying basic office supplies in quantity once a year.

There is a lot of overlap under the heading of Office Needs, so be sure to look through all three sections. Also refer to Audio & Video Equipment for listings applicable to business and professional offices.

Office Furniture, Machines & Supplies

A-JACK COMPANY — NEW LISTING
Kent: 6822 S. 190th ☎ 251-0571
Hours: Mon-Sat 10-6, Sun 11-4

By purchasing close-outs, discontinued styles and manufacturers' specials, the owner passes the savings on to customers. Even new merchandise sells at "used" prices. During sales, used chairs start at $5, desks at $25, new photo copiers and FAX machines at $595, and new oak veneer desks and credenzas at $365 each. Located in the back room of Alliance Furniture.
Checks, Credit cards

ACME OFFICE FURNITURE
Seattle: 1230 1st Ave. S. ☎ 682-6565 *South of Kingdome*
Hours: Mon-Fri 8:30-4

Acme sells new, used and abused office furniture. They keep prices low on new merchandise by buying overstock and discontinued styles. Used furniture goes for less than wholesale, and there's a big selection. Most items are in good condition since the owner does furniture cleaning and repair work for other companies. Enter through the sliding door on the east side of the building, facing Occidental.
Checks

ACTION OFFICE INTERIORS — NEW LISTING
Seattle: 212 3rd Ave. S. ☎ 382-9818 *Pioneer Square*
Hours: Mon-Fri 8:30-5:30

Action offers a complete range of budget-priced furniture, including premier lines. Because they belong to the largest office furniture buying service in the country, they charge distributors prices. Plus, they own the building, which makes them even more competitive. Office machines for rent or sale include typewriters, overhead projectors, transcribers, copiers and paper shredders. Save up to 80% on both furniture and machines. Call for a full-color catalog to compare prices.
Checks, Credit cards

Office Needs, Furniture, Machines & Supplies 133

BANK AND OFFICE INTERIORS WAREHOUSE OUTLET
Seattle: 5990 1st Ave. S. ☎ 767-9452 *South of Kingdome*
Hours: Mon-Fri 8-4

This huge warehouse services the well-known B&OI store down the street, which specializes in interior decor for offices. Merchandise is generally high-quality, and best buys are on used and damaged goods from trade-ins and rentals. Call 768-8000 to make an appointment with a salesman, who will come over from the main store to wait on you.

Checks, Credit cards

BUDGET OFFICE FURNITURE   NEW LISTING
Seattle: 2244 1st Ave. S. ☎ 447-0393 *South of Kingdome*
Hours: Mon-Fri 8:30-5:30, Sat 11-4

Over 75% of the inventory in this large, low-rent showroom warehouse is used. If you find just what you need, chances are it will be at a price you can afford. We bought a handsome contemporary-style roll-top desk for a song and stackable metal file drawers for $15 each. Discounts on new merchandise vary. Trade-ins welcome.

Checks, Credit cards

BELLEVUE, SEATTLE, & WESTLAKE OFFICE FURNITURE
Bellevue: Bellevue Office Furniture; 13219 N.E. 20th St. ☎ 641-8500
Seattle: Seattle Office Furniture; 3035 1st Ave. ☎ 728-5710 *Downtown*
   Westlake Office Furniture; 222 Westlake Ave. N. ☎ 623-9222 *East of Seattle Center*
Hours: Mon-Fri 8-5

All of these stores are owned by the same company. As high-volume dealers, they can sell new merchandise at 10% to 40% off. Bargain hunters check out factory seconds and freight-damaged goods. About 25% of the inventory in the Seattle stores comes from rentals, trade-ins and buy-backs.

Checks, Credit cards

DATA PRINT RIBBONS   NEW LISTING
Seattle: P.O. Box 66211 (98166) ☎ 241-1143
Hours: Mon-Fri 8-4:30

This company stocks over 50,000 styles of computer printer ribbons and laser supplies. All orders are by mail or phone. Call for price quotes and inquire about volume discounts.

C.O.D., Credit cards or terms upon approval

DISCOUNT OFFICE FURNITURE MART
Seattle: 3825 1st Ave S. ☎ 682-6811 *South of Kingdome*
Hours: Mon-Fri 8:30-5:30

You'll find a well-rounded inventory of basic office furniture by leading manufacturers at the budget outlet for this 5-store chain. Look for especially good prices and a good selection on file cabinets. Some items are discounted as much as 50%. Get on their mailing list for big sales.

Checks, Credit cards

DUCKY'S OFFICE FURNITURE — NEW LISTING
Seattle: 1832 Yale Ave. ☎ 623-1010 *Downtown*
500 W. Boren Ave. N. ☎ 623-7777 *Downtown*
Hours: Mon-Fri 8-6; Yale store, Sat 9-5

The owner puts some fun into the boring business of shopping for office furniture by posting wacky signs on his colorful building like "Duck into our place and you'll go quackers over the prices." The atmosphere is informal, and salesmen make a point of educating customers on how to look for quality. Inventory varies from "el cheapo" to expensive lines, both new and used. Prices are incredibly low because of low overhead and volume buying. Posted prices apply to cash-only purchases. Rentals available. Umbrellas, calendars, pencil sharpeners and other items carry out the duck motif.

Checks, Credit cards

FOSTER'S USED OFFICE FURNITURE — NEW LISTING
Kent: 840 S. Central ☎ 854-9482
Hours: Mon-Fri 9-6, Sat 10-4

Low overhead keeps prices down on new and used furniture at Foster's. The big warehouse is filled with terrific buys on desks, credenzas, chairs, tables, file cabinets, safes and computer furniture, plus a limited selection of office supplies and equipment. Most of the used merchandise comes from banks. Everything is reconditioned before it goes out on the floor, so many items look brand new. The store also re-upholsters office furniture for other businesses.

Checks, Credit cards

NORTHWEST LIQUIDATION & SALES — NEW LISTING
Seattle: 1050 W. Nickerson ☎ 623-7440 *North Queen Anne*
Hours: Mon-Fri 8-5

General office furnishings are bought and sold here, along with architectural and engineering equipment. Wall panels and work stations are always in stock, plus a full range of office machines from computers to copiers, FAX machines, transcribers, typewriters and microfiche. Most merchandise is used, and prices can be incredibly low.

Checks

OFFICE CLUB — NEW LISTING
Bellevue: 100 108th N.E. ☎ 453-2900
Seattle: 1751 Airport Way S. ☎ 587-CLUB *South of Kingdome*
Tukwila: 290 Andover Pkwy. E. ☎ 248-2582
Hours: Mon-Fri 8-7, Sat 9-5

Individuals, small businesses and big corporations shop side-by-side at these huge membership warehouses. The 40-store West Coast chain guarantees the lowest prices everyday on a complete range of quality name-brand office supplies, machines and furniture. You'll find

continued >

everything from steno pads to file cabinets, computer furniture and FAX machines. Look for big savings on bulk disks and paper for your copier, computer or laser printer. Office machines by *Canon, Panasonic, Texas Instruments, Packard Bell* and other leading manufacturers. Prices average 40-50% below retail. Discounts on some items go as low as 70%. Anything not in stock can be ordered at 25% off retail with next-day availability. Membership is $10/year. No fee for non-profit organizations. The public is welcome to shop, but pays 10% above the posted price. Stop by the warehouse nearest you to pick up a membership application and free merchandise catalog.

Checks, Credit cards

NINE TO FIVE BUSINESS FURNITURE & OFFICE FURNITURE EXPRESS

Bellevue: Nine To Five; 13407 N.E. 20th, #1 ☎ 462-9595
Office Furniture Express; 13211 N.E. 20th ☎ 747-5577
Hours: Generally, Mon-Fri 9-5, Sat 10-3

Both stores are owned by the same company, but carry different lines. Merchandise focuses on low-end and budget designs. They boast, "Nobody comes close to our prices", and when you check out their show rooms, you'll find prices are close to wholesale on many items. Truckloads are bought and sold in volume to big businesses, so small offices and individuals benefit from the same discount.

Checks, Credit cards

OFFICE FURNITURE DISCOUNTERS

Tacoma: 1908 Pacific Ave. ☎ 383-4505
Hours: Mon-Fri 8:30-6, Sat 9-5

With hundreds of items stored on five floors, this is one of the largest discount office furniture companies in Western Washington. Look for huge savings on merchandise ranging from generic to designer lines. New furniture averages 40% below retail. Overstock, floor models and discontinued lines come from a top Seattle/Tacoma dealer. Bargains galore on used furniture from trade-ins and the store's rental department.

Checks, Credit cards

OFFICE FURNITURE CO-OP NEW LISTING

Bellevue: 13223 N.E. 16th ☎ 454-1710
Hours: Mon-Fri 9-5:30, Sat 10-3

Wow, does this place look like a money-saver for Eastsiders! The 20,000 square foot warehouse/showroom displays new and used furniture and office supplies. Merchandise is dirt cheap because it's drawn from close-outs, samples, factory seconds, freight-damaged or liquidation goods. Desks run the gamut from traditional to executive styles fit for a CEO

continued >

Office Needs, Furniture, Machines & Supplies

Shelving units, drafting stools and computer tables are best selling items. Computer and copy paper sometimes dips below $18/case. Inventory and prices vary tremendously, so call for price quotes and to find out what's new.

Checks, Credit cards

R AND S SALES, INC.
Seattle: 1221 E. Pike ☎ 323-5966 *Capitol Hill*
Hours: Mon-Fri 8:30-5

Although the retail showroom displays new furniture for the home and office, the 2nd and 3rd floors warehouse a huge inventory of used merchandise from rental returns and business liquidations. Staff attempts to give budget-minded customers the lowest price possible. Save big bucks by renting used furniture or take advantage of their trade-in policy if you buy new furniture.

Checks, Credit cards

UNIVERSITY OFFICE PRODUCTS & WACKY WAREHOUSE   NEW LISTING
Seattle: University Office Products; 5263 University Way N.E. *U-District*
  Wacky Warehouse; 2209 Rainier Ave. S. ☎ 325-9450 *Mt. Baker*
Hours: U-District Mon-Sat 10-7; Mt. Baker Mon-Fri 11-5:30

These are great places to pick up office supplies and equipment at dirt-cheap prices, if you aren't intimidated by the disorganized jumble of merchandise crowded into every nook and cranny. Most everything comes from offices and stores going out of business, so inventory changes constantly. Office furniture and machines may be vintage or well-used, but who cares at these prices? Paper and stationary products, from basics to specialty items, start at 30% off. Pay $1.50 for a roll of 3/4" scotch tape instead of $2.25. And here's the best deal of all! University Office Supply charges only 2¢ /copy, the lowest price we've encountered. Wacky Warehouse carries mainly furniture and equipment.

Checks

VIKING DISCOUNT OFFICE PRODUCTS
Los Angeles, CA ☎ 800/421-1222
Hours: Mon-Fri 7-6, Sat 8-2

With six distribution centers nationwide, Viking is the largest mail order office supply company in the country. We know an accountant who purchases everything from furniture to calculators to post-its from the extensive list of products displayed in Viking's colorful catalogs. Not only do the prices beat most local discounters, but also delivery is free with orders of $25 or more. Catalogs come out six to eight times a year. Frequent sale supplements offer fantastic discounts on a complete range of paper products, office machines and basic office furniture. They stock toners, laser cartridges, print wheels and ribbons for typewriters and computers. Call for a free catalog.

Checks, Credit cards

WINTER'S OFFICE FURNITURE
Seattle: 6169 4th Ave. S. ☎ 763-2677 *Georgetown*
Hours: Mon-Fri 9-5, Sat 9-11

Check out Winters' for bargains on used, close-out and damaged office furniture and equipment. They often buy up whole offices, so the selection is all-inclusive. Used *Steelcase* 5-drawer files start at $129. Used computers are bought and sold— *Compaq Deskpro* 286 and 286s preferred. Other IBM-compatibles will be considered. Microfiche machines sell for $39. The day we visited they had just received a shipment of stylish used furniture. New furniture, which is 1/3rd of the inventory, starts at 20% off list.

Checks, Credit cards

Computer Hardware & Software

The key to buying computer equipment at a good price is to know what you want before you set out to buy it. A few hours of research now can save you hundreds of dollars later. Uninformed buying has resulted in early retirement for hundreds of thousands of computer systems. Start your research at the library or at any of the area's larger bookstores. Look for recent copyright dates as technology is changing quickly. A five-year-old book on computers is out-of-date. As we go to press, "The First Book of Personal Computing" by Wang and Kraynak (1990) is highly recommended.

When buying new equipment, shop with a reputable local dealer to ensure reliable service, protect your warranty, and receive some training. Name brands are not as important as dealer reliability; over 20% of computer stores close within their first year. If you feel intimidated by computer terms and technology, good place to start is Ballard Computer, which is known for its service, both before and after the sale. They have a very large selection of IBM-compatible and Apple hardware, plus associated software. The staff is helpful and knowledgeable, and their prices are competitive. Hardware is often 25% below list, and some software items are heavily discounted.

Used computer goods are available from: computer brokers (see yellow pages under Computers-Used.), computer repair services (unclaimed equipment), and classified sections of major newspapers under Computers/Software. Also check with computer dealers for user groups that trade, buy and sell equipment among themselves.

Computer Hardware

AM COMPUTER SWAP MEET
Kent: ☎ 874-8711
Periodic sales

Buyers and sellers converge at this unique event, usually held in the Kent Commons' Exhibition Hall in March, July, September and December. Over 100 vendors rent space, the majority of them small retailers selling brand-new merchandise at discount prices. Individuals clearing out their offices often offer great buys on used equipment.

Office Needs, Computer Hardware & Software

BALLARD COMPUTER
Seattle: 5424 Ballard Ave. N.W. ☎ 782-8591 *Ballard*
Hours: Mon-Sat 8-8, Sun 10-6

Novices need not fear entering this store. A large selection of hardware and software and a staff that offers personal help have made Ballard Computer a success. Their extended warranty service (at additional cost) provides service for one year after the manufacturers' warranty expires and includes loaners until repairs are completed. Ballard Computer prides itself on desktop publishing expertise and offers training. They'll mail you a price list.

Checks, Credit cards

COMPU-TECH
Tacoma: 2107 S. 12th St. ☎ 383-6346
Hours: Mon-Fri 9-6, Sat 10-3

Here's a good place to buy, sell or trade computers and accessories. They carry new IBM-compatibles and are the authorized *Epson and Commodore* repair center, with 24-hour turn-around on most repairs.

Checks, Credit cards

COMPUTERS & APPLICATIONS
Bellevue: 10623 N.E. 8th St. ☎ 451-8077
Hours: Mon-Fri 8-6, Sat 10-5, Sun 12-5

This retail store is backed up by a warehouse stocked with over a million dollars worth of equipment and software. They regularly discount *IBM, Hewlett Packard, Epson, AST* and others. No Apples here. Special sales are frequent and prices are very competitive. Free classes offered. Prices shown are for cash or check. Add 3% for bank cards, 5% for American Express.

Checks, Credit cards

COMPUTER EXCHANGE NORTHWEST
Kirkland: 12006 98th Ave. N.E., #103 ☎ 820-1181
Hours: Mon-Fri 9-5

All transactions are by telephone with this brokerage firm for new and used computer equipment. They've a large clientele and an excellent reputation. Buyers pay a fair market price and have the security of a 48-hour inspection period. Cash, cashier's checks or money orders are held in escrow during the inspection period.

COMPUTERS 'N' THINGS
Tacoma: 3640 S. Cedar ☎474-1383
Hours: Mon-Fri 8-6, Sat 10-5

You'll usually find a big inventory of used equipment and low prices on IBM-clones and accessories here. Used computers are sold on consignment or purchased outright. Their $45/hour fee for on-site maintenance and service is one of the lowest in the Puget Sound area.

Checks, Credit cards

Office Needs, Computer Hardware & Software

COMPUTER CITY
Bellevue: 13622 N.E. Northrup ☎ 641-2983 *Apple Tree Plaza*
Tukwila: 17900 Southcenter Pkwy. ☎ 575-8737 *Pavilion Mall*
Hours: Bellevue Mon-Sat 10-6; Tukwila Mon-Fri 9:30-9:30, Sat 9:30-7, Sun 11-6

One of the largest liquidators of computer hardware, software and peripherals in the country, Computer City offers prices 30% to 85% off retail. A local trade journal describes the inventory as "strange, exotic and cheap." Incredible buys on software are the norm at the Pavillion Mall store, which stocks over 1,000 programs. The Bellevue location carries more hardware and peripherals.

Checks, Credit cards

FLO COMPUTING
Seattle: 18332 Aurora Ave. N. ☎ 542-9600 *Richmond Highlands*
Hours: Tues-Fri 10:30-6, Sat 10-4

Flo Computing mainly sells used computers and hardware on consignment. Bargain hunters and hackers love the low prices. Bring in your old system, and if it sells within 60 days, you receive 30% of the selling price.

Checks, Credit cards

HI-TECH RENTALS
Redmond: 3908 148th Ave. N.E. ☎ 881-1113
Hours: Mon-Fri 10-6, Sat 12-4

Here's a good place to start if you want to try different systems before buying. The company rents *Apple* and IBM-compatible systems, plus printers, scanners and CD ROM's for short or long-term use. Call for current rates. They also sell used rental equipment with warranties.

Checks, Credit cards

PACIFIC COMPUTER EXCHANGE, INC.
Seattle: 2825 Eastlake Ave. E. #120 ☎328-8800 *East Lake Union*
Hours: Mon-Sat 9-6

An authorized dealer for *Acer, Mitsubishi, Everex and Leading Edge,* Pacific Computer Exchange also buys, sells and trades used equipment.

Checks, Credit cards

PACIFIC COMPUTER NORTHWEST
Fife: 4905 Pacific Highway East, Suite 1 ☎ 922-5490
Hours: Mon-Sat 8:30-5:30

This Tacoma-area dealer features 386-40 megabyte IBM-compatibles for under $1,500. Call or fax (922-7674) your specifications and they'll quote today's price. *Epson and Panasonic* printers are also discounted.

Checks, Credit cards

See area locator index for this section on page 226

THE PRINTER STORE

Bellevue: 1014 116th Ave. N.E. ☎ 453-0151
Hours: Mon-Fri 9-6, Sat 10-3

Here you'll find the largest selection of printers in Greater Seattle. Prices are low, and even lower during their frequent sales. There's a surcharge for credit cards.

Checks, Credit cards

SEATTLE MICRO

Seattle: 2308 4th Ave. ☎ 441-9111 *Downtown*
Hours: Mon-Fri 9:30-5:30

Used computer rental and demo's turn up at Seattle Micro, a discount retailer of IBM-compatibles, printers and accessories.

Checks, Credit cards

SEATTLE TELECOM & DATA, INC.

Redmond: 2735 152nd Ave. N.E. ☎ 883-8440
Hours: Mon-Fri 8-5

All of the big consumer computer journals have favorably reviewed this hardware manufacturer. They make complete systems and upgrades for *Compaq and IBM AT's and XT's*, and they've a reputation for technical reliability and outstanding user support. Factory-direct prices are very competitive. Call or fax (881-7391) your requirements for a personal quotation.

Checks

SUN COMPUTERS

Seattle: 2521 3rd Ave. ☎ 728-2828 *Downtown*
Bellevue: 881 Bellevue Way N.E. ☎ 451-2828
Hours: Mon-Sat 9-6

Sun Computers, a Western states chain, is among the largest *Apple* computer and accessory retailers. Prices are competitive, and advertised sales are frequent. If you live on the East side or near downtown, this is a good place to start your *Apple* comparison shopping. IBM-compatibles and printers are also stocked.

Checks, Credit cards

TRINITY TECH INC.

Renton: 879 Rainier Ave. N. ☎ 772-7774
Periodic sales

A local assembler of IBM-clones, Trinity Tech clears out inventory of computers and components during factory sales in July and December. At the annual Renton factory sale, you'll find hard drives, keyboards, monitors and systems at clearance prices below cost. Retail stores in Seattle, Renton and Bellevue offer bargain basement prices on their *Genesis* line of IBM-compatibles and *Star* printers.

Checks, Credit cards

Office Needs, Computer Hardware & Software 141

UNITED PRODUCTS
Seattle: 1123 Valley St. ☎ 582-5025 *East of Seattle Center*
Hours: Mon-Fri 9-6, Sat 9-5

If you're into building your own computer or tinkering with old ones, this is the place to buy parts and equipment. Prices are low because they buy close-outs, surplus lots and outdated systems. Used printers, terminals, monitors and parts for *Deck and Epson* always in stock. New components can be purchased at low bulk prices. There are tools, chemicals and testing equipment and motor drive kits (manufactured by United for educational purposes). Check the latest books on computer electronics, robotics and laser applications. Call 472-7518 for info on how to hook up your modem to their on-line parts list. Put your name on their mailing list to receive notice of special sales. United will ship anywhere with a $20 minimum order.

Checks, Credit cards

U.S. MICRO EXPRESS
Bellevue: 10216 N.E. 8th ☎453-4046
Tacoma: 2502 S. 38th ☎ 475-2000
Hours: Generally, Mon-Fri 9-7, Sat 10-5, Sun 10-5

Washington's largest maker of IBM-compatible computers for business or personal use claims the best prices in Washington. Prices are factory-direct, and you can count on quick warranty service. They also offer a network hot-line, free seminars and mail order. Call for one of their free quarterly catalogs, which includes easy-to-understand information, price-comparison charts, and a great question and answer section.

Checks, Credit cards

Computer Software

AMERICAN SHAREWARE
Burien: 223 S.W. 152nd ☎ 433-1926
Hours: Mon-Fri 10-6, Sat 10-4

This company offers 350 IBM-compatible Shareware programs. Some are as low as $1.75, with big savings on bulk disks. All commercial software programs are discounted 20% to 40%. Free software catalog upon request.

Checks, Credit cards

DISCOUNT COMPUTER SOFTWARE
Burien: 641 S.W 152nd ☎ 431-0180
Hours: Mon-Fri 10-7, Sat 10-5

For 10% of the asking price, you can preview programs before you buy, and the rental cost applies to the purchase.

Checks, Credit cards

EGGHEAD DISCOUNT SOFTWARE
Bellevue: 14330 N.E. 20th ☎ 644-4545   1105 Bellevue Way N.E. ☎ 451-3701
Lynnwood: 4201 196th S.W. ☎ 672-9397

continued >

142 Office Needs, Computer Hardware & Software

Seattle: 1122 4th Ave. ☎ 623-4851 *Downtown*
2111 Northgate Way ☎ 361-5002 *Northgate*
Tacoma: 2505 S. 38th ☎ 473-5195
Tukwila: 17326 Southcenter Pkwy. ☎ 575-0445 *Parkway Plaza*
Hours: Generally, Mon-Sat 10-7, Sun 12-5

Egghead, the largest software chain in the country, advertises "eggstraordinary selection," "eggceptional service" and "eggcellent savings." Stores stock over 1300 programs, plus a full range of accessories for *IBM and Apple*. Prices are 10-50% below suggested retail. Private-label ribbons, disks and supplies are good buys.

Checks, Credit cards

FAIR SHARE

Duvall: 210 Main Street ☎ 800/848-2384
Hours: Mon-Fri 8:30-5:30

Visit the retail store in picturesque Duvall or call for a free catalog listing hundreds of software programs from this distributor of public domain software for *IBM* and compatibles. Program disks run $2.99 each, and the price drops for larger quantities. Shipping and handling is only $3/order.

Checks, Credit cards

GEMINI SHAREWARE

Bellevue: 12404 S.E. 38th St. ☎ 746-7671
Everett: 5108 Evergreen Way ☎ 339-1366
Federal Way: 1706 S. 320th St. ☎ 941-8244 *Sea-Tac Village*
Seattle: 10331 Aurora Ave. N. ☎ 524-0701 *North Park*
Catalog requests: 800/346-0139
Hours: Mon-Sat 11-6

Winner of Computer Shopper's Magazine "Best Buy Award" for 1989, this company offers thousands of programs in every category imaginable for *IBM, Apple, Macintosh, Commodore and Atari*. Prices on multiple orders can be as low as $1.25 per program. Mail order, telephone, or retail sales.

Checks, Credit cards

HALF PRICE SOFTWARE

Seattle: 4709 Roosevelt Way N.E. ☎ 547-7620 *U-District*
Tacoma: 6409 6th Ave. ☎ 566-1238
Hours: Daily 10-10

Buy, sell and trade hardware and software in the same way used books are sold next door at the parent company, Half Price Books. You'll find terrific prices on new and used inventory purchased from individuals, retail stores going out of business, and office liquidations. All new products are discounted 35%.

Checks, Credit cards

Office Needs, Computer Hardware & Software

RAINWARE SOFTWARE
Mercer Island: ☎ 232-5376 or **800/441-1458**
Hours: Mon-Fri 7-6, Sat 8-5

The newest mail order Shareware public domain distributor in the Puget Sound area, Rainware's library contained over 500 titles when we called and, according to staff, was growing every day.

Checks, Credit cards

SHAREWARE OUTLET
Bellevue: 713 110th N.E., #207 ☎ 646-3571 *Wayne Building*
Catalog requests: 800/388-3475
Hours: Mon-Fri 9-7, Sat 9-5

An approved vendor for the Association of Shareware Professionals, this company carries over 800 programs, all of which have been tested and evaluated by a staff of capable professionals who offer telephone technical support. Only the latest in disk duplication is used, and all disks are IBM-compatible. Current versions with complete descriptions cost only $3.50 each. Free bi-monthly catalog.

Checks, Credit cards

SOFTWARE CONNECTION
Seattle: P.O. Box 45226, Seattle, WA 98145 ☎ 524-9394
Hours: Daily, 24 hours

Shop this mail-order-only company, and never pay retail prices again. After working for well-known software companies locally, the owners decided they could sell the same programs for 25-50% less by eliminating the high cost of a retail operation. For $2 they'll send you their catalog, listing over 3,000 titles, including one of the largest selections of *IBM* software in the Puget Sound area. Free shipping and handling on all orders.

Checks, Credit cards

UNIVERSITY SOFTWARE
Seattle: 4719 University Way N.E., #203 ☎ 527-2167 *U-District*
Hours: Mon-Sat 10-7

Specializing in accessories, modems and software, University Software has a "try-before-you-buy" policy.

Checks, Credit cards

Mail-order Computer Goods

If you know the specifications of the IBM-clone you want, good mail-order prices are offered by Dell Computer and CompuAdd; both come highly recommended. Should you have a problem with a product made by either of these companies, you can call a toll-free number and receive service from a local representative. There are no Apple clones made for sale in this country, but dealer pricing is very competitive at several local outlets and via mail-order. Here's a starter list of mail-order computer companies that will provide catalogs or price lists for comparison shopping.

144 Office Needs, Computer Hardware & Software

COMPUADD
Austin, TX ☎ **800/627-1967**
Hours: Mon-Fri 8-9, Sat 9-5 (Central time)

DELL COMPUTERS
Austin, TX ☎ **800/426-5150**
Hours: Mon-Fri 7-7, Sat 9-2 (Central time)

47TH STREET PHOTO
New York, NY ☎ **800/221-7774**
Hours: Mon-Thur 8-7, Fri 9-2, Sun 10-5 (Eastern time)
See full listing under Photographic Supplies & Equipment.

PC CONNECTION
Marlowe, NH ☎ **800/243-8088**
Hours: Mon-Fri 9-1(a.m.), Sat 9-5 (Eastern time)

UNDER-WARE ELECTRONICS
Wichita, KS ☎ **800/442-1408**
Hours: Mon-Fri 7-8, Sat 9-4 (Central time)
See full listing under Audio & Video Equipment.

Computer Publications

"Computer Shopper", a national classified tabloid-size magazine for direct buyers and sellers, offers great buys for the knowledgeable and selective shopper on both new and used goods. It's available on most newsstands.

The local computer marketplace is served by the "Puget Sound Computer User", a monthly tabloid newspaper distributed free of charge at most retail computer stores, and at Safeway and Albertson's in the greater Seattle area. Subscriptions are mailed free to businesses that send a request on their letterhead. Informative articles, a calendar of events, listings of user groups, advertisements by big discounters, and a classified section make this newspaper a must for bargain hunters. They also sponsor a modem-linked electronic bulletin board and publish an annual comprehensive user-directory in January. Call 547-4950 for information or write 3530 Bagley Ave. N., Seattle, WA 98103.

"Northwest Computer News" is a regional tabloid geared more to business than users. Pick up complimentary copies at 7-11 stores, Payless, and computer stores. They publish a pocketbook-sized directory that includes an index of supplier information. To order by mail, send $1 (for postage) to 440 N.E. 73rd, Seattle, WA 98105.

Office Needs, Paper Products

☑ Consumer Tips:

☞ If you are considering a computer for any purpose other than simple word processing or basic accounting, the rule of thumb is to double what you think you will need in terms of hardware capability. When asked if they would like more features and more power, most new computer users answer yes to both questions after their first two years of experience.

☞ The latest copy of PC Magazine will contain ads for hundreds of mail-order sources. If you are not an expert, be careful where you buy because most mail-order services offer no recourse other than returning the machine should trouble arise. It's always a good idea to order with a credit card, which gives you extra protection in case of problems with delivery, breakage or returns.

☞ Used equipment may be the best option for beginners and those on a strict budget. Until you know your exact needs, don't become fanatic about keeping up-to-date with the latest application or power-user capability. The good news is that a lot of people "trade up". When they do, they're often happy to part with their old machines at 25 cents on the dollar, so if you don't need a state-of-the-art machine, their loss is your gain. Even recent-model name-brand used machines should be at least 50% off the original cost. Newer models of such major brands as IBM, Apple, Hewlett Packard and Compaq tend to hold their value longer, but good buys can be made on other leading brands offering similar features, including AST, Epson, Hyundai, NEC, Toshiba and Zenith.

☞ Some dealers will offer one-week written guarantees or exchange agreements on used equipment. Be sure appropriate manuals and documentation are included on all computers and peripherals. Printers are much more prone to breakdowns than other equipment because they are primarily mechanical rather than electronic. A 90-day service guarantee is worth a few extra dollars when buying a used printer.

☞ Used software can be found at bargain basement prices, but beware of pirated copies. Look for the manufacturers' labels on all disks and make sure documentation is original. Old versions of software are often much less capable than the latest update. Some shops will let you rent software to see if it fills your need.

Paper Products for Home & Office

The cost of paper products adds up fast, especially if you run to the drugstore, neighborhood card shop, or retail office supplier every time you need something. Get in the habit of buying in volume for both home and office. The big paper distributors— Arvey, The Paper Merchant and The Paper Pick-up— will quote prices over the phone and deliver. Keep in mind that a number of the companies listed in the Office Furniture section also carry paper products, just as some of the listings here stock business machines and furniture.

ARVEY PAPER & OFFICE SUPPLIES
Bellevue: 1910 132nd Ave. N.E. ☎ 643-4333
Seattle: 2930 1st Ave. S. ☎ 622-9232 *South of Kingdome*
Hours: Mon-Fri 8-5:30, Sat 9-5

continued >

146 Office Needs, Paper Products

Arvey's is part of a 38-store nationwide chain that stocks everything you could possibly need to outfit an office. Envelopes, labels, file folders, graphic, copier and computer paper are the big sellers. Office supplies and equipment runs the gamut from paper clips to bulk disks, calculators, typewriters, telephones, copiers, Fax machines and furniture. Arvey's even stocks janitorial and graphic art supplies. Savings average 10% to 50%. Shop monthly specials and buy in quantity for even bigger discounts. Get on their mailing list to receive notice of major sales. Free delivery with $100 purchase if you're in their designated delivery area.

Checks, Credit cards

CURRENTS   NEW LISTING
Colorado Springs, CO ☎ **800/525-7170**
Hours: Daily, 5am-midnight (Mountain time)

Call for a complimentary catalog and samples from this mail-order company that produces creative paper products. Prices are often 50% below Hallmark's, and the offerings include calendars, stationery, gift-wrapping materials and cards for all occasions. You can order personalized checks at a better price than charged by your local bank. If you include payment with your orders, shipment is free.

Checks, Credit cards

DISCOUNT PAPER PRODUCTS
Lynnwood: 4601 200th S.W. ☎ 771-2944 *Lynnwood Square*
Hours: Mon-Fri 9-7, Sat 10-6, Sun 11-4

Businesses, churches and schools shop here for office supplies and paper products. The big selection of party goods include everything you'd need for a wedding, birthday, or company picnic. Good buys on ribbon, giftwrap, fancy boxes and bags. Art supplies and seasonal decorations also available. Visit the special cash and carry department set up for caterers. You'll love the matching tumblers, napkins, placemats, and tablecloths. Aluminum foil and plastic wrap sold in 1,000 foot rolls. Prices average 10-30% below retail. Best buys are on closeouts, usually displayed on separate tables.

Checks, Credit cards

EVERETT WHOLESALE PAPER COMPANY
Everett: 2914 McDougal Ave. ☎ 252-2105 or **800/448-9314**
Hours: Mon-Fri 8-5

Save on cleaning supplies, stationery items and packaging products sold mainly to offices, restaurants, janitorial services and disposal companies. Ribbon and giftwrap comes in big rolls. Packing boxes of all sizes are available for moving or storage. Not all items must be purchased in large quantities, but keep in mind that this is a wholesale operation and shop accordingly.

Checks

Office Needs, Paper Products

PAPER FACTORY OUTLET

Tacoma: 1565 Center ☎ 272-2181
Hours: Mon-Fri 9:30-6:30, Sat 9:30-5, Sun 12-5

Here's a great place to shop if you're planning a wedding or a large party. Two floors are filled with paper products and decorative items just like you'd find at Hallmark, only for much less. Look for outstanding buys on gift wrap and ribbon purchased by the foot from huge rolls— 26¢/ft. for printed paper, 22¢/ft. for foil paper, 2¢/ft. for ribbon. Helium-filled balloons, greeting cards, and seasonal decorations are other items on which you can always save money. Buy in bulk for the lowest prices.

Checks, Credit cards

THE PAPER MERCHANT

Seattle: 2700 4th Ave. S. ☎ 622-8225 *South of Kingdome*
Hours: Mon-Fri 7:30-5

This retail outlet for Barber-Ellis Fine Papers sells everything from the finest quality paper products to basic stock for copiers, computers, and laser printers. They have an extensive line of stationery and envelopes made from recycled paper. You'll discover big reductions on discontinued stock. Buy merchandise by the case, carton, or ream. Free delivery for cash accounts with a purchase over $50.

Checks, Credit cards

THE PAPER PICK-UP

Everett: 9423 Evergreen Way ☎ 355-7703
Redmond: 3838 148th Ave. N.E. ☎ 883-0273
Seattle: 1911 1st Ave. S. ☎ 682-8644 *South of Kingdome*
Hours: Mon-Fri 8-5

West Coast Paper is the parent company for these three outlets that sell a wide variety of paper products for the office, plus fine art paper, party goods, janitorial, packaging and restaurant supplies. Prices are wholesale both to businesses and individuals. You'll realize the biggest savings on discontinued items and quantity purchases. Pick up flyers at the beginning of the month to find out about specials and check in-store promotions. No minimum for UPS delivery.

Checks, Credit cards

THE SALVAGE BROKER

Seattle: 13760 Aurora Ave. N. ☎ 365-7771 *Haller Lake*
Hours: Mon-Sat 10-5

The owner buys close-outs, cancelled orders, and goods which were destined for printers but damaged in shipment from paper manufacturers. Computer paper costs only $15 per case here. Artists buy acid-free paper for painting and drawing, and schools pick up butcher paper and poster board.

continued >

148 Office Needs, Paper Products

You'll find everything you need for packaging or wrapping— from containers to twine, tape, plastic bags and shrink-wrap film. And what a great resource for paper napkins, tablecloths, party goods and greeting cards. Even drugs and sundries turn up now and then.

Checks, Credit cards

Moving? U-haul will send you an excellent booklet on how to compute the number of boxes and size of truck you'll need if you're planning to move. Save as much as 50% on boxes of all sizes for shipping, moving, or storage by buying seconds and overstock from one of these companies: (Call first to make sure they have what you need.)

ACE BOX COMPANY
Tukwila: 18200 Olympic Ave. S. ☏ 243-7181
Hours: Mon-Fri 8-5

CARTON SERVICE
Tukwila: 1141 Andover Park W., Bldg. C ☏ 575-9111
Hours: Mon-Fri 8-4

Recreation & Hobbies

Sporting Goods & Recreational Clothing

The Puget Sound area is "Bargain City" when it comes to sporting goods and clothing. The growth of local manufacturers, many of them nationally known, has given rise to a proliferation of factory outlets, discount stores and annual sales where overstock, irregulars and close-outs are sold at clearance prices year-round. Also, because Seattle is a port of entry for goods made in the Orient, many distributors and retailers import and sell merchandise at factory direct prices, frequently under their own label.

AA RENTALS
Seattle: 12700 Lake City Way N.E. ☎ 362-5547 *Lake City*
Annual sales
Every year after Labor Day, AA Rentals sponsors a big "Year-End Summer Fun Sale," where the majority of items rented out for camping, backpacking and mountain climbing go on sale. Savings may amount to 50% and sale merchandise stays in the stores until mid-October. Snow ski equipment is marked down in April.
Checks, Credit cards

ALPINE HUT
Redmond: 7875 Leary Way N.E. ☎ 883-7669
Hours: Mon-Fri 10-8, Sat 10-6, Sun 12-5
The Alpine Hut always has good buys on used equipment from the store's rental supply or consignment stock. In the winter it's skis, in the summer, bikes. If you decide to sell your equipment here, the store gives you half of the selling price or 75% toward in-store credit. Mid-October is the best time to shop for skis. In the summertime, Alpine Hut sponsors a factory direct sale for *O'Brien*, a local manufacturer of sailboards.
Checks, Credit cards

ATHLETIC EXPRESS
Bellevue: 4027 128th S.E. ☎ 643-8976 *Factoria Square*
Everett: 1402 S.E. Everett Mall Way ☎ 353-1161 *Everett Mall*
Federal Way: 1804 S. 320th St. ☎ 839-2838 *Sea-Tac Mall*
Redmond: 2184 148th ☎ 643-4862 *Overlake Fashion Plaza*
Tacoma: 10509 Gravelly Lake Dr. S.W. ☎ 584-0904 *Lakewood Mall*
Hours: Generally, Mon-Fri 10-9, Sat & Sun 10-6

continued >

150 Recreation and Hobbies, Sporting Goods & Clothing

Athletic Express, a large national chain, offers promotional prices on huge inventories of recreational and athletic shoes by such familiar names as *Nike and Reebok*. They outfit the whole family and stress good fit for kids. Sports apparel and accessories also in stock. Get on the mailing list.

Checks, Credit cards

B & I SPORTS SHOP
Tacoma: 8012 S. Tacoma Way ☎ 584-3207
Hours: Mon-Fri 9-9, Sat 9-7:30, Sun 10-6

For almost 50 years B & I has been supplying outdoor enthusiasts with any and everything they need. The store takes up a city block, so it's no surprise that it's the largest volume ski dealer in Western Washington. Don't miss the annual tent sale the first three weeks in July when a mountain of goods gets marked down. Look for bargains on *Coleman* appliances (B & I is an authorized repair center) and used rental equipment reduced 50% or more.

Checks, Credit cards

BACKWOODS SUPPLY CO.
Tacoma: 711 S. 48th ☎ 473-4095
Hours: Mon-Fri 10-6, Sat 10-5

Thanks to low overhead, prices on all-purpose outdoor clothing and equipment for camping and hiking are competitive at this small out-of-the-way store. Gore-Tex outerwear is the #1 seller. If you're taking up cross country skiing, check into their package deal. Sales of display models and rentals take place the last week in August for camping and hiking gear, before and after Christmas for ski equipment.

Checks, Credit cards

BIG 5
Bellevue: 156th & N.E. 8th ☎ 746-9407 *Crossroads*
Factoria: 4055 128th S.E. ☎ 747-5230 *Factoria Square*
Burien: 125 S.W. 148th ☎ 246-2707
Everett: 1201 S.E. Everett Mall Way ☎ 353-9100 *Everett Mall*
Federal Way: 1916 S. 320th ☎ 941-9991 *Sea-Tac Mall*
Kirkland: 12520 120th N.E. ☎ 821-4366 *Totem Lake*
Lynnwood: 18600-A 33rd ☎ 771-8066 *Alderwood Plaza*
Renton: 503 S. 3rd ☎ 271-6900
Seattle: 1140 N. Aurora Village Place ☎ 546-4443 *Richmond Highlands*
      1740 N.W. Market ☎ 783-0163 *Ballard*
      4315 University Way N.E. ☎ 547-2445 *U-District*
West Seattle: 2500 S.W. Barton ☎ 932-2212
Hours: Generally, Mon-Fri 10-9, Sat 9-7, Sun 10-6

continued >

Recreation and Hobbies, Sporting Goods & Clothing

Recreational and athletic equipment of every kind can be found at local outlets for this 125-store chain. Name-brand merchandise is often available at below market prices because they buy close-outs and promotional goods in huge quantities. Recently the company advertised half a million pairs of *Fila* leather sport shoes at 50% off retail price. Ski equipment and products manufactured exclusively for the stores are often good buys.

Checks, Credit cards

BIGFOOT OUTDOOR OUTLET
Tukwila: 17810 West Valley Hwy. ☎ 251-0663
Hours: Mon-Fri 9-8, Sat 9-6, Sun 11-5

Northwest outdoor enthusiasts will love the terrific, low-priced selection of quality camping and hiking equipment at this big warehouse. The owners guarantee savings of up to 50% on goods purchased factory direct from 40 different manufacturers. They stock lots of ski clothes in the winter. Jackets and tents made especially for Bigfoot are always good buys.

Checks, Credit cards

BRENCO   NEW LISTING
Kent: 7877 S. 180th ☎ 251-5020
Periodic sales

Ski buffs take note! Visit this distributer during close-out sales of discontinued alpine and cross country skis made in Austria by *Kneiss* and Italian boots by *Munari*. Prices hover at wholesale or below.

Checks, Credit cards

CALVERT MANUFACTURING CO. INC. *Black Bear*   NEW LISTING
Seattle: 1964 4th Ave. S. ☎ 467-1003 *South of Kingdome*
Periodic sales

This distribution center for men's and women's ski apparel has big sales in the fall and winter to clean out factory overruns and irregulars. Wholesale prices go up to $150 on generic as well as fashion-oriented merchandise. Pacific Coast Feather, another local manufacturer, sells down pillows, comforters, robes, etc. during these events.

Checks

THE CLOSE OUT   NEW LISTING
Tacoma: 1614 S. Mildred ☎ 564-1609 *James Center*
Hours: Mon-Sat 10-7:30, Sun 11-5

The Close Out is one of the few discount active wear outlets in Tacoma that stocks casual as well as athletic clothing for biking, tennis, swimming, working out and other sports-related activities. T-shirts and sweats from *Speedo, Big Dog* and *Frank Shorter* are in stock year-round. Ski apparel is the big seller in the winter. Athletic shoes are a bargain here, and if they don't have what you want, they'll order them and still charge 20% below retail. Merchandise is drawn from factory close-outs, samples and local stores' surplus.

Checks, Credit cards

152 Recreation and Hobbies, Sporting Goods & Clothing

DIRECT TRADE INTERNATIONAL — NEW LISTING
Tacoma: 505 S. Broadway ☎ 383-2922
Annual sale

Soccer is the main focus, but DTI wholesales clothing and equipment for numerous recreational and athletic activities. You can find balls for every sport imaginable. Teams order factory-direct for 35% to 50% savings. Individuals pick up first-quality goods at wholesale or below during the annual close-out sale in December. Choose from over 2,000 jerseys. Soccer shoes for children and adults sell for $15 to $30. Mailing list.

Checks, Credit cards

DISCOUNT SPORTS
Seattle: 14058 Aurora Ave. N. ☎ 367-5345 *Haller Lake*
Hours: Open August through March only. Call for hours.

The store sells only snow ski equipment and clothing. Look for big discounts on name-brand merchandise and ski packages. Don't miss their two-for-one and end-of-season sales.

Checks, Credit cards

THE DOWN FACTORY
Seattle: 1101 E. Pike ☎ 322-0800 *Capitol Hill*
Hours: Mon-Fri 7:30-4:30, Sat 9-4

If it's made of down, you'll find it at this factory, which has been in business since 1932 and manufacturers only first-quality goods at substantial savings. Outerwear includes stylish coats for Mom, vests for kids and survival gear for Dad. Down comforters that normally retail for over $400 are discounted 25% or more. Save even more by buying their popular comforter kit: you do the basic sewing, the factory blows in the down and finishes the quilting. Pillows, hats, booties, houserobes, long johns and sleeping bags are also in stock. Prices are lowest in summer. Call for a brochure or to order.

Checks, Credit cards

EASY RIDER CANOE & KAYAK CO.
Tukwila: 15666 W. Valley Hwy. ☎ 228-3533
Hours: Mon-Fri 9-6, Sat 10-3

Buy a canoe, kayak, or rowing shell factory-direct from the West Coast's largest manufacturer. Seconds, which have blemishes on the finish, are 25% to 35% off retail. Canoes can be outfitted for rowing, sailing, fishing or whitewater outings. Kayaks range from economy-priced, entry-level versions to deluxe expedition styles.

Checks, Credit cards

EDDIE BAUER
Seattle: 1330 5th Ave. ☎ 622-2766 *Downtown*
Hours: Mon-Sat 9:30-6, Sun 12-5

continued >

Recreation and Hobbies, Sporting Goods & Clothing

Since Eddie Bauer opened his first store in Seattle in 1920, his name has become synonymous with quality outdoor merchandise. All clothing is manufactured exclusively for the Eddie Bauer chain and catalogs, and fans flock to the clearance outlet in the basement of the downtown location for bargains on overstock, close-outs, samples and seconds shipped in from factories and stores around the country. Prices start at 40% off retail and go even lower on certain items every Tuesday and Wednesday during weekly managers' specials. Flaws on factory rejects are marked with a piece of tape. At the beginning of the season, the stores have major sales to promote new merchandise and in the late fall all goose down products are substantially reduced. Pick up a free catalog at one of the local stores or call 800/426-6253 to get on the mailing list.

Checks, Credit cards

EVERETT STEEL NEW LISTING
Everett: 3126 Hill Ave. ☎ 258-4505, 682-3166
Kirkland: 504 7th Ave. S. ☎ 821-9491
Hours: Both stores, Mon-Fri 8-4:30; Kirkland, Sat 8-4

Commercial fishermen and smart boaters buy used and surplus marine hardware, rope, anchor and chains at this no-frills outfit. Used merchandise is rebuilt and tested before being sold. Anchors range from 12 to 40,000 lbs.

Checks, Credit cards

GERRY SPORTSWEAR *Tempo, Farwest, Colorado Classics, Outer Limits*
NEW LISTING
Seattle: 1051 1st Ave. S. ☎ 623-4194 *South of Kingdome*
Annual sale

The newest addition to Seattle's family of outerwear manufacturers offers clothing for ski or winter wear at tremendous savings! Prices are 50% to 75% off retail on pants, bibs, ski suits, insulated and shell jackets for men, women and children. Come early for the best selection, and bring your own shopping bag.

Checks

GOLDEN EGG SKI AND SPORT
Woodinville: 13300 N. E. 175th ☎ 487-9755 *Woodgate Mall*
Hours: Mon-Wed 10-7, Thurs & Fri 10-9, Sat 10-6, Sun 12-5

If you enjoy any activity related to water or snow, terrific buys on equipment and clothing await you at the Eastside's largest factory outlet. Prices start at 40% off on overstock, discontinued items and close-outs purchased from manufacturers all over the country in sizes Toddler to adult's XXL. Gore-Tex and goosedown clothing are best sellers. Other off-price items you may find are tents, sleeping bags, biking gear, backpacks, boots, poly-propylene underwear and famous-maker sunglasses.

Checks, Credit cards

154 Recreation and Hobbies, Sporting Goods & Clothing

GOLFLAND DISCOUNT PRO SHOP
Tacoma: 4701-1/2 Center St. ☎ 564-7155
Hours: Mon-Sun. 10-10

Beginners on a budget can buy a full set of clubs made especially for this chain for under $300 or check out the selection of used clubs. Top-of-the-line *Ping* irons go for $416, woods for $235. Receive five private lessons from one of the store's golf pros when you purchase a full set of irons. Have fun on the 20-stall covered driving range and 9-hole pitch and putt.
Checks, Credit cards

HARRIS CONLEY DISCOUNT GOLF SHOP
Bellevue: 1440 156th ☎ 747-2585 *Crossroads*
Hours: Mon-Sat 10-10, Sun 10-9

Clubs to suit a golfer's age, size and ability can be custom-assembled on the premises. A starter set ranges from $70 to $150. A knock-off of *Ping* irons goes for $115 to $160. Name-brand equipment is discounted. PGA-qualified pros help you get the right fit and teach lessons on the 32-stall, covered and lighted driving range or putting green.
Checks, Credit cards

JAN SPORT FACTORY OUTLET
Everett: 10931 32nd Place W. ☎ 743-2862, 353-0200
Periodic sales

Twice a year this well-known local manufacturer of sporting goods opens its warehouse to the public. Excess inventory and seconds, plus merchandise returned from stores is sold at close to wholesale prices. Backpacks, sleeping bags and apparel abound. Call to put your name on the mailing list.
Checks, Credit cards

JERRY'S SURPLUS
Everett: 2031 Broadway ☎ 252-1176
Hours: Mon-Fri 9-9, Sat 9-6, Sun 11-5

Fishing and hunting enthusiasts will find clothing, guns, tackle, tents, backpacks, coolers and sleeping bags at discounted prices because everything is factory-direct or irregulars. Look for good buys on first-run merchandise from name manufacturers like *Coleman* and bargains galore on seconds from *Levi and Helly Hanson*. You'll also find reasonably priced heavy-duty workclothes.
Checks, Credit cards

MARMOT MOUNTAIN WORKS   NEW LISTING
Bellevue: 827 Bellevue Way N.E. ☎ 453-1515
Hours: Mon, Thurs, Fri 10-8; Tues, Wed, Sat 10-6, Sun 12-6

This is one of three retail outlets in the country for state-of-the-art camping, hiking, skiing and mountain climbing gear manufactured by Marmont for their mail-order business.

continued >

Clearance and close-out merchandise available year-round starts at 20% off. Seconds are the best buy if you don't mind cosmetic defects. Get on the mailing list to find out about the big spring and fall sales. Marmot has a huge supply of rental equipment, and half of the rental fee can be applied to the purchase price. Call for a free catalog.

Checks, Credit cards

MOUNTAIN PRODUCTS

Everett: 2801 Colby St. ☎ 259-7954
Seattle: 160 S. Jackson ☎ 624-2748 *Pioneer Square*
Hours: Mon-Fri 10-5, Sat 9-5; Closed in June

Fashionable and functional skiwear for the whole family fills these popular manufacturers' outlets. First-quality goods, mainly overstock and close-outs, come from leading national manufacturers. Last time we visited, ladies stretch pants were only $24.95, down and polyfil jackets went from $40 to $80, and a bin filled with Gore-Tex gloves beat retail prices by 40%. Bibs in assorted colors and sizes are always a good buy, as well as accessories. Seconds in a "reject box" go fast. Outlets also located in Wenatchee and Bellingham.

Checks, Credit cards

MT. PILCHUCK SKI & SPORT   NEW LISTING

Everett: 10822 Hwy. 99 ☎ 743-5752
Hours: Mon-Sat 10-9, Sun 10-6

Summertime best buys are on waterskis and sailboards purchased factory-direct from popular local manufacturers *Jobe, O'Brien and Ho*. In the winter, the emphasis switches to snow. Check out prices on skis by *Elan, Dyna Star and Atomic* . The store buys close-out equipment and clothing at the end of the season and holds a "Gangbuster" sale every year the first week in October. Selection varies from high-end to budget. The mailing list is a must.

Checks, Credit cards

NEVADA BOB'S DISCOUNT GOLF

Bellevue: 12015 N.E. 8th ☎ 453-7378
Lynnwood: 4601 200th S.W. ☎ 778-3921
Renton: 101 S.W. 41st St. ☎ 251-1486
Silverdale: 9445 Silverdale Way N.W. ☎ 692-9539
Tacoma: 2917 S. 38th ☎ 474-8288 *Cascade Plaza*
Hours: Mon-Fri 10-8, Sat 10-6, Sun 11-5

With over 240 stores nationwide, Nevada Bob's is the biggest discount golf chain in the country. Their incredible buying power puts goods in their stores at prices they claim can't be beat. Make one of their stores a first stop for comparison shopping.

Checks, Credit cards

156 Recreation and Hobbies, Sporting Goods & Clothing

OUTDOOR CLOTHING OUTLET — NEW LISTING
Bellevue: 2241 148th Ave. N.E. ☎ 562-9094
Hours: Mon-Wed 11-6, Thurs & Fri 11-8, Sat 10-6, Sun 12-5

Much of the merchandise is factory-direct overruns or last season's goods from Eddie Bauer, L.L. Bean, REI and Lands End catalogs, salesmen's samples on consignment or factory seconds. Men's, women's and some children's sizes. Prices verge on wholesale or dip below, and smart shoppers visit often. Skis, tennis rackets, sleeping bags, backpacks and tents are sometimes available. Add your name to the mailing list for advance notice of sales that offer incredible buys.

Checks, Credit cards

OUTDOOR EMPORIUM
Seattle: 420 Pontius N. ☎ 624-6550, 624-6642 *Downtown*
Hours: Mon-Sat 8-5

Check this 10,000 sq. ft. warehouse for low prices on camping and fishing gear and outdoor clothing. You'll find over a dozen different styles of tents, *Hollofil* sleeping bags and backpacks, the biggest coolers in town and lots of fishing tackle, rods and marine equipment.

Checks, Credit cards

PENNER GOLF PRODUCTS, INC. — NEW LISTING
Seattle: 12333 Lake City Way N.E. ☎ 362-4455 *Lake City*
Hours: Mon-Fri 9:30-7, Sat 10-6, Sun 12-5

Penner's factory outlet store makes its own clubs from components, so custom fitted irons are a specialty. Bags and balls also available. Prices run $30% to 50% below national brands.

Checks, Credit cards

PRO GOLF DISCOUNT
Lynnwood: 19125 33rd Ave. W. ☎ 525-5518
Redmond: 15015 N.E. 24th ☎ 641-6766
Seattle: 10746 5th Ave. N.E. ☎ 367-3529 *Northgate*
Tacoma: 5015 Tacoma Mall Blvd. ☎ 473-4290
Tukwila: 301 Tukwila Pkwy. ☎ 431-0100
Hours: Mon-Fri 10-9, Sat 10-6, Sun 11-5

A 21 year old entrepreneur started this local discount chain in 1977, and today the superstore in Tukwila houses every major brand of golf equipment on the market. Prices are kept low with volume buying and they like to compare their service with Nordstrom's. Every year after Thanksgiving the chain holds a huge tent sale. Merchandise is brought in by the truckload and sold at a small markup. Practice cages, putting greens, club repair, trade-ins and league discounts are other incentives to shop Pro Golf.

Checks, Credit cards

Recreation and Hobbies, Sporting Goods & Clothing

PUETZ GOLF CENTERS
Bellevue: 1645 140th Ave. N.E. ☎ 747-0664
Seattle: 11762 Aurora Ave. N. ☎ 362-2272 *North Park*
Hours: Generally, Mon-Sat 9-9, Sun 9-8

Puetz keeps prices low on a complete selection of name-brand equipment and apparel. "Popular-styled clubs" at affordable prices and a big inventory of custom-fit variables have kept customers coming back for 44 years. Used and returned equipment is a good buy. The Aurora store has an outdoor driving range where you can test your new clubs or learn the game. Get on the mailing list for annual sales held in February and September.

Checks, Credit cards

REI (Recreational Equipment, Inc.)
Bellevue: 15400 N.E. 20th ☎ 643-3700 *Sherwood Center*
Federal Way: 2565 S. Gateway Ct. Place ☎ 941-4994 *Gateway Center*
Seattle: 1525 11th Ave. ☎ 323-8333 *Capitol Hill*
Hours: Mon, Tues, Sat 10-6, Wed-Fri 10-9, Sun 12-5

This landmark co-op, founded in 1938 by a group of Seattle mountaineers, is considered by many to be the most comprehensive, quality-conscious store in the nation for backpacking, mountaineering, kayaking and bicycling equipment. Thirteen locations on the West Coast serve over 2 million members, who pay a $10 lifetime membership fee and receive a 10% dividend on purchases, seasonal and specialty catalogs, sales notices and voting rights. Non-members can shop at REI but receive no dividends. Pick up free catalogs or call 1-800-426-4840 to have them mailed. Smart shoppers hold out for big sales held the last weekend in May and the first two weeks in October when pre-season and end-of-season sporting goods and used rental equipment are sold at reduced prices. Clearance clothing and footwear are sold in the upper level of the Capitol Hill store.

Checks, Credit cards

R & E 2ND GEAR   **NEW LISTING**
Seattle: 1314 N.E. 56th Ave. ☎ 527-1536 *U-District*
Hours: Mon-Fri 9-8, Sat 9-6, Sun 11-5

At last! A discount store for cyclists. Most bikes have at least $80 lopped off the retail price. Clothing and bike accessories average 30% to 50% below retail. Inventory is mostly name-brand close-outs and seconds, last year's styles, or left-overs from the R & E up the street on University Way, one of the area's leading cycle shops. If you're interested in selling your bike, inquire about their consignment program or post a notice on the bulletin board. Get on R & E's mailing list for supersales and classes. Once a year they sell out their entire stock of rental and demo bikes (including *Terra Tech* mountain bikes) at killer prices.

Checks, Credit cards

158 Recreation and Hobbies, Sporting Goods & Clothing

SECOND BASE NEW LISTING
Seattle: 1101 E. Pine ☎ 325-2273 *Capitol Hill*
Hours: Mon & Tues 11-6, Wed-Fri 10-8, Sat 9:30-5, Sun 11:30-5

What a great place for the whole family to browse for secondhand recreational and athletic equipment. Croquet sets, dart boards, wet suits, baseball mitts, sleeping bags, bike helmets, golf clubs, exercise equipment and balls for every sport are just a few of the items that fill the store. Parents will save on children's ski equipment and soccer shoes. Merchandise is taken on consignment or purchased from garage sales, auctions and individual sellers. Consignees get a whopping 60% of the selling price.

Checks, Credit cards

SIERRA TRADING POST NEW LISTING
Sparks, NV ☎ 702/355-3355
Hours: Mon-Fri 7-6 (Pacific time)

This mail-order catalog specializes in first-quality overstock, close-outs and irregulars from such famous outdoor clothing lines as *Patagonia, Jansport, Hanes, The North Face, Terramar, New Sportif USA, Woolrich and Asolo* are priced at 40% to 50% below retail. The catalogs, which are similar in design to Banana Republic's distinctive style, are free upon request.

Checks, Credit cards

SKI BONKERS
Seattle: 2601 Elliott *Seattle Trade Center*
Annual sale

For over a decade families have gone bonkers over the low prices and huge selection of athletic wear and sporting goods at this Labor Day Weekend supersale sponsored by Olympic Sports! Pay 20% to 70% off the normal price on name-brand clothing and ski equipment of all kinds. Most of the merchandise is special promotions, close-outs, or clearance items from the local chain stores. Watch the newspapers for big ads.

Checks, Credit cards

SKI RACK SPORTS
Seattle: 2118 8th Ave. ☎ 623-5595 *Downtown*
Hours: Mon-Fri 10-6, Thurs 10-8, Sat 10-5, Sun 12-5

Skiers on a budget may want to check out the big inventory of used boots and skis, all of which meet current safety standards. Prices start at half off and go down, depending on the condition of the equipment. If you decide to recycle your used skis, you get 55% of the selling price.

Checks, Credit cards

SNIAGRAB and SPORTS BLAST
Seattle: Seattle Center Exhibition Hall ☎ 728-8999
Periodic sales

continued >

Northwest sports enthusiasts flock to these annual bargain festivals sponsored by Osborn and Ulland. Since 1947, Sniagrab (bargains spelled backwards) has been attracting skiers who like to stock up on equipment and clothing at the beginning of the season. The event is held the 3rd or 4th weekend in September. Sports Blast, held the first weekend in June, is a sale and show that features merchandise for outdoor summer activities, plus celebrity appearances, fashion shows, clinics and exhibitions. The goods sold at both of these events will be close-outs, discontinued styles, demos, or last year's models (all new, first-quality) at 30% to 70% below retail prices. You're never going to find such a large selection under one roof. Watch the newspapers, radio and TV for ads.

Checks, Credit cards

SPORTCO — NEW LISTING

Fife: 4702 20th St. E. ☎ 922-2222
Hours: Mon-Fri 9:30-6, Sat 9-5

As a local distributor of sporting goods, this company warehouses over 15,000 items from 480 different manufacturers. In the last few years, they've opened their doors to the public. For a $15 membership fee, customers can save a bundle on recreational and athletic equipment of all kinds. Non-members pay 5% over the posted price.

Checks, Credit cards

SPORTS EXCHANGE

Seattle: 2232 15th Ave. W. ☎ 285-4777 *West Queen Anne*
Hours: Mon-Fri 10-6, Sat 10-5, Sun 12-5. Open until 8 weeknights in winter

Although you'll find camping supplies and clothing at this discount outlet, the big draw is a terrific selection of equipment for snow skiing and watersports, which sells for 40% below retail. *Ray Ban* sunglasses are discounted year-round. Ditto bikes, including heavy terrain models. Merchandise is mainly close-outs, discontinued styles and consignment goods from factories and individuals. The store liquidates its rental equipment at sales held in March and mid-September.

Checks

SPORTS REPLAY

Lynnwood: 5421 196th St. S.W., #7 ☎ 775-4088 *Parkview*
Hours: Tues-Fri 10-7:30, Sat 10-5:30

Terrific deals on new as well as used equipment and athletic clothing are at this location! Half of the inventory is close-outs, samples and seconds purchased from local manufacturers *Sunbuster, Snuggler and Seattle Sports Apparel*. The day we shopped they had a "ton of tents" and quoted us $95 for a 6-man dome that normally sells for $178. Sleeping bags and biking apparel were other good buys. Prices average 40% below retail on most items. With over 1800 consignees, the store has a great selection of used items. Consignees get 60% of the selling price.

Checks

WEST MARINE PRODUCTS — NEW LISTING
Seattle: 6317 Seaview Ave. N.W. ☎ 789-4640 *Shilshole*
1000 Mercer ☎ 292-8663 *South Lake Union*
Hours: Mon-Sat 8-6, Thurs & Fri 9-8, Sun 9-5

This big West Coast chain sells quality boating gear for fishing, racing, cruising and water skiing at discount prices. Clothing and the latest in electronics keep pleasure boaters coming back. Do-it-yourselfers find products needed for building or repairing boats. An incredible variety of ropes and pulleys lines the walls. Call 800/538-0775 for free catalogs.

Checks, Credit cards

WILEY'S WATERSKI SHOP — NEW LISTING
Seattle: 1417 S. Trenton St. ☎ 762-1300 *South Park*
Hours: Mon-Fri 10-6, Sat 10-4

With the biggest selection in six states and some of the lowest prices in town, Wiley's sells more skis in one day than most sporting goods stores sell in an entire season. Water sport devotees flock to this place. Inventory includes watersuits, dry suits, ropes and life preservers. They'll custom-make bindings. Prices hover close to wholesale on many items.

Checks, Credit cards

☑ Consumer Tips:

☞ Wait for annual sales sponsored by local retailers, many of which take place on Labor Day and Memorial Day weekends.

☞ Visit the Capitol Hill area where discount, consignment and factory outlets are clustered around REI.

☞ Good used equipment offers the best value for your money.

☞ Army-Navy surplus stores are great places to find camping gear and outdoor clothing at reduced prices. See the yellow pages for listings.

☞ Recreational clothing, now a driving force in high fashion, is less expensive in sporting goods stores than in the department stores.

Audio & Video Equipment

For audio, video, telephone and fax equipment, consistent low pricing can be found at Silo, Office Club, Costco and Price Savers. If you have no idea where to start or exactly what you want, the best place to get a handle on the better-quality, state-of-the-art equipment is at one of the five Magnolia Hi-Fi & Video outlets. Regular prices are not always the lowest, but frequent sales turn up good buys. In Tacoma, check out The Stereo Shoppe for similar research. Hawthorne Stereo in Bellevue and Definitive Audio in Seattle offer top-of-the-line audio equipment at competitive prices, and sales are frequent. A catalog from 47th Street Photo in New York City (See listing under Photographic Equipment & Supplies) will provide basic information on a wide selection of telephone and facsimile equipment at low mail-order prices. Also refer to Household Appliances.

Recreation and Hobbies, Audio & Video Equipment

DICK'S CAMERA AND VIDEO
Burien: 15421 1st Ave. S. ☎ 244-1101
Hours: Mon-Fri 9-7, Sat 9-5

You'll find a large stock of video cameras, recorders and accessories at discounted prices here. Camcorder rental and instruction is offered. They can make color prints from still video frames, and they provide duplication service.

Checks, Credit cards

LEE'S VIDEO-AUDIO-FAX-CELLULAR
Bellevue: 1424 156th N.E. ☎ 643-5555, 643-0562
Hours: Mon-Fri 10-8, Sat 10-6, Sun 11-6

Few local discounters can match their selection of current-model name-brands, and Lee's claims they'll beat any local dealers' prices. Choose from dozens of VCR's, TV's, and camcorders. Over 30 different fax machines are priced at 40% to 50% off list. Stereo equipment, compact disc players, laser disks, tape decks, radar detectors, answering machines and mobile phones are also in stock. Prices shown are for cash or check; add 2% for credit cards. Shipping available anywhere in the U.S. or Canada.

Checks, Credit cards

OLD TECHNOLOGY SHOP NEW LISTING
Seattle: 7712 Aurora Ave. N. ☎ 527-2829 *Green Lake*
Hours: Wed-Sat 12-6, Sun 2-6

Step into this fascinating store and you'll feel like you've entered a museum. An odd assortment of obsolete electronic parts, radio equipment, and scientific instruments attracts amateur inventors, radio operators and hobbyists. It's one of the few places where you can find replacement parts for vintage TV's, radios, and bicycles. Fine carpenters' hand tools are another specialty.

Checks

T-DEE APPLIANCE NEW LISTING
Seattle: 13339 Lake City Way N.E. ☎ 361-7368 *Lake City*
Hours: Mon-Thurs 9-6, Fri, Sat 9-5

T-Dee rents major household appliances, televisions, VCR's, video cameras, and PA systems to apartment owners, trade shows, and businesses. When the items come back to the store, the owner puts "old" inventory on sale at bargain prices. Big-screen TV's rented to restaurants go on sale every once in a while. A big selection of refrigerators, washers, and dryers starts at $125. Monday is the day to shop because that's when new inventory arrives. Or, you can put your name on a waiting list for specific items. Service-oriented for 35 years, T-Dee stands behind its products. The company also offers installation and cabinet work.

Checks, Credit cards

UNDER-WARE ELECTRONICS — NEW LISTING
Wichita, KS ☎ 800/442-1408
Hours: Mon-Fri 7-8, Sat 9-4 (Central time)

This Kansas discounter has an eclectic mix of video cameras, stereo components, facsimile machines and computers. Some are discontinued models, some not. Prices are very low on brands such as *JVC, Kenwood, Sony, Brother, Leading Edge* and *Zenith*. Call for free catalog.

Checks, Credit cards

VIDEO ONLY — NEW LISTING
Bellevue: 14339 N.E. 20th ☎ 644-9400 *Ross Plaza*
Federal Way: 1706 S. 320th ☎ 946-4600 *Sea-Tac Village*
Seattle: 707 Westlake Ave. N. ☎ 623-3388 *South Lake Union*
Tacoma: 2941 S. 38th ☎ 472-3838 *Cascade Plaza*
Tukwila: 17620 Southcenter Parkway ☎ 575-6665
Hours: Generally, Mon-Fri 10-9, Sat 10-6, Sun 11-5

Here's another big discount chain that stays competitive by focusing on a narrow range of products. TV's, VCR's, and camcorders are all they sell, but inventory includes many different styles and leading brands. Blank cassettes and videotapes sell at low prices in case lots of ten. Nintendo games are also stocked.

Checks, Credit cards

ZOBRIST CONSUMER ELECTRONICS
Seattle: 1214 1st Ave. ☎ 624-2424 *Downtown*
Hours: Mon-Fri 10-6:30, Sat 10-5:30

For over 60 years Zobrist has been offering discount prices on electronic products for the car, home, or boat. Check them out if you're in the market for a CD, TV, VCR, stereo, telephone, shortwave radio, computer, CB radio or antenna. All major manufacturers are represented, and staff will quote prices over the phone. Look for big discounts on radio and TV tubes and component kits. They also trade and pay cash for quality goods, so you can pick up some real buys on used merchandise. Knowledgeable sales staff will give advice on home repairs or do-it-yourself projects.

Checks, Credit cards

Audio & Video Recordings

To save money on new releases, music lovers frequent the University District where Peaches, Tower Records and the Wherehouse share the territory with half a dozen independent and used record stores. The big chains discount new recordings because they buy in volume and need to generate sales to recoup their investment if the item is a flop. A month later the same recording may cost 30% more. Mass merchandisers like Fred Meyer, Best and Target keep prices competitive with the big record

continued >

store chains. Always check stores' bargain bins for overstock, promos and discontinued labels. Watch for special discounts on current and old releases when recording artists come to town.

Used recordings— if they're in good condition— offer the best value. Current and mainstream music are often marked half price at independent stores. It's hard to comparison shop country, classical, jazz and blues, since price depends on demand and many items are one-of-a-kind. Used bookstores, second-hand and thrift shops sell "recycled" recordings. If you're selling old records, tapes and CD's, call for an appointment first and don't expect to make a lot of money. Stores in the U-district often pay the least. Take advantage of trades and credits for a better return on your money. Refer to Used Books for entries that also carry recordings.

Over 65% of the homes in America have VCR's, and the number continues to increase as record stores devote more space to video sales and rental stores spring up on every corner. If you want to buy a movie, the longer you're willing to wait, the less you pay. The price goes down 50% once a video drops off the current release list. Mass merchandisers and grocery stores sometimes sell at a loss just to get people in the store, hoping they'll buy something else. Keep up with where the best buys are by reading "Video Watch," a column that appears in the Seattle Times Arts and Entertainment section every Sunday. Used videos may be of lesser quality, but at $9 to $19.98, you can't beat the prices. For the best selection, look to volume renters like Tower, Wherehouse, Blockbuster and Critic's Choice. For the lowest prices, check out flea markets and swap meets, where video rental stores dump a lot of tapes.

When renting, comparison shop in your own neighborhood for the lowest prices. Why drive an extra mile when the cost of gas will eat up a $1 savings? Check grocery stores and mini-markets where selection may be limited, but prices will be cheaper. Don't forget your local library, which offers popular, informational and children's videos at no charge.

Some video rental stores sell memberships, which include special incentives for those who rent a lot of movies. Look for discount coupon books, two-for-one rentals, or free rentals after you rent a certain number of videos. During our research, we discovered two unique bargain places: 75¢ Video in Bothell sells lifetime memberships for $100. You then pay 75¢ for any video in stock for the rest of your life (or as long as the company is in business). Or purchase a punch card and rent 10 movies for $15 or 22 for $30. Blockbuster Video's 3-night rental policy and midnight closing time allow you to stock up for the weekend in one trip and not worry about the 24-hour return policy. Rental fees average $1-$3. Community service videos are free. (Check the yellow pages for current addresses.)

See area locator index for this section on page 226

164 Recreation and Hobbies, Audio & Video Recordings

BACKTRACK VIDEOS AND RECORDS
Seattle: 5339 25th Ave. N.E. ☎ 524-0529 *Ravenna*
Hours: Mon-Fri 11-6:30, Sat 12-5

Ever wondered where you could rent or buy cult classics like "Amazon Women on the Moon" and "Attack of the Killer Tomatoes"? Backtrack specializes in psychotronic and Golden Turkey videos in the horror, science fiction and rock 'n' roll genre. Music recordings are mostly pop, folk and rock from the 1950s, '60s and '70s. Backtrack pays up to $1 or gives $2 credit for old records.

Checks, Credit cards

BOP STREET RECORDS AND TAPES
Seattle: 5512 20th Ave. N.W. ☎ 783-3009 *Ballard*
Hours: Mon-Sat 12-6

Bop Street offers one of the best selections in town of 1950s and '60s American and British vintage rock, plus current jazz and big band sounds. Half the inventory is in storage, so if you can't find what you want, just ask. CD's are stocked in smaller quantities. Prices negotiable on everything. Qualify for a discount card just by walking in the door. The owner loves to track down hard-to-find recordings.

Checks, Credit cards

BUBBLE RECORDS & VIDEOS
Kent: 10451 S.E. 240th ☎ 854-7788
Hours: Mon-Fri 12-8, Sat 12-6, Sun 1-5

Shop here for the most extensive selection of current and used records, CD's and cassettes in the South end. All new recordings are discounted. Collectors and radio DJ's often find what they want in the huge out-of-print section, which covers everything from jazz to classical.

Checks, Credit cards

BUD'S JAZZ RECORDS
Seattle: 102 S. Jackson ☎ 628-0445 *Pioneer Square*
Hours: Mon-Sat 11-7, Sun 12-6

This store focuses on breadth rather than depth, so ardent fans will find jazz in all its forms from ragtime to avant garde, and everything in between. Eighty percent of the merchandise is new, and prices are kept low to turn over the 5,000 titles in stock. Compact disc prices are competitive with Tower Records. Vintage recordings attract collectors.

Checks, Credit cards

BUDGET TAPES AND RECORDS
Puyallup: 11707 Meridian E. ☎ 845-2117
Renton: 534 Rainier Ave. S. ☎ 228-8298
Silverdale: 10408 Silverdale Way ☎ 398-3868 *Ross Plaza*

continued >

Prices are low because Budget carries a lot of "cut-outs" and used recordings. Used CD's average $7.99. Current Top-40 releases are sometimes discounted when they first come into the store. The selection of pop, rock, soul, jazz and country varies from store-to-store.

Checks, Credit cards

CELLOPHANE SQUARE

Bellevue: N.E. 8th & Bellevue Way ☎ 454-5059 *Bellevue Square*
Seattle: 1315 N.E. 42nd ☎ 634-2280 *U-District*
Hours: Mon-Sat 10-midnight, Sun 12-10

A popular hangout for those interested in contemporary, independent and local rock, Cellophane Square stocks a big inventory of new and used records, CD's and tapes. Used current releases go for half price, and rare rock is a specialty.

Checks, Credit cards

COMPACT DISC CONNECTION   NEW LISTING

Lynnwood: 4201 196th St. S.W. ☎ 774-4538
Hours: Mon-Sat 11-10, Sun 11-7

New and used CD's are sold here. Pay $7.99 to $9.99 for current used releases.

Checks, Credit cards

DON'S HOUSE OF RECORDS   NEW LISTING

Tacoma: 3111 6th Ave. ☎ 759-3194
Hours: Mon-Sat 12-6

Find lots of 45's at dirt cheap prices plus a few 78's in the "oldies but goodies" category. Used tapes and CD's lean toward rock and folk. Elvis memorabilia for fans.

Checks, Credit cards

DRASTIC PLASTIC RECORDS

Tacoma: 3005 6th Ave. ☎ 272-2886
Hours: Mon-Sat 11-6:30

Thousands of used albums, cassettes and CD's are sold here, with rock and jazz the main focuses. The owner only buys or trades items in good condition.

Cash only

EXOTIQUE IMPORTS   NEW LISTING

Seattle: 2400 Third Ave. ☎ 448-3452 *Downtown*
Hours: Mon-Sat 11-9, Sun 12-6

New and used records, tapes and CD's in the import, domestic, independent and progressive/electronic categories are bought, sold and traded. Some collectibles and classics from the 60's. With a local DJ on staff, Exotique specializes in the latest dance music. Mail order catalog available.

Checks, Credit cards

Recreation and Hobbies, Audio & Video Recordings

FALLOUT RECORDS & SKATEBOARDS
Seattle: 1506 E. Olive Way ☎ 323-2662 *Capitol Hill*
Hours: Mon-Fri 11-8, Sat & Sun 12-6

Fallout specializes in independent, experimental, underground and punk in records, tapes and CD's. Prices are equal to or lower than big stores on major labels. Occasional sales advertised via flyers in the store.
Checks, Credit cards

GOLDEN OLDIES RECORDS & TAPES
Bellevue: 156th N.E. & N.E. 8th ☎ 641-9820 *Crossroads Mall*
Lynnwood: 3925 196th St. S.W. ☎ 778-7722
Everett: 1902 Hewitt Ave. ☎ 252-0707
Kirkland: 356 Park Place Center ☎ 827-9580 *Park Place Mall*
Renton: 924 S. 3rd St. ☎ 228-0866
Seattle: 201 N.E. 45th St. ☎ 547-2260 *Wallingford*
Tacoma: 8024 S. Tacoma Way ☎ 581-7947
Hours: Generally, Mon-Fri 10-7, Sat 10-6, Sun 11-5

This local chain sells an incredible selection of out-of-print 45's. Albums and tapes from the 1940s, '50s, '60s and '70s fill the shelves. Although vintage rock 'n' roll is a big draw, country, jazz, western and big band sounds are also stocked in depth. Rare recordings, used CD's and re-issues of popular rock music round out the inventory. Merchandise varies from store to store, so if you know what you want, call first. The staff hunts nationwide for hard-to-find requests, and the store has an international mail order clientele.
Checks, Credit cards

M & L ASSOCIATES
Seattle: 6504 Ravenna Ave. N.E. ☎ 522-8189 *Ravenna*
Hours: Mon-Fri 1-7, Sat 10-8

If you treasure rare or vintage jazz, check out the extensive collection of 45's, 78's and LP's at this low-profile store. Customers also praise their outstanding inventory of second-hand rock, country and movie sound tracks. Used CD's may run as low as $8.00. Send $3 to receive a 40-page computerized listing of collectible jazz recordings. Send $1 for separate listings of other categories. For $8.00 you can purchase a 2-inch-thick catalog that includes everything in stock.
Checks, Credit cards

MOVIE MASTERS   NEW LISTING
Tukwila: 17900 Southcenter Pkwy. ☎ 575-0717 *Pavilion Mall*
Hours: Mon-Fri 10-9, Sat 10-6, Sun 11-6

The largest selection and lowest prices around on video movies make this exciting for film buffs. New and used videos average $20 or less, with classics and science fiction the specialties. Current releases and re-issues come from distributors who dump surplus merchandise. Used videos are purchased from libraries, individuals and rental stores. The owner will track down hard-to-find titles.
Checks, Credit cards

Recreation and Hobbies, Audio & Video Recordings

NORTHWEST RECORD & COMPACT DISC CONVENTION
Seattle: ☎ 228-3537
Periodic sales

Think of this as a swap meet for recordings. Thousands of records, tapes, CD's and memorabilia are brought in by collectors, dealers and retail stores from as far away as Oregon and Eastern Washington. The convention usually takes place at the Seattle Center. Call or watch for ads in record stores.
Checks, Credit cards

ORPHEUM   NEW LISTING
Seattle: 618 Broadway E. ☎ 322-6370 *Capitol Hill*
Hours: 10-midnight

This small shop reflects the diverse tastes of its neighborhood and competes price-wise by taking a lower markup on new releases. Although they stock a little bit of everything, alternative rock and dance music are the main focuses. DJ's shop here because 12" singles are a specialty. Used CD's and LP's available.

PARK AVENUE RECORDS
Seattle: 532 Queen Anne Ave. N. ☎ 284-2390 *West of Seattle Center*
Hours: Mon-Sat 10-10, Sun 12-8

Check out the secondhand imports, oldies and collectibles here. Although inventory covers all categories, rock and jazz sections attract the most customers. Special-orders are filled, and shipping is available.
Credit cards

PENNY LANE RECORDS & TAPES
Tacoma: 11013 Bridgeport Way S.W. ☎ 588-1777
Hours: Mon-Fri 10-9, Sat 10-8, Sun 12-6

If you live near Fort Lewis and like R&B, jazz, British rock, or current popular music, check out Penny Lane's new and used LP's and cassettes. The store is big on 12" singles. New CD's are often discounted.
Checks, Credit cards

REBELLIOUS JUKEBOX   NEW LISTING
Seattle: 506 E. Pine ☎ 329-7847 *Capitol Hill*
Hours: Mon-Sat 11-8, Sun 11-6

You'll find low prices and a good selection of imported and independent rock, underground and industrial sounds. Future plans call for adding jazz, blues and world beat.
Checks, Credit cards

RECORD PLANET   NEW LISTING
Seattle: 6 Mercer St. ☎ 283-4446 *North of Seattle Center*
Hours: Tues-Thurs 12-6, Fri, Sat 12-8

continued >

168 Recreation and Hobbies, Audio & Video Recordings

Thousands of vintage 45's were brought out of storage by Park Avenue Records to start this shop. Collectors can spend hours going through stacks of classic rock, R&B, country, folk, pop and vocals from the 1950s and later. Prices start as low as $1 and go to $100.

Checks, Credit cards

RUBATO'S
Bellevue: 10672 N.E. 8th ☎ 455-9417
Hours: Mon-Fri 12-9, Sat 12-7, Sun 12-5

You can count on finding bargains on quality used jazz, soul, classical, recent pop and movie sound tracks at Rubato's. Check out their large selection of CD's.

Checks, Credit cards

SECOND TIME AROUND RECORDS, STEREO & VIDEO
Federal Way: 32015 23rd Ave. S. ☎ 839-0649 *Sea-Tac Mall*
Seattle: 4209 University Way N.E. ☎ 632-1698 *U-District*
Tacoma: 2505 S. 38th ☎ 472-0623 *Lincoln Plaza*
Hours: Generally, Mon-Thurs 10-9, Fri & Sat 10-11, Sun 11-7

This classic used record store focuses on collectible rock LP's from the 1960s, although they stock everything from pop to big band sounds. Prices are low on new and used CD's, cassettes and music videos. Recordings by local groups turn up here first. Secondhand stereo equipment is always a good buy, as well as used guitars, TV's, camcorders and rock clothing.

Checks, Credit cards

SOUNDWAVES   NEW LISTING
Burien: 630 S.W. 153rd ☎ 248-3959
Hours: Mon-Sat 11-8, Sun 12-5

Burien record collectors celebrated when this small but comprehensive shop opened. Prices are less on current releases than at the Fred Meyer down the street. Much of the inventory is imported rock. They'll special-order records or track down hard-to-find music.

Checks, Credit cards

SUN COAST VIDEO   NEW LISTING
Federal Way: 1824 S. 320th St. ☎ 941-2842 *Sea-Tac Mall*
Hours: Mon-Fri 10-9, Sat 10-6, Sun 11-6

You'll be amazed at how many movies are available for so little money. Sun Coast is the biggest national chain in sales-only video tapes, stocking over 6,000 titles, most in the $29.95 category. Hundreds sell for $10 and under. If you're trying to build a collection, the staff can provide a list of all the movies ever made by your favorite actor or comedian.

Checks, Credit cards

TOWER RECORDS & VIDEO
Bellevue: 10635 N.E. 8th ☎ 451-2557
Seattle: 500 Mercer ☎ 283-4456 *Northeast of Seattle Center*
           4321 University Way N.E. ☎ 632-1187 *U-District*
Tacoma: 2941 S. 38th ☎ 475-9222
Hours: Daily, 9-midnight

continued >

Tower leads the pack when it comes to selection and discount prices on recordings and videos. Volume is the name of the game here. (The Mercer Street store is the largest in the Pacific Northwest.) Top-25 current releases, CD's and cassettes are always on sale, and in-store promotions change constantly. Watch the newspapers for big sales two or three times a year. Used rental movies sold in their Red Tag section are the cheapest in town.

Checks, Credit cards

THE WHEREHOUSE

Bellevue: 1100 Bellevue Way N.E. ☎ 454-2235
2301 148th Ave. N.E. ☎ 746-7022
Everett: 1203 S.E. Everett Mall Way ☎ 353-1201
Federal Way: 31861 Gateway Ctr. Blvd. S. ☎ 941-3221
Lynnwood: 3000 184th St. N.W. ☎ 776-5099 *Alderwood Mall*
19800 44th Ave. W. ☎ 670-2827
Seattle: 4501 Roosevelt Way N.E. ☎ 633-4072 *U-District*
206 Broadway E. ☎ 324-2140 *Capitol Hill*
Tacoma: 6409 6th Ave. ☎ 564-2336
10115 Gravelly Lake Dr. ☎ 584-1156
Hours: Generally, Daily 10-10

Every week something different goes on sale at this chain. Save on tapes, CD's, videos, software and computer games. Prices go down 20% to 30% during big quarterly sales (advertised via colorful bulk mailings) on computer games and videos for the kids, audio and video accessories, plus blank videos and cassette tapes. Used videos from the rental department are incredibly cheap. Inquire about their Frequent Renter Video Program and earn points that can be applied towards free products. A catalog is available every month in the stores with a complete listing of video rentals in stock and sale prices for previously viewed movies.

Checks, Credit cards

Photographic Equipment & Supplies

Seattle has a group of competitive camera retailers who make bargain shopping easy for amateur photographers. Most firms will quote over the phone, and all advertise their specials regularly. After determining the exact camera model or lens you want, you may also want to check the back pages of photographic magazines for lowest mail-order prices.

If you've ever dealt with some of New York City's discount mail-order dealers, you already know that not all crime in Manhattan is committed in the streets. Their prices often don't include cases, and some even replace the manufacturer's lens with a cheaper after-market brand. On the other hand, there are some reliable dealers with good prices. 47th Street Photo in New York publishes an extensive catalog with prices and terms of sale.

Recreation and Hobbies, Photographic Equipment & Supplies

All mail-order dealers charge extra for packaging and handling, and shipping charges are usually marked up. Read the fine print carefully and figure out your lowest "realistic" delivered cost before ordering. Always purchase with a credit card instead of a check.

For price quotes in the Seattle area, call Kits, Tall's, Warshal's and Cameras West. Remember that local dealers will likely take care of any future problems much faster than the mail-order folks, and for only a little more than mail-order prices they provide hands-on demonstrations and basic instructions. Ken's Cameras has pledged to meet any locally advertised price on items in stock, and Bellevue's Crown Camera is a fairly competitive Eastside discounter.

Most professionals frequent Glazer's or Optechs Camera Supply to scout their wide selections of new and used professional-level equipment and supplies. Ballard Camera, Camera Show on Aurora and Clyed's downtown have large stocks of used 35mm equipment at or below average market prices.

If you want to save money on amateur film or developing, Costco and Price Savers boast the cheapest prices in town. Film selection is limited, but popular sizes of Kodak and Fuji slide and print film are stocked. Drug stores and supermarkets have frequent 50%-off specials on developing and enlargements.

CAMERA SHOW   NEW LISTING
Seattle: 7509 Aurora N. ☎ 782-9448 *Green Lake*
Hours: Tues-Sat 12-6

Only used photo equipment and accessories are sold here. Professionals and collectors drop in frequently to check out everything from late model Nikons to museum-quality antique cameras. We hear the owner has been known to negotiate, especially if you're buying in volume. The store buys outright, trades, or will sell your equipment on consignment for a 10% fee.

Checks, Credit cards

47th STREET PHOTO
New York, NY ☎ 800/221-7774 **Hours:** Mon-Thurs 8-7, Fri 9-2, Sun 10-5

This giant mail-order firm has five retail stores in New York City. They sell name-brand audio-video equipment, cameras, computers, fax machines, microwaves, stereos, television sets, vacuum cleaners and watches at very competitive prices. A comprehensive catalog published several times a year is available upon request. Latest (and often lowest) prices can be found in their weekly two-page ads in the Sunday New York Times, available throughout the Seattle area. Orders can be placed via phone or fax.

Credit Cards

OPTECHS CAMERA SUPPLY
Seattle: 133 Dexter Ave. N. ☎ 443-1737 *East of Seattle Center*
Hours: Mon-Fri 8:30-6, Sat 9-5

Recreation and Hobbies, Photographic Equipment & Supplies 171

This family-run business offers a complete section of film, quality equipment and darkroom supplies for beginner through professional photographers at prices that average 25% to 30% below the market. Only top-brand cameras and accessories are stocked, and you'll find a selection of good used cameras.

Checks, Credit cards

PACIFIC COLOR, INC.   NEW LISTING

Seattle: 7101 Woodlawn Ave. N.E. ☎ 524-7200 *Green Lake*
Hours: Mon-Fri 8:30-5

A full-service professional laboratory catering primarily to the portrait and wedding photographer, Pacific Color is a fine resource for large quantities of color enlargements (up to giant 48" x 96" murals) or great numbers of duplicate slides (25¢ each in lots of 100).

Checks, Credit cards

QUANTITY PHOTOS, INC.   NEW LISTING

Hollywood, CA ☎ 800/843-9259
Hours Mon-Fri 8:30-5

This is where movie stars and rock musicians have had their 8" x 10" black & white glossies made for over 40 years. Prices are as low as 10¢ per print. Brochure with price list and ordering information available by calling the toll-free number.

Checks

RAINIER PHOTOGRAPHIC SUPPLIES

Seattle: 8730 Rainier Ave. S. ☎ 722-8700 *Rainier Beach*
Hours: Mon-Fri 9-6, Sat 9-2

Rainier wholesales film, videotapes, mailers, photo albums, studio and darkroom supplies to professionals, retail stores and big accounts like the University of Washington. They sell to the public for 30% to 40% below list. Look for some of the lowest prices in town on film and broadcast-quality videotape. Pick up a price list in the store or call to have one sent by mail. They offer same-day UPS shipping for orders of $10 or more received by 2 P.M.

Checks, Credit cards

SHUTTERBUG   NEW LISTING

Titusville, FL, P.O. Box 1209, (32781) ☎ 407/268-5010

We recently discovered this monthly photo equipment buyer/seller publication with over 200 pages of classified and display advertising plus product buying information. Most advertised items are used and are systematically graded from mint through fair condition. This is a good place to start your search for common to exotic new or used equipment. Subscription is $16.00 a year.

Checks, Credit cards

172 Recreation and Hobbies, Arts and Crafts & Sewing

WARSHAL'S SPORTING GOODS AND PHOTOGRAPHIC SUPPLY CO.
NEW LISTING

Seattle: 1000 1st Ave. ☎ 624-7303 or 800/545-6675 *Downtown*
Hours: Mon-Sat 9-5:30

Over the years Warshal's has become a downtown institution noted for its low film prices and broad selection of cameras and photographic supplies. A large film inventory attracts commercial photographers as well as amateurs. Fuji, Kodak and Ilford Film is heavily discounted when you buy more than six rolls at a time. Prices are at or below most East Coast mail-order suppliers. One-hour free parking validation at nearby Republic lots with purchase. Warshal's offers same-day shipping and free delivery on mail-orders of $100 or more, in-or-out-of-town. A published photographic film and paper price list is available.

Checks, Credit cards

Arts and Crafts & Sewing

Even if you only make such simple items as elastic-waist skirts and decorative pillows or learn to do your own minor alterations, sewing is a good way to stretch the family budget. Many fabric stores have expanded their arts and craft departments and added home decorator fabrics as interest in these areas continues to grow. Free classes, demonstrations, and inexpensive seminars provide incentive to purchase merchandise. Call the stores, get on mailing lists, and watch the newspaper for announcements. Refer to Appliances for stores that sell sewing machines. Look under Window Coverings for drapery fabrics and Paper Products for art supplies.

B & B HOBBIES AND CRAFTS
NEW LISTING

Bellevue: 14506 N.E. 20th ☎ 641-9722
Kent: 317 S. Washington Ave. ☎ 859-1585
Hours: Mon-Fri 10-8, Sat 10-6, Sun 11-5

This nationwide chain may not have the biggest stores, but they carry the best variety of arts and crafts supplies, especially if you like to make candles, dolls, miniatures, jewelry, Christmas ornaments, or flower arrangements for fun or profit. They beat competitor's prices by 20% because they buy by the truckload and manufacture many of their own products. Acrylic paints, macramé and papier-mâché supplies are big sellers.

Checks, Credit cards

BEST FABRIC OUTLET
NEW LISTING

Everett: 5303 Evergreen Way ☎ 355-7373 *Everett Plaza*
Kirkland: 12546-A Totem Lake Blvd. N.E. ☎ 821-7187 *Totem Lake Mall*
Kent: 25742 104th Ave S.E. ☎ 859-1143 *Kent Hills Plaza*
Lynnwood: S.W. 196th & N. Hwy. 99 ☎ 778-0007 *James Village*

continued >

Recreation and Hobbies, Arts and Crafts & Sewing

Renton: 2819 N.E. Sunset Blvd. ☎ 271-1733 *Highland Shopping Ctr.*
Seattle: 15236 Aurora Ave. N. ☎ 362-8072 *Shoreline*
Silverdale: 13276 N.W. Plaza Rd. ☎ 692-7243 *Kitsap Plaza*
Spanaway: 14916 Pacific Ave. S. ☎ 535-3241
Tacoma: 5943 6th Ave. ☎ 564-3081 *Highland Hills Shopping Ctr.*
Hours: Mon-Fri 9:30-9, Sat 9:30-6, Sun 12-5

Inventory is strong on inexpensive fabrics, with calico a specialty. Prices run from $3 to $10 a yard. Patterns are always half off, and you can save 10% to 50% on notions and craft items. *Singer and Brother sewing machines sold at discounted prices.*

Checks, Credit cards

CALICO CORNERS

Bellevue: 104 Bellevue Way S.E. ☎ 455-2510
Lynnwood: 3225 Alderwood Mall Blvd. ☎ 778-8019 *Alderwood Towne Center*
Hours: Generally, Mon-Sat 9:30-6, Wed 9:30-8, Sun 12-5

The array of gorgeous decorator fabrics and creative displays will inspire you to re-do your whole house, and at these prices you can afford to! Most of the fabrics, which come from Waverly, a leading name in home fashions, have slight imperfections in color or design. Seasoned seamstresses can work around most of these flaws and all yardage is examined carefully before sold to make sure a project is viable. Big sales in April and August. Call the Bellevue store for a schedule of sewing classes or to inquire about custom labor.

Checks, credit cards

CLOTILDE   NEW LISTING

Fort Lauderdale, FL ☎ 305/761-8655
Hours: Mon-Fri 8:30-5 (Eastern time)

For over 20 years home sewers have been shopping by mail with Clotilde, whose colorful catalogs feature everything you'd find in a fabric store except fabric— all discounted 20%. Complementary catalogs, issued quarterly, include the latest products on the market, many of which are not available in local stores.

Checks, Credit cards

DAISY KINGDOM / DK SPORTS   NEW LISTING

Portland, OR ☎ 800/288-5223
Hours: Mon-Fri 7-5

Send for free catalogs filled with nursery, craft and outerwear kits designed and manufactured exclusively by Daisy Kingdom and save 20% off the going price at their Oregon retail stores. The outerwear catalog features stylish ski and activewear apparel for the whole family. Fabrics and notions for these types of garments can be ordered separately.

Checks, Credit cards

See area locator index for this section on page 227

174 Recreation and Hobbies, Arts and Crafts & Sewing

DANIEL SMITH — NEW LISTING
Seattle: 4130 1st Ave. S. ☎ 223-9599 *South of Kingdome*
Hours: Mon-Sat 9-6, Sun 12-5

Daniel Smith stocks the largest selection of fine art supplies on the West Coast, and everything is sold at discounted prices. Once a year the company publishes a beautiful 200-page color catalog showcasing 20,000 products and offering information on how to use them. Smaller catalogs, which include a lot of sale items, are free upon request.

Checks, Credit cards

ELÉGANCE FABRICS — NEW LISTING
Seattle: 2030 5th Ave. ☎ 448-9355 *Downtown*
Hours: Mon-Sat 9:30-5:30

The finest European fabrics are sold exclusively in this store at 25% or more off the regular $50 to $100 price tags. Natural fibers are a specialty with lots of gorgeous silks and woolens. Elegance goes nationwide with their mail-order business, and the parent company publishes a fashion magazine by the same name.

Checks, Credit cards

EVERETT TENT & AWNING CO.
Everett: 2916 Hewitt Ave. ☎ 252-8213
Hours: Mon-Fri 8-4:30

Canvas yardage and bolt ends are available starting at $5.50/yd., but inventory depends upon recent work-orders. If you can use little pieces of canvas for craft projects, a box of free scraps sits inside, near the door.

Checks, Credit cards

FABRICLAND, INC. — NEW LISTING
Portland, OR, P.O. Box 20235, (97220) ☎ 800/255-5412
Hours: Mon-Fri 8-5, Sat 9-3

Fabricland's chain of stores has frequent sales. Small manufacturers, independent retailers, and home-based businesses can buy direct from their warehouse and save 40% off the retail price. There is a $50 minimum order, so fabric, trim, notions and craft items must be purchased by the bolt or box. No buttons or patterns. Delivery is within 48 hours. Send $2 for a complete product price list.

Checks, Credit cards

HANCOCK FABRICS
Kirkland: 12030 N.E. 85th St. ☎ 827-3020
Lynnwood: 3815 196th S.W. ☎ 774-4414
Renton: 2810 N.E. Sunset Blvd. ☎ 226-7071 *Greater Highlands Ctr.*
Seattle: 112 N. 85th ☎ 783-2434 *Greenwood*

continued >

Tacoma: 10401 Gravelly Lake Dr. S.W. ☎ 581-2619 *Lakewood Mall*
3121 S. 38th ☎ 474-8681
5401 6th Ave. ☎ 756-9696 Sixth Avenue Plaza
West Seattle: 3922 S.W. Alaska ☎ 932-1110
Hours: Mon-Fri 9:30-9, Sat 9:30-6, Sun 12-5

Make Hancock's your first stop for fabrics to suit every need from filmy chiffon for an evening gown to calico prints for a quilt, fake fur for a Halloween costume or fabric for home decorating. Budget-conscious seamstresses make a beeline for the tables piled high with remnants and bolts of discontinued fabric marked at 50% or more below retail. Some are seconds, so check carefully for flaws. Put your name on the mailing list for special sales— great opportunities to stock up on notions, patterns, and arts and craft supplies at incredible savings.

Checks, Credit cards

JANTZEN FABRIC OUTLET

Renton: 17820 W. Valley Hwy. ☎ 251-0067
Tacoma: 3720 S. G St. ☎ 472-2394
Hours: Mon-Sat 9:30-5:30, Sun 12-5

You'll find a terrific selection of knits for swimsuits, T-shirts, sweatshirts, and sweaters, plus collars and cuffs to match since everything is coordinated. Prices vary from $1.49 to $4.50/yd., and many of the samples can't be found anywhere else. Bargain hunters pick up the best buys when fabric is sold by the pound. Unused notions turn up at greatly reduced prices. Call for a monthly sales schedule.

Checks, Credit cards

MACPHERSON LEATHER CO.

Seattle: 519 12th S. ☎ 328-0855 *Capitol Hill*
Hours: Mon-Fri 8-4:30

McPherson's sells top quality leather and suede skins. Half a cowhide at only $80 will make a skirt or pair of pants. Remnants are priced "as is", and some are large enough for a vest or purse. Check out the scrap bins where leather sells for $4.50 to $6.00/lb. Scout troops shop here for their arts and crafts projects. You'll also find tools, special thread, patterns and instruction books.

Checks, Credit cards

PACIFIC FABRICS WAREHOUSE OUTLET

Seattle: 2230 4th Ave. S. ☎ 628-6237 *South of Kingdome*
Hours: Mon-Sat 9-6, Sun 11-6

Most of the home sewing and decorating fabrics at this outlet come from Pacific Fabric's retail stores after they have been marked down 30% to 50%. Something different goes on sale every week and prices have been known to drop as low as 99¢/yd. Designer-look fabrics get snatched up fast— it pays to rummage through the remnants. Patterns are half-price if you spend $5. You can purchase a Halloween and Christmas crafts year-round at discount prices.

Checks, Credit cards

176 Recreation and Hobbies, Arts and Crafts & Sewing

PERFECT FIT / McDONALD CO.
Seattle: 414 Boren N. ☎ 682-7161 *East of Seattle Center*
Hours: Mon-Fri 8-4:30

McDonald's sells foam and batting to upholstery shops and furniture manufacturers. Foam comes in huge sheets, so it has to be cut to order. Call ahead. Scraps of foam for stuffing pillows or toy animals are sometimes available in 50 to 100-pound bales at 50¢ per lb.

Checks

PLENTY OF TEXTILES
Seattle: 2909 N.E. Blakely ☎ 524-4383 *U-District*
Hours: Mon-Sat 10-6, Thurs 10-9, Sun 12-5

Specializing in natural fibers and one-of-a-kind cuts from designer showrooms, Plenty of Textiles offers seamstresses something different. Their selection of woolens and silks is outstanding, as are the prices, which range from $2 to $40/yd. Once a year they get in fine wool suiting remnants. Quarterly newsletters announce sales.

Checks, Credit cards

SEATTLE FABRICS
Seattle: 3876 Bridge Way N. ☎ 632-6022 *Fremont*
Hours: Mon-Fri 9-5:30, Sat 10-2

With the lowest prices and best selection in town on outdoor and recreational fabrics, this company sells to small manufacturers of windsocks, kites, banners, tote bags and outerwear, as well as to the marine industry and people who make their own tents or sleeping bags. Inventory includes outdoor patterns, hardware and the notions necessary to complete your project.

Checks, Credit cards

SHAMEK'S BUTTON SHOP
Seattle: 1201 Pine St. ☎ 622-5350 *Downtown*
Hours: Mon-Fri 10-5, Sat 11-4

For only $3.50 you can buy a gross of white Indian blanket buttons and have a lifetime supply for kids' clothes, men's shirts and PJ's. Or pick through a jar and pay only 5¢ to 10¢ apiece. Shamek's will custom-make buttonholes and belts if you bring in the fabric. Belts can be shortened or lengthened for $4. The minimum fee for punching holes is $1.50.

Checks, Credit cards

SILK GREENHOUSE, INC.
Kirkland: 9755 Juanita Dr. N.E. ☎ 821-4444
Lynnwood: 4027 198th S.W. ☎ 771-6600
Seattle: 5959 Corson Ave. S. ☎ 762-0900 *Georgetown*
Tacoma: 4510 95th St. S.W. ☎ 582-0314
Hours: Mon-Fri 9-9, Sat 9-6, Sun 11-6

continued >

Recreation and Hobbies, Arts and Crafts & Sewing 177

These huge warehouses offer a staggering array of floral, craft and party supplies. Prices are unbelievably low on some items, but it pays to comparison shop. In their extensive wedding department, invitations are always 40% off list price, and once a year they host a bridal fair. Silk flowers, plants, and artificial trees make up a big part of the inventory. Christmas items are available year-round, and you'll find the stores packed with other seasonal goodies.

Checks, Credit cards

SOFT COVERINGS
Seattle: 999 Western Ave. ☎ 340-0398 *Downtown*
Hours: Mon-Fri 9-5:30, Sat 10-3

By buying direct from the mill, Soft Coverings offers super buys on quality decorator fabrics. Some are mill-ends or discontinued patterns, in which case you're getting one-of-a-kind styles. Other fabrics can be ordered in quantity. Most are natural fibers that sell for $4 to $18/yd. Get on the mailing list for their big October anniversary sale.

Checks, Credit cards

SUPER YARN MART
Bellevue: 2251 140th Ave. N.E. ☎ 746-0309
Seattle: 15208 Aurora Ave. N. ☎ 364-9276 *Parkwood Plaza*
Hours: Mon-Fri 10-8, Sat 10-6, Sun 11-5

Prices are low in these chain discount yarn shops because they buy mill ends and have yarn specially manufactured for them. Most of the stock is acrylic, orlon, or synthetic blends. The best buy is 3-oz. skeins of 100% Dupont Acrylic 4-ply yarn at 79¢. Pattern books, kits and other knitting products are also discounted. Mailing list for special promotions and close-outs.

Checks, Credit cards

TACOMA TENT & AWNING
Tacoma: 121 N. G St. ☎ 627-4128
Hours: Mon-Fri 8-5

This company constructs various outdoor products from canvas, tarp, and tent fabrics. Selection varies from full rolls to bolt ends, and prices range from $2.50 to $18/yd. Scraps for appliqués or patchwork sell for 50¢/lb.

Checks

TANDY LEATHER
Burien: 14611 1st Ave. S. ☎ 244-0351
Seattle: 20003 Aurora Ave. N. ☎ 542-1677 *Richmond Highlands*
Tacoma: 5429 S. Tacoma Way ☎ 474-1777
Hours: Mon-Fri 9:30-6:30, Sat 9-5

continued >

178 Recreation and Hobbies, Arts and Crafts & Sewing

Scraps of leather for making wallets, pouches, knife sheaths and beading projects sell for about $3/lb. Garment leather is not as well-priced here as at McPherson's, but Tandy's carries a wider variety of commercial items and related accessories for the hobbyist. Leather-making classes are free every Saturday as long as you buy the supplies here.

Checks, Credit cards

TEXTILE NETWORK MARKETING — NEW LISTING
Woodinville: P.O. Box 1072 (98072) ☎ 487-0675
Periodic sales

Throughout the year, this organization sponsors consumer shows geared to sewing, crafts and the needle arts trade. Retailers clear out old or excess merchandise, and individuals sell leftover or unused fabric, trim, yarns, and craft items for fun and profit. Call for details or pay $15 to join and receive a quarterly newsletter.

WEAVING WORKS — NEW LISTING
Seattle: 4717 Brooklyn N.E. ☎ 524-1221 *U-District*
Hours: Mon-Fri 10-6, Thur 10-8, Sat 11-5, Sun 11-3

If you're looking for a good buy on natural fibers or imported yarns, check the bargain table at Weaving Works or put your name on their mailing list to find out about the terrific bin sale each June. Yarn, fleece, basketry supplies, spinning, knitting, and dying equipment get marked down 50%.

Checks, Credit cards

WELLWORTH'S
Everett: 4818 Evergreen Way ☎ 252-3293
Hours: Mon-Fri 9:30-6, Sat 9:30-5

Creative seamstresses may be interested in the 26-inch drapery fabric samples sold at this custom workroom. At 55¢ each you can buy dozens for pillows or patchwork quilts.

Checks, Credit cards

If you're interested in fur scraps, we've found three downtown Seattle furriers who will sell leftovers by the pound for doll clothes or craft projects. Price depends on the pelt and size. Call first to find out what's available and make an appointment. Bob Manders (622-3076) and Jonas Artur (622-4807), both located at 1424 4th Ave, offer Persian lamb, mink, and beaver scraps. Alaska Arctic Furs (622-6116) at 1407 5th Ave. has mostly coyote scraps used for ruffs, parkas, and coats sold in Alaska.

Looking for inexpensive paper for art work, tablecloths, banners, box packing, bird cage liners or puppie puddles? The following newspapers sell roll ends of newsprint for $1 to $5 per roll, depending on how much is left: (Roll widths vary, but common sizes are 18-inch, 34-inch, and 45-inch. It's best to call first. What a great resource for preschool groups and Sunday school classes!)

THE EVERETT HERALD
Everett: Grand & California ☎ 339-3000

THE JOURNAL AMERICAN
Bellevue: 1701 132nd N.E ☎ 455-2222

THE SNOHOMISH COUNTY TRIBUNE
Snohomish: 114 Ave. C. ☎ 776-7546

THE TACOMA NEWS TRIBUNE
Tacoma: 1950 S. State ☎ 597-8511

Used Books

Seattle has long been among the top ten cities in the country in bookstores per capita, so it's no wonder there's a flourishing business in used hardbound books. Selling or trading books is a good way to continually replenish your reading material. Prices depend on condition and demand, but generally you can count on saving 50%. Prices may be even less at thrift shops, secondhand stores, rummage and estate sales.

Stores that sell only paperbacks are not included in this section because their businesses are so similar and numerous. Collectibles, used magazines and comics have not been listed because they are so specialized. The yellow pages will give you ample choices in your neighborhood.

AARDBOOKS
Seattle: 2016 2nd. Ave. ☎ 441-1620 *Downtown*
Hours: Mon-Sat 12-5

Aardbooks promotes "good books for people with reasonably good minds." The selection of titles is relatively small, but the books are in excellent condition. Fiction, history, art, photography, travel, adventure and literature predominate.

Checks

BEATTY BOOK STORE
Seattle: 1925 3rd. Ave. ☎ 728-2665 *Downtown*
Hours: Mon-Sat 11-5

Spend hours browsing through rooms of moderately priced paperback and hardback books at Seattle's second largest used bookstore, where you'll find everything but romance novels and textbooks. Art, cookbooks, fiction, philosophy, poetry, theology and military and regional history are their strong points. Beatty's is reputed to have one of the best bibliography sections on the West Coast, and they pay well for used books.

Checks

BEAUTY AND THE BOOKS
Seattle: 4213 University Way N.E. ☎ 632-8510 *U-District*
Hours: Mon-Sun 10-10

continued >

Recreation and Hobbies, Used Books

After 20 years on "the Avenue", B&B has acquired an eclectic selection of books and collectibles and a funky atmosphere that includes several cats. If you're looking for science fiction, poetry, history, literature, the occult, vintage pornography or books on the Northwest, check them out. Visit the sale annex in the basement, where over 15,000 titles sell for 1/4 the original price.

Checks

BIBELOTS AND BOOKS
Seattle: 112 E. Lynn ☎ 329-6676 *East Lake Union*
Hours: Tues-Sat 12-5:30

What a great resource for children's books from "Mother Goose" to "Treasure Island," including out-of-print and rare editions! Mysteries, classics and illustrated books, mostly hardcover, are specialties.

Checks, Credit cards

BOOK AFFAIR
Seattle: 15203 Military Road S. ☎ 241-0629 *Sea-Tac*
Hours: Mon-Fri 10-5:30, Sat 10-4

Book Affair offers a general selection of used paperbacks and hardbacks with an emphasis on military history and metaphysical subjects.

Checks, Credit cards

CATCHPENNY BOOKS
Seattle: 9101 Roosevelt Way N.E. ☎ 527-4530 *Northgate*
Hours: Tues 10-9, Wed-Sat 10-6

Half of this store, which is located in an old house, contains hardbacks, children's books and rare classics. Look for good selection on art, the classics, poetry, science fiction, the Civil War, westerns, travel, World War II history and politics. Catchpenny is one of the few bookstores that stocks foreign language novels and study books.

Checks

COMSTOCK'S BINDERY AND BOOKSHOP
Auburn: 257 E. Main ☎ 939-8770
Hours: Mon-Sat 10-6

Used and out-of-print books cover every subject you can think of, with strengths in aviation, railroading and military history. Special interest magazines on these subjects are bought and sold. If you have a rare book, Bible, or family heirloom that needs restoration, Comstock still does hand-bookbinding.

Checks, Credit cards

EDMONDS OLDE BOOKSTORE
Edmonds: 9679 Firdale Ave. ☎ 542-8636 *Firdale Village*
Hours: Mon-Sat 11-6, Sun 1-5. Tues 11-9

The emphasis here is on Northwest and Alaska history, cookbooks, the classics, children's literature, nautical and military subjects. Some rare books are in stock.

Checks, Credit cards

Recreation and Hobbies, Used Books 181

FILLIPI BOOK AND RECORD SHOP
Seattle: 1351 E. Olive Way ☎ 682-4266 *Capitol Hill*
Hours: Tues-Sat 10-5

For over a half-century this venerable old bookstore has served as a collection site for books, sheet music, postcards, old photos, piano rolls, phonograph records and ephemera of all kinds. Serious collectors of recordings from jazz to opera rate Fillipi's as one of the best resources on the West Coast. An astounding inventory of first and rare editions attracts those with an interest in art, history and literature. Prices may be slightly higher, but everything is well organized, in above-average condition, and the staff is service-oriented.
Checks

FORTUNA BOOKS
Kirkland: 113 Lake ☎ 827-7294
Hours: Mon-Sat 10-6, Sun 12-4

A good general selection and a great cat reside at Fortuna Books, a small corner shop that is noted for its strong foreign language section.
Checks, Credit cards

FOX BOOK COMPANY
Tacoma: 737 St. Helens ☎ 627-2223
Hours: Mon-Sat 10-6

For 50 years this family-owned book store has supplied Tacoma readers with one of the largest selections of used, rare and out-of-print books in the area. Their Northwest history section is outstanding.
Checks, Credit cards

FRIENDS OF THE SEATTLE PUBLIC LIBRARY   NEW LISTING
Seattle: Lincoln High School, N. 44th & Woodlawn ☎ 386-4636
Biannual sales

These sales during the last weekends in March and August attract thousands of booklovers, who often buy a year's supply of reading material in one day because prices are so low. The spring sale is the larger, and the books sold are donated by patrons at branch libraries all over the city throughout the year. In August, books discarded by the library go on sale. Proceeds from these two events help finance special projects and purchases. Anyone can join Friends of the Seattle Public Library for $10 and receive a monthly newsletter, notice of the sales, and a chance to shop the sales a day in advance.
Checks, Credit cards

GLOBE BOOKS
Seattle: 5220 University Way N.E. ☎ 527-2480 *U-District*
Hours: Mon-Sat 11-6

The arts, humanities and world literature are the focus at this small shop, which also stocks blues, folk, jazz and classical recordings. Books are both new and used, with cookbooks, travel, nature and women's studies the strong-suits.
Checks

Recreation and Hobbies, Used Books

HALF PRICE BOOKS RECORDS MAGAZINES
Bellevue: 15600 N.E. 8th ☎ 747-6616 *Crossroads Shopping Ctr.*
Seattle: 4709 Roosevelt Way N.E. ☎ 547-7859 *U-District*
Hours: Mon-Sat 10-9, Sun 10-6. U-District, Daily 10-9

These well-organized shops are part of a 30-store franchise that buys and sells anything printed or recorded. They stock a huge selection, with prices starting at half-off. About 35% of the inventory is remainders and closeouts. Look for best buys in the bargain book section, where mysteries, science fiction and general fiction sell for 48¢ to $5.

Checks, Credit cards

HORIZON BOOKS
Seattle: 425 15th E. ☎ 329-3586 *Capitol Hill*
Hours: Mon-Fri 10:30-10, Sat & Sun 10-9

Books on every subject imaginable are stacked to the ceiling in a maze of nine small rooms at this old house. Look for antiquarian and scholarly titles, secondhand records, and a collection of science fiction that hold its own with any store on the West Coast.

Checks, Credit cards

JANE'S BOOKS
Seattle: 12348 Lake City Way N.E. ☎ 362-1766 *Lake City*
Hours: Mon-Sat 11-4

Cookbooks are the specialty of the house at Jane's. Every chef in town should find something to savor among the 3,000 titles. Other well-represented categories include gardening, art, the Northwest and children's books. Many hardbound books are recent publications in mint condition.

Checks, Credit cards

LEISURE BOOKS   NEW LISTING
West Seattle: 4461 California S.W. ☎ 935-7325
Hours: Mon-Sat 9:30-6, Sun 11-5

Travel books and anything published in the 1940s and '50s are areas of specialization here. They're building up their selection of classics and world literature.

Checks

MAGUS BOOKSTORE & DAVE BELL BOOKSELLER
Seattle: Magus; 1408 N.E. 42nd ☎ 633-1800 *U-District*
Dave Bell; 5525 University Way N.E. ☎ 523-3277 *U-District*
Hours: Magus, Mon-Wed 10-8, Thurs & Fri 10-10, Sat 11-6, Sun 1-5;
Dave Bell, Tues-Fri 12-8, Sat 12-6

Magus has been catering to the diverse interests of the U-District crowd for twenty years, so inventory leans heavily towards modern fiction, the humanities and sciences. They're also strong on gardening, sports, cooking, science fiction and mysteries. Expensive technical computer books can be picked up here at half-price. Good buys often get snapped up within a day. Dave Bell, the owner, opened the second, smaller store in 1988. It stocks a similar mix, with a bigger antiquarian selection.

Checks, Credit cards

O'LEARY'S BOOKS
Tacoma: 3828 100th S.W. ☎ 588-2503
Hours: Mon-Fri 9-9, Sat 10-6, Sun 12-5

O'Leary's boasts they're one of the largest bookstores in the Northwest. Stock is evenly divided between comics, paperbacks and hardback books with emphasis on the history of North America.

Checks, Credit cards

QUIET COMPANION BOOKS
Tacoma: 21 Tacoma N. ☎ 272-2929
Hours: Mon-Sat 10-6

This residential bookstore normally stocks around 25,000 paperbacks and hardbound covers that include business, economics and Northwest history. Used records and tapes, some current, are available. The day we called they had a good selection of 1960s rock, classical and movie sound tracks.

Checks

SHAKESPEARE & MARTIN
Seattle: 1914 2nd Ave. ☎ 448-2665 *Downtown*
Hours: Mon-Sat 11-5

New and used hardbacks lean heavily toward feminist literature, general fiction and first editions. Mysteries and classics are favored, as well as books on architecture and an excellent selection of illustrated books for children.

Checks

SHOREY BOOKSTORE
Seattle: 110 Union ☎ 624-0221 *Downtown*
Hours: Mon-Sat 9-6, Sun 12-6

Seattle's oldest bookstore (1890) is the first place many people look for antiquarian books, old magazines, maps, posters, prints and museum-quality ephemera relating to the Puget Sound area. Thirty rooms contain 200 separate categories from antiques to western Americana. Prices tend to be high, but Shorey's has satisfied customers all over the world and uses every means possible to track down hard-to-find titles, even if it takes years. Thousands of used books go for half-price during their famous annual New Year's sale, which always starts on December 26th and lasts two weeks. Don't miss it! Shorey's is planning a move in 1991, so call for the new address.

Checks, Credit cards

TACOMA BOOK CENTER
Tacoma: 324 E. 26th ☎ 572-8248
Hours: Mon-Fri 11-5:30, Sat 12-5:30

Since this store moved next to the Tacoma Dome parking lot, it has become one of the city's largest used, rare and out-of-print booksellers. A good general selection includes childrens' books, mysteries, science fiction and literature.

Checks, Credit Cards

TITLEWAVE BOOKS
Seattle: 7 Mercer St. ☎ 282-7687
Hours: Tues-Sat 10:30-8, Sun 12-5

Shop here if you want to find used books in tip top condition at 50% off the cover price. A general selection favors art, biographies and fiction.

Checks

☑**Consumer Tip:**
☞If you're selling a rare book or collectible, have it appraised by a reputable dealer. You will have to pay a fee, but it will be worth the money. Some dealers will take more expensive items on consignment if they can't afford to buy outright.

Museums, Films & Performing Arts

We love to save money on entertainment for the whole family, so we decided to share a few ideas. For starters, the following museums do not charge an admission fee except during special exhibits: Center for Wooden Boats, Frye Art Museum and the Burke Memorial Museum. Free admission at the Museum of History and Industry on Tuesdays, Tacoma Art Museum on Wednesdays and the Wing Luke Asian Museum, Bellevue Art Museum and Seattle Art Museum on Thursdays. Become a member and qualify for reduced fees at special events as well as daily admission.

Every Friday the Seattle Times runs a list of "Reel Bargains" in the Arts and Entertainment section listing the lowest prices on movies for the week, including freebies. Libraries and community centers sponsor children's movies free of charge. Pick up a brochure at one near you for dates.

If you enjoy the theater, some companies sell subscriptions for previews, which cost less than matinees or week nights. Single tickets are even cheaper but usually only available in small numbers, so call ahead and make a reservation. Most theaters offer discounts for groups of ten or more, so get a bunch of friends together and save 10%. What a great idea for day care groups that want to attend children's presentations! Inquire about discounts if you're a student or a senior citizen or volunteer to usher— you can see the show for free at some theaters. The Intiman Theater offers the best deal in town for live theater. Attend the last matinee of any of the five plays presented during their June thru November season and pay only $1. Call two weeks before to reserve a ticket. And, check the classifieds for people selling tickets to theater productions and expensive big-name events.

50 HOUR CLUB NEW LISTING

Seattle: ☎ 328-5548

Donate your time and qualify for free tickets to On the Boards, ACT, Intiman, The Group, Northwest Chamber Orchestra, Empty Space Theater, Allegro Dance Festival and Northwest Asian American Theater. Jobs include helping with public relations, phone sales, mailings, computer entry, or technical assistance at concerts. For every six hours you work, pick up two tickets to the event of your choice.

TICKET TICKET NEW LISTING

Seattle: 401 Broadway E. ☎ 324-2744 *Capitol Hill*
Hours: Tues-Sun 10-7

This walk-up-only service is a great place to save money on theater, music and dance performances. Tickets average half price plus a service charge for almost every show in town, local as well as national. All events are posted on a big board, and tickets can only be purchased the day of the show, unless it's a matinee, in which case they are sold the day before. Parking in the building is free if you make a purchase. Check out the entertainment section of newspapers and pick out a couple of events in case your first choice is sold out or not on the list.

Cash

Dining Out

The amount of money spent on food consumed outside of the home continues to rise as more people frequent restaurants for convenience as well as pleasure. According to the National Restaurant Association, Americans eat out an average of 3.7 times a week. Whether you spend $5 at McDonald's or $50 at the Palm Court, the cost can add up fast.

If you dine out frequently, you can save a bundle by checking the weekly entertainment section of local newspapers for discount and 2-for-1 coupons. Or, invest in coupon books (See Coupon Books) for 2-for-1 offers that vary from fast food to haute cuisine.

Among the best kept secrets around are the community college food facilities, whose formal dining rooms we've listed below. Prices are incredibly low when compared to the going rate at restaurants because they only charge enough to break even. Meals average $6, and you must pay in cash.

Food is prepared fresh on the premises by students in the Culinary Arts Departments, and the menu changes throughout the quarter depending on what the class is doing. Call to make reservations as seating is limited or the facility may be closed for instruction or quarter breaks. Private banquets can sometime be arranged for groups or organizations. Also, food can be special-ordered for take-out, which may be a life-saver if you're planning a last minute dinner party.

Recreation and Hobbies, Dining Out

Every year the Food Technology program at Everett Community College sponsors an Hawaiian Luau in the Spring and a Sugar Plum Festival in December. Seating is limited to 275 people and tickets go fast since they're usually under $10 for adults. Call for specific dates.

South Seattle and Seattle Central also have bakeries. Products are made by students, so be prepared for some irregular sizes. Cookies, pastries, and breads are priced below grocery stores, but it's hard for school bakeries to compete with big supermarkets. Cakes usually run about 20% less. If you want to special-order bakery products, give the staff a week's notice. Allow more than a week for wedding cakes.

EDMONDS COMMUNITY COLLEGE — NEW LISTING
Lynnwood: 2000 68th Ave. W. ☎ 771-7405 Brier Hall
Hours: Mon-Fri 11:30-1, Open Mon-Thurs during the Summer Quarter

EVERETT COMMUNITY COLLEGE — NEW LISTING
Everett: 801 Wetmore Ave. ☎ 259-7151 Ext. 497 or 483 *Parks Memorial Bldg.*
Hours: Mon-Thurs 11:30-1, Closed Summer Quarter

NORTH SEATTLE COMMUNITY COLLEGE — NEW LISTING
Seattle: 7600 College Way N. ☎ 527-3779 *College Center Bldg.*
Hours: Mon-Thurs 11:30-12:45, Closed Summer Quarter

SEATTLE CENTRAL COMMUNITY COLLEGE — NEW LISTING
Seattle: 1701 Broadway; Bakery ☎ 587-6917, Dining ☎ 587-5427
Hours: Bakery, Mon-Thurs 7:45-5:30, Fri 7:45-2:30;
Dining Room, Mon-Fri 11-12:30, Closed Summer Quarter

SOUTH SEATTLE COMMUNITY COLLEGE
West Seattle: 6000 16th Ave S.W.; Bakery ☎ 764-5821, ET Bldg.;
Dining ☎ 764-5344, Food Service Bldg.
Hours: Bakery, Mon-Fri 10-6; Dining Room, Mon-Fri 11-1

South Seattle has a reputation for turning out chefs and bakers who end up in the best restaurants in town, so here's your chance to sample their talents before they graduate to higher-priced institutions. European pastries and breads sold in the bakery reflect the influence of the Swiss and Austrian chefs who teach here. Wedding cakes are acclaimed as works of art. The culinary school also teaches candy making, so hand-dipped chocolates are sold as well. Fruit or liqueur truffles go for the low price of $10/lb. Edible chocolate boxes filled with goodies are a specialty.

continued >

Students practice continental and classic-oriented cuisine in informal dining rooms where entrees might include fresh poached sea bass with capers and brown butter or veal tenderloin with raspberry Madeira wine. Once or twice a quarter the department schedules one of their famous connoisseurs' luncheons or four-star gourmet dinners, which feature the finest in food preparation and presentation. Advance tickets are required and space is limited. Call or write to receive information on special events.

Checks, Credit cards

Coupon Books

We know people who save hundreds of dollars a year investing in coupon books! They don't plan a vacation, family outing or night on the town without checking to see if there's a bargain available. Savings add up fast for those who eat out frequently because the majority of coupons are two-for-one offers at restaurants. Most books include goods and services, as well as recreational and cultural activities. Although listings will vary, many of the same businesses appear in all the books. You may want to buy more than one book since prices are so low that you only have to use a few coupons to recoup your cost. They also make great gifts.

Coupon books are usually sold by non-profit organizations for fundraising purposes. Call the main office to find out where you can purchase a book. Some publishers sell direct through the mail for the cost of postage and handling. Most have informational brochures they'll send if you wish to buy or sell their book.

COLLEGE COUPONS, LTD.   NEW LISTING

Seattle: 600 1st Ave., #410 ☎ 621-7528
Hours: Mon-Fri 9-5

This company publishes free coupon books offering discounts from businesses located near college campuses. Although they're geared to students, anyone can use them. They're distributed through student government organizations and at student bookstores a few days before classes start. Over 75 coupons guarantee savings on goods and services that range from Domino's Pizza to haircuts and video rentals.

ENTERTAINMENT PUBLICATIONS, INC.   NEW LISTING

Bellevue: 14110 N.E. 21st St. ☎ 641-8025
Hours: Mon-Fri 8:30-5

Sold at a cost of $40, with over 600 listings, this is the largest and most expensive coupon book on the market. Similar books are published by the same company in 80 other cities in the U.S. and if you buy one book, it automatically qualifies you for a 50% discount on any others. Restaurants vary from four-star establishments to fast food outlets. Menus are sometimes included. The line-up of cultural activities is impressive. For sports enthusiasts, discounts include tickets to the racetrack and professional events.

188 Recreation and Hobbies, Coupon Books

A Seattle Parks section offers fun for the whole family. The Travel Club can save you hundreds of dollars on hotels, condos, resorts, car rentals, cruises, airfares and tours all over the country. A special section includes popular tourist attractions in California, Oregon and British Columbia.

FOR FAMILIES AND FRIENDS NEW LISTING
Redmond: 17637 N.E. 30th Place ☎ 885-3218
Hours: Mon-Fri 9-5

With almost 300 listings at the price of only $11, you'll find 10%-50% discount coupons for classes, recreational activities, clothing, gifts, toys and educational products from leading department and specialty stores. Family dining includes lots of two for one coupons at popular fast food chains and kid-oriented restaurants. The "Parents' Night Out" section offers reduced prices at restaurants, hotels and theaters. The next time you take a trip, save on the cost of car rentals, hotels and tourist attractions in Washington, Oregon and California. Services cover everything from hair cutting to interior design consultation to market appraisal for your home. Some coupons offer freebies. The index includes an informative resource guide for parents.

GIFT CHECKS/WARDCO, INC. NEW LISTING
Bellevue: 300 120th Ave. N.E., Bldg. 5 Suite 100 ☎ 453-1509
Hours: Mon-Fri 9-5

Kids will love Gift Checks, which sell for $5 or $10. Fifty to a hundred coupons are printed to look like real checks and most are two for one's at favorite fast food eateries. Discounts on recreational activities and entertainment are also included. You can buy books that cover Seattle, South King County, the Puget Sound area, Snohomish or Pierce County, plus other parts of Washington state. Similar books are available for Alaska, Oregon, Idaho and Montana.

GOLD "C" SAVINGS SPREE NEW LISTING
Bellevue: 14110 N.E. 21st ☎ 644-7331
Hours: Mon-Fri 8-5

This family-oriented coupon book includes two for one coupons for popular fast food chains and family style restaurants, plus discounts on entertainment, merchandise and services— all for $8. Recreational activities include participatory as well as spectator sports. Kids 8 to 18 will have a ball using coupons in the special Youth section. Gold "C" is a subsidiary of Entertainment Publications, Inc. and similar books can be purchased in 26 cities throughout the U.S.

GOLDEN AMERICAN NEW LISTING
Seattle: 2142 8th N., Suite 205 ☎ 284-1139, 800/562-2112
Hours: Mon-Fri 9-5

continued >

Recreation and Hobbies, Coupon Books

If you're over 55, for $16 you can join Golden American and save 20% on meals at over 250 Seattle area restaurants. The yearly membership fee also includes discounts on travel, eye wear and prescriptions, plus free membership in Price Savers! (see Membership Buying Clubs) When you dine out, the membership card can be used for a maximum of three guests as long as they're 55 or older. Golden American hosts social functions throughout the year and sponsors a single's club.

LET'S EAT ETHNIC   NEW LISTING
Seattle: 3123 Eastlake E. ☎ 726-0055 *East Lake Union*
Hours: Mon-Fri 8:30-5

Purchase this two-for-one coupon book for $15 and explore over 40 ethnic restaurants that give the Seattle area its international flavor. Proceeds support programs sponsored by the Ethnic Heritage Council of the Pacific Northwest, an organization dedicated to preserving cultural diversity.

METRO PASS SAVERS   NEW LISTING
Seattle: 821 2nd Ave. ☎ 624-PASS *Downtown*
Hours: Mon-Fri 8:30-5

When you buy a Metro Pass, you automatically qualify for discounts of 10% to 20% at over 100 of Seattle's downtown business establishments. Call and they'll send you a Pass Savers book free in the mail. All you have to do is show your valid Metro pass (1-Day Visitor Pass, Monthly, 3-Month or Annual Pass) to any of the stores, restaurants or services listed in the book. Visitors will love the big selection of waterfront tourist attractions. Metro pass holders ride the street car free.

PAVILION MALL SUPER SHOPPER   NEW LISTING
Tukwila: 17900 Southcenter Pkwy. ☎ 575-8090 *Pavilion Mall*
Hours: Mon-Fri 8-5

The Pacific Northwest's largest enclosed off-price mall provides shoppers with a free coupon book featuring discounts at 25 participating merchants. Call and they'll send the book through the mail, or you can pick one up in the office, located on the 2nd floor.

SEATTLE SUPPER CLUB   NEW LISTING
Seattle: P.O. Box 12099, (98102) ☎ 322-5061

The majority of coupons in this $17 book are two for one's at over 100 restaurants in the Puget Sound area. You'll also find discounts on cultural and recreational activities for the whole family, including the Seattle Opera. Coupons are also available for hotels, restaurants and tourist attractions in Oregon, California, Hawaii, British Columbia and other parts of Washington. Books are published twice a year and only sold through the mail.

Luggage

BERGMAN LUGGAGE
Bellevue: 9900 102nd N.E. ☎ 643-2344
Lynnwood: 320 Alderwood Mall ☎ 774-9533
Redmond: 15116 N.E. 24th ☎ 643-2344
Seattle: 1930 3rd Ave. ☎ 448-3000 *Downtown*
         I-5 & N.E. Northgate Way ☎ 365-5775 *Northgate Mall*
Silverdale: 10315 Silverdale Way N.W. ☎ 698-0499 *Kitsap Mall*
Tacoma: Tacoma Mall Blvd. & S. 38th ☎ 473-4855 *Tacoma Mall*
Tukwila: 17900 Southcenter Parkway ☎ 575-4090 *Pavilion Mall*
Hours: Generally, Mon-Fri 10-9, Sat 10-9, Sun 12-5; Downtown Mon-Sat 9:30-6

Volume buying keeps prices low on moderately priced as well as top-of-the-line luggage. The staff recommends *Boyt and Andiamo*. Bergman's also carries briefcases, handbags, wallets and travel accessories, plus backpacks and nylon totes made especially for the stores. Discontinued stock is sent to Tukwila, where prices are lowest.

Checks, Credit cards

T.W. CARROL & CO.   NEW LISTING
Tukwila: 350 Upland Dr. ☎ 575-1064
Hours: Mon-Fri 8:30-4:30, Sat 9-12

Visit the showroom of the largest wholesale distributor of luggage in the Pacific Northwest and pay way below retail. Choose from dozens of leading name-brands, including *Haliburton*. Briefcases, garment bags, and related travel goods round out the inventory. Look for super buys on surplus and close-out goods.

Checks

TACOMA LUGGAGE & OFFICE SUPPLY
Tacoma: 2941 S. 38th ☎ 473-3044 *Best Cascade Shopping Plaza*
Hours: Mon-Fri 8:30-5:30

This store sells luggage and business cases at 25% to 50% below the normal retail price, and slightly irregular goods go for less. Watch for monthly specials. *Skyway and Atlantic* are their main lines. Since our last edition they've expanded inventory to include general office supplies and paper products, including greeting cards. Prices are competitive.

Checks, Credit cards

Children's Toys

ACE NOVELTY CO.
Bellevue: 13434 N.E. 16th ☎ 644-1820
Hours: Mon-Fri 9-5

continued >

Recreation and Hobbies, Children's Toys

Everything you'd ever need for a birthday party, school carnival, or company picnic! Ace Novelty imports paper products, glassware, decorations, adult jokes, games, and inexpensive toys in volume and wholesales them to drugstores and specialty shops all over the U.S. and Europe. Prices on many items average 25% off retail. Stock up on seasonal goodies at Christmas, Easter, and Halloween. A great place to buy party favors.

Checks, Credit cards

ARNIE'S DISCOUNT TOYS
Woodinville: 14045 N.E. 175th ☎ 481-2464
Hours: Mon-Fri 9:30-8, Sat 9:30-9, Sun 11-5

Here's a toy store where you can turn the kids loose and not go home broke. Customers drive miles for the big selection and good prices, especially around Christmas time. Low mark-up on best sellers like *Barbie and Nintendo* keeps Arnie's competitive with Toys'R'Us. *Playmobile* is discounted year-round. Save 30% to 70% on inventory purchased from stores going out of business and discontinued items. Free gift-wrapping

Checks, Credit cards

BUFFALO BILL'S SPORTING GOODS AND TOYS   NEW LISTING
Issaquah: 1480 N.W. Gilman Blvd. ☎ 392-0228
Hours: Mon-Thurs 10-7, Fri 10-8, Sat 10-6, Sun 10-5

Comparison tags verify savings of 10% to 20% on current merchandise and 30% or more on close-outs and samples. Kids will love the big selection of toys and the model and hobby supplies. As the store name implies, sporting goods make up half the inventory. Fishing gear, athletic supplies and camping equipment (*Coleman Products'* complete line) are great buys.

Checks, Credit cards

KAY-BEE TOYS, INC.   NEW LISTING
Bellevue: Bellevue Way & N.E. 8th ☎ 453-0505 *Bellevue Square*
Federal Way: 2001 S. 320th ☎ 839-4454 *Sea-Tac Mall*
Tacoma: Tacoma Mall Blvd & S. 38th ☎ 474-3730 *Tacoma Mall*
Tukwila: I-5 at I-405 S. ☎ 248-2215 *Southcenter Mall*
Hours: Generally, Mon-Sat 9:30-9, Sun 11-6

The next time a birthday rolls around, check out the discounted prices on famous-name toys and incredible buys on close-outs and samples at this national chain. You can't beat their prices on goods marked "Special Value" or "Blockbuster", many of which are not sold anywhere else. Most close-out games end up here at 50% or more off their original cost.

Checks, Credit cards

See area locator index for this section on page 227

Recreation and Hobbies, Children's Toys

KIDS CRAFT

Seattle: 1711 N. 45th ☎ 632-5160 *Wallingford*
Hours: Mon-Fri 9-6, Sat 9-5

This is a popular spot for pre-school and kindergarten teachers or moms looking for something constructive for kids to do. The main focus is art supplies and educational toys for children age ten and under. Hands-on materials include a huge paper and paint selection, lots of puzzles and stickers. Everything is priced 10% to 30% below retail. Save even more at the big inventory clearance sale held between Christmas and mid-January.

Checks, Credit cards

PLAY IT AGAIN TOYS   NEW LISTING

Redmond: 16003 Redmond Way ☎ 881-6920
Hours: Mon-Sat 10-5

A great name for a second-hand toy shop and a great place to save money on toys! Everything is consigned, so prices start at 50% off retail. The biggest selection is for infants thru five-years-olds, who will find lots of books and *Fisher Price* toys. *Legos, Barbie and My Little Ponies* are popular items. Trikes and bikes don't stay around very long.

Checks

TOYS 'R' US

Bellevue: 103 110th Ave N.E. ☎ 453-1901
Federal Way: 31510 20th Ave. S. ☎ 946-0433
Lynnwood: 18601 Alderwood Mall Blvd. ☎ 771-4748
Silverdale: 3567 N.W. Randall Way ☎ 698-1882
Tacoma: 4214 S. Ferry St. ☎ 472-4568
Tukwila: 16700 Southcenter Parkway ☎ 575-0780
Hours: Mon-Sat 9:30-9:30, Sun 10-6. Holidays & Christmas open Mon-Sat until midnight, Sun until 10

Toys 'R' Us dominates the market because of everyday low prices and aisles stacked to the ceiling with every toy imaginable. The baby department is stocked with everything from diapers to nursery furniture. Clothing goes up to 6X. Also find party favors, giftwrap, crafts, records and seasonal items. They'll assemble bicycles, *Big Wheels*, play furniture and gym sets for only $8 on 24-hour notice. With 450 stores nationwide averaging over 40,000 sq. ft. each, the company not only buys in quantity, but also has merchandise made exclusively for them. Discounts vary from item-to-item, but since they do so much advertising it's easy to compare prices. Nothing ever goes on sale, so sometimes a mass merchandiser will beat their price by a couple of dollars on special promotion goods.

Checks, Credit cards

TOY WORLD

Mercer Island: 3028 78th S.E. ☎ 232-8306
Tukwila: 17900 Southcenter Parkway ☎ 575-1076 *Pavilion Mall*
Hours: Mercer Island, Mon-Sat 10-6, Sun 11-4; Tukwila, Mon-Fri 9:30-9:30, Sat 9:30-6, Sun 11-6

Toy World offers very competitive prices on name-brand toys and games for children and adults. Many items, including *Playmobile*, are discounted year-round. Look for the lowest prices on merchandise picked up at bankruptcies and liquidation sales. Free gift-wrapping, except at Christmas.

Checks, Credit cards

If your rec room isn't quite complete, consider shopping at one of these outlets that sell coin-operated machines to arcades. Brand-new video games (more complex than Nintendo and Atari) cost $3,000, but one that has been in use for a year goes for about $600. Reconditioned machines sell for $200 to $300, "as is". You'll also find secondhand pinball machines, foosball games, jukeboxes and pool tables. Inventory fluctuates, so put your name on a list if you want something special.

GENERAL COIN DISTRIBUTERS

Seattle: 3901 1st Ave. S. ☎ 625-1474 *South of Kingdome*
Hours: Mon-Fri 8-5

MUSIC VEND DISTRIBUTING CO.

Seattle: 1550 4th Ave. S. ☎ 682-5700 *South of Kingdome*
Hours: Mon-Fri 8-5

Automotive

In addition to the sources listed below, refer to Auctions and see the index for Boeing Surplus (vehicles), Costco and Price Savers (parts, accessories and tires), Greenshield's Industrial Supply and Your Tool House, Inc. (tools).

New & Used Automobiles

According to the National Automobile Dealers' Association, the median price for a new car in 1990 was $15,200 with an average rebate of $1,000. Although cars represent the most expensive item a person will buy in his lifetime next to a home, studies show that consumers are often guided more by emotional than economic factors. They spend little time investigating the market place, which happens to be the most complicated, confusing and competitive around. You can save big bucks and be assured of a better quality vehicle if you take the time to educate yourself first.

Check out bookstores and libraries for unbiased consumer buying guides. Consumer Reports magazine publishes a yearly buying guide that includes reports on new models and the repair history of used cars. The Auto series by Consumer Guide magazine is also good. Read prior reports on new and used vehicles in library copies of Car & Driver, Motor Trend and Road & Track magazines.

For basic "list" and "cost" figures, buy a copy of "Edmonds New Car Prices" at a bookstore or magazine stand. This small annual paperback book gives a good idea of U.S. prices for new domestic and foreign vehicles. Members of Amway's Motoring Plan can request, for a small fee, computer printouts of wholesale prices on new cars. Many credit unions offer their members the same service free of charge.

TRADER PUBLICATIONS

Familiarize yourself with the local auto market prices by picking up a copy of Auto Trader. This weekly tabloid magazine, features hundreds of photos and listings of new and used cars and trucks for sale or trade by owners and dealers. Copies are available at grocery and convenience stores throughout the area or from the Trader Publications offices.

CAR/PUTER INTERNATIONAL

Hollywood, FL: ☎ 800/221-4001 **Hours:** Mon-Fri 9-5 (Eastern time)

For $20 plus $2 shipping and handling this Florida-based company will send you a computer printout listing the manufacturer's retail price, factory invoice price, plus the cost of options on any car you're interested in buying.

Checks, Credit cards

CONSUMER REPORTS AUTO PRICE SERVICE
Novi, MI: P.O. Box 8005, (48050)

Constantly updated list price and dealer costs on more that 1100 models of domestic and foreign cars and trucks. Send the make, model and exact style (Example: Chrysler, LeBaron, Premium 2-door) of the car you're considering and receive a computer printout of the dealer cost for the car, plus all available factory-installed options. $11 for one quote, $20 for two, $27 for three and $7 for each additional.

Checks

Auto Buying and Referral Services

Going through a broker can save time and money. Tell them exactly what you want and they'll track it down for a fee and you'll never have to set foot in a showroom. State law requires that brokers be bonded and licensed just like car dealers, so make sure you're dealing with a legitimate business before you pay up front. Beware of any brokers who try to talk you into buying another make. They may be free-lance commission salesmen for a regular dealer.

AUTO ADVISOR, INC.
Seattle: 3123 Fairview E. ☎ 323-1976, 800/326-1976
Hours: Mon-Fri 9-5

Auto Advisor is one of the oldest, most reputable brokers in the nation. Originally founded in 1977 as a consulting service on how to buy the best car for your needs, a car buying program was soon added. Ashley Knapp, the owner, quickly became a noted authority and consumer advocate. For many years he has written a column for AAA Motorist.

The company's philosophy, "A good deal on a bad car is no deal at all," is reflected in their policy of test driving cars before recommending them, staying on top of the latest technology, and putting safety first. They also guarantee the lowest prices and have access to any make or model you want— foreign or domestic. Clients from all over the country utilize this agency. All vehicles are picked up on local dealer lots. Trade-ins can be arranged.

Consultation fees are $2 per minute with a $30 minimum charge. Average time spent is one half hour and it can be done by phone. The staff has even been known to recommend forgoing the purchase of a car. The buying service costs $300 to $1,000, depending on whether you use their 24-hour, 2-week, or 4-week service. There's a 10% discount if you're paying cash. A free brochure, which includes a fee schedule, is available.

Checks, Credit cards

AUTO INSIDER
NEW LISTING
Van Nuys, CA ☎ 800/446-7433
Hours: Mon-Fri 8:30-5:30

continued >

Automotive, Used Vehicles

Check to see if you belong to a credit union or an organization such as Costco or Price Savers that subscribes to this private referral service. Their ads appear in newsletters, trade publications and house organs. AAA is one of their clients. Participating dealers will sell to members at fleet prices or 10% over factory invoice.

Used Vehicles

Don't buy a used vehicle without first having it inspected by a knowledgeable mechanic. If you are a good customer at a local garage, they may agree to do it free. AAA members qualify for limited free diagnostic service. Firestone stores charges approximately $40 for this service, Goodyear $65.

If you're an informed mechanical-type and understand all the legal transactions involved in purchasing a vehicle, the best buys on used cars often come from private individuals, who advertise mainly in the newspaper classifieds and Auto Trader publications. Want-ads in small publications such as "The Little Nickel" and "Buy and Sell" are also a favorite with individuals and low-price dealers, since they're much less expensive than major newspaper advertising.

If you're planning to buy a late model used car, a good place to start is car rental agencies. They buy cheap and sell often. Rental vehicles are generally well-maintained and less than one year old. Mileage is usually under 20,000 with warranties still intact. Bank repossessions also can be good buys, although the background of the car is more questionable. Most are sold "as-is." Re-po's often have windshield stickers listing mileage, options, wholesale and retail value. Offers are submitted via sealed bid, which the bank has the right to refuse. Most vehicles sell for $500 to $800 over the wholesale price. At SeaFirst you can call in every day to find out where you stand on your bid. Only vehicles marked "special" are sold below wholesale and are open to outright offers. They may need some repair, have been on the lot for a long time, or be considered soft on the market. If your bid is accepted, you have three days to check out the car and obtain financing. The two banks give out general information sheets and bidding rules when you visit.

SEAFIRST BANK VEHICLE SALES FACILITY

Seattle: 2409 N. 45th ☎ 358-1990 *Wallingford*
Hours: Mon-Fri 9-6, Sat 9-3

SECURITY PACIFIC BANK VEHICLE LIQUIDATION WAREHOUSE

Seattle: 10830 East Marginal Way S. ☎ 431-4381 *Sea-Tac*
Hours: Mon-Fri 8-6, Sat 10-4

The following list includes dealers disposing of rentals. Budget is the largest dealer, plus it's the only agency offering financing and trade-ins. Note that the majority of these lots are located out by Sea-Tac Airport's Rental Row on Pacific Highway South. Smaller auto rental agencies have not been listed, but are worth checking.

Automotive, Parts & Accessories

ALL STAR RENT-A-CAR
Seattle: 2402 7th ☎ 443-3368 *Downtown*
Hours: Daily 7:30-6

AVIS USED CARS SALES
Bellevue: 11969 Bellevue-Redmond Rd. ☎ 455-1535
Seattle: 18811 16th Ave. S. ☎ 433-5858 *Sea-Tac*
Hours: Mon-Fri 9-9, Sat 9-6, Sun 10-5

BEST RENT-A-CAR
Seattle: 6501 Aurora Ave. N. ☎ 784-2378 *Green Lake*
Hours: Mon-Fri 8 30-6, Sat 9-3

BUDGET RENTAL CAR SALES
Seattle: 2655 S. 188th ☎ 248-2088 *Sea-Tac*
Hours: Mon-Fri 8 30-8, Sat & Sun 9-6

DOLLAR RENT A CAR SALES
Seattle: 176th & Pacific Hwy. S. ☎ 433-6776 *Sea-Tac*
Hours: Mon-Thurs 9-8, Fri & Sat 9-6, Sun 12-5

HERTZ USED CAR SALES
Seattle: 18625 Des Moines Memorial Dr. ☎ 243-3210 *Sea-Tac*
Hours: Mon-Thurs 9-8, Fri 9-7, Sat 9-6, Sun 10:30-5:30

NATIONAL CAR RENTAL
Seattle: 197th & Pacific Hwy. S. ☎ 433-5500 *Sea-Tac*
Hours: Mon-Sat 8-7, Sun 12-5

THRIFTY CAR RENTAL
Seattle: 18836 Pacific Hwy. S. ☎ 244-9700 *Sea-Tac*
Hours: Daily 9-7

Parts & Accessories

Big discount chains dominate the automotive parts and accessories market. No one dealer delivers the best buy on everything, so watch for specials and compare prices via newspaper ads. Many stores will give price quotes over the phone, but be sure you can state exactly what you want before calling. It's hard for smaller independent chains and stores to beat the big discounters, but that doesn't mean they won't be competitive if asked to meet prices.

Schucks is the most visible parts store, with a whopping 33 locations throughout the Puget Sound area. The Ballard store is the biggest. Also check Al's Auto Supply, with half as many stores spread from Bothell to Auburn; they have a better selection than Shuck's and stay open until midnight seven days a week. Bellevue and Richmond Highlands have the largest inventory. Look in the yellow pages for a location near you.

continued >

Automotive, Parts & Accessories

Parts that fall into one of the three following categories will always be cheaper: re-manufactured original parts, which are rebuilt by independent firms to the original factory specifications; rebuilt and reconditioned parts, which combine used components to produce a part that works; and used parts, which are available at auto wreckers. Guarantees will vary from place to place, so ask.

Some outlets specialize in used parts from certain makes or countries of origin. Others only sell particular items such as hub caps and wheels. Prices will be lowest at wrecking yards and even lower if you remove the part from the junked car yourself.

COST SAVERS, LTD.   NEW LISTING
Seattle: 5514 24th Ave. N.W. ☎ 784-8140 *Ballard*
Issaquah: 710 N.W. Gilman Blvd. ☎ 392-0585 *Heritage Square*
Hours: Mon-Fri 10-6, Sat 9-5

Here's a great resource for mechanical tools and audio equipment for your car. The owner used to be in the wholesale end of the business, so he knows how, when and where to buy to get the best deal. Hand and air tools go for 30% to 60% off retail. Inventory includes heavy duty equipment like floor jacks, bench grinders, drill presses and wire feed welders. Shop accessories— work gloves, tape measures and safety goggles at super-low prices. Look for terrific buys on speakers, car stereo systems and blank cassettes.

Checks, Credit cards

SHEEPSKIN STATION FACTORY OUTLET   NEW LISTING
Seattle: 2933 4th Ave. S. ☎ 467-1966 *South of Kingdome*
Hours: Mon-Fri 10-6

Save 20% to 30% on seatcovers, steering wheel covers, wash mitts and leather driving accessories because the items didn't meet the manufacturer's standards of quality. Don't miss their annual "Black Sheep Sale" every June when all seconds, rejects, discontinued items and overstock go on sale at rock-bottom prices. You can also save on wool mattress pads, sheepskin boots, slippers and rugs.

Checks, Credit cards

Batteries

BUDGET BATTERIES
Bremerton: 140 N. Callow ☎ 373-1778
Burien: 14805 Ambaum Blvd. ☎ 246-7075
Everett: 5111 Evergreen Way ☎ 339-2289
Federal Way: 272nd & Pacific Hwy. S. ☎ 839-5880
Fife: 7900 Pacific Hwy. E. ☎ 922-3737
Lynnwood: 6306 196th S.W. ☎ 778-8684
Seattle: 1501 Elliott W. ☎ 285-4075 *Ballard*
2006 Rainier Ave. S. ☎ 322-2075 *Rainier Valley*
7110 East Marginal Way S. ☎ 767-3075 *Georgetown*
15001 Bothell Way N.E. ☎ 365-8015 *Lake City*
Tacoma: 3518 Center St. ☎ 572-8075
Hours: Mon-Fri 9-6, Sat 9-5

continued >

Automotive, Parts & Accessories

This local chain sells new, reconditioned and factory-second batteries for cars, trucks, boats, tractors, golf carts and motorcycles. Alternators, solenoids and starters are also available. No charge for installation.

Checks, Credit cards

STANDARD BATTERIES

Seattle: 5200 4th Ave. S. ☎ 763-1244; 763-9125 *Georgetown*
Hours: Mon-Fri 8-5, Sat 9-1

Standard sells batteries, new and used, for all types of vehicles. They're part of a big West Coast chain. If you live close by, call for a price quote. Free testing and installation.

Checks, Credit cards

Tires

For price quotes on name-brand tires, call the Discount Tires or Advantage Tire Services store near you. Each chain has a dozen stores in the area. Both offer free mounting, rotation and flat repair with any new tire purchase. Be sure to include the cost of required wheel balancing when getting quotes. Changing brands from the original vehicle equipment is no problem. The same tires may be more expensive at other dealers, but balancing might be included in the cost, so always inquire. Here are a few smaller dealers you might want to check out.

BILL'S TIRE EXCHANGE

Seattle: 4910 Leary Ave. N.W. ☎ 789-4759 *Ballard*
Hours: Mon-Fri 8:30-5:30, Sat 9-4

FACTORY DIRECT TIRE SALES

Edmonds: 22617 76th Ave. W. ☎ 774-5131
Hours: Mon-Fri 8:30-5

4 DAY TIRE STORES

Seattle: 3245 S. 146th St. ☎ 244-0742
Hours: Wed-Fri 8:30-8, Sat 8:30-5

RICK'S TIRE & CHEVRON

Seattle: 8506 5th N.E. ☎ 525-9392 *Northgate*
Hours: Mon-Fri 7-9, Sat 8-6

TIRES PLUS

Kirkland: 12540 N.E. 124th St. ☎ 821-9200
Hours: Mon-Fri 8-6, Sat 8-5

Used tires or retreads are economical purchases for spares or to replace tires that wear out before you're ready to buy an all new set. Although many dealers sell used tires, the following specialize in them, so they offer a bigger selection.

continued >

Automotive, Road Services

SAGERS' GEORGETOWN TIRE & RETREAD — NEW LISTING
Seattle: 5623 Airport Way S. ☎ 763-9994 *Georgetown*
Hours: Mon-Fri 8:30-5:30, Sat 9-4

USED TIRE & WHEEL CO. — NEW LISTING
Lynnwood: 15304 N. Hwy. 99 ☎ 742-4810
Seattle: 14038 Lake City Way ☎ 364-0565
Hours: Mon-Sat 8-6, Sun 10-5

USED TIRE WHEREHOUSE — NEW LISTING
Federal Way: 35516 Pacific Hwy S. ☎ 838-TIRE
Hours: Mon-Sat 9-7, Sun 10-5

Road Services

AMERICAN AUTOMOBILE ASSOCIATION (AAA)
Bellevue: 13201 Bellevue-Redmond Rd. ☎ 455-3933
Bremerton: 5700 Kitsap Way ☎ 377-0081
Everett: 1520 Broadway ☎ 258-3581
Lynnwood: 4100 200th S.W. ☎ 775-3571
Renton: 3900 E. Valley Hwy. #105 ☎ 251-6040
Seattle: 330 6th Ave. N. ☎ 448-5353
Tacoma: 1801 S. Union ☎ 756-3050
Hours: Generally, Mon-Fri 8:30-5

Founded in 1902, AAA was the first auto club in the country. Today it's the largest with over 30 million members throughout the U.S. and Canada. Nonprofit status keeps prices low and amazingly enough, membership fees have not changed in five years. New members pay $39 the first year, $30 thereafter. A spouse or unmarried independent children (age 23 and under) can become associate members for $15 and receive the same services, which include:

1 Free towing for the first five miles to the nearest repair facility. Those who spend a lot of time on the road or in isolated places, like ski slopes or camping sites, pay an extra $24/year and extend the service to 100 miles.
2 Emergency road service 24 hours a day anywhere in the nation, which is great if your battery dies on you, you run out of gas, have a flat tire, or lock yourself out of your car.
3 A trained staff who will help you plan any trip from a weekend getaway to a cross country trek and prepare a detailed easy to follow itinerary with their exclusive "Triptic" map system.
4 Travel arrangements anywhere in the world including reservations and ticketing for air, ship and rail; bookings for tours, cruises, hotel accommodations and car rentals.
5 A personal accident insurance policy worth up to $4,000; access to AAA's own insurance agency.
6 Discounts on rental cars, credit cards, passport photos, AAA approved lodgings and travel books. U.S. and Canadian maps, tour books and camping guides that include AAA inspected accommodations free of charge. Call for a membership brochure.

AMWAY MOTORING PLAN

Amway has put together a membership program that offers complete motorist road protection and fleet purchasing power via local participating auto dealers. This program is similar to AAA. The basic plan covers husband and wife for $99.95 a year. Dependents aged 16 to 22 with a license who reside at the same address can be added for $20 each. Contact the Amway distributor in the business listings of your phone directory for information and membership application.

AUTO AMERICARD

Seattle: P.O. Box 88259, WA 98138 ☎ 241-7833
Hours: Mon-Fri 8-5

Save 10% to 30% on auto services and products when you join Auto Americard, a unique concept that originated in the Northwest. The $29.95 cost includes a membership card and directory listing over 400 participating merchants who sell everything from cars to parts and accessories at a discount. You even qualify to buy cars at dealer or fleet prices. Services include repair work, tune-ups, lube jobs and brake replacements by well-known chains like Minit Lube, Walt's Radiator and Muffler and 60 Minute Tune. Members also receive Travel Americard, the nation's leading hotel discount program. The card can be purchsed only by mail.

LEWIS & HART NATIONAL INFORMATION AND REFERENCE SERVICES, INC.

King County: ☎ 340-2269 or 800/635-4636
Hours: Daily, 24 hours

This nonprofit organization refers consumers, free-of-charge, to automotive specialists. Services include everything from standard maintenance to engine rebuilding, detailing, painting and body repair. Business must be free of complaints and pass certification to be recommended.

☑ Consumer Tips:

☞ When negotiating a price for a new car, we recommend starting at $250 above dealer cost. While this doesn't seem like much of a profit, dealers receive additional bonuses from manufacturers based upon their sales volume. Manufacturers sell cars to dealers for the base price plus the cost of factory installed options and freight. Large American cars are marked up more than foreign or small domestic models, so expect greater savings on the big ones.

☞ Dealer-added options or special services (which must be listed separately from factory options on the window sticker) are usually a bad buy as they can be purchased for much less elsewhere. Watch out for added-dealer-markups on some exotic models. This signals that so many people want this car that the dealer has added extra profit on top of his normal full mark-up. Unless you are crazy (about the car) or rich, this is not smart shopping.

Something for Everyone

Factory Outlet Malls

A relatively new addition to the discount retail scene, the factory outlet mall is made up of a dozen or more stores owned and operated by manufacturers. Over half of the tenants sell clothing and related items. Stores are smaller than big off-price chains and look more like specialty retailers. To avoid competition with department stores that carry the same brands, factory outlet malls locate alongside major interstate highways at some distance from big retail areas and seldom advertise.

At factory outlets you may find a few labels that are new to the Pacific Northwest and products unavailable anywhere else. Merchandise varies from store to store. Some have a good selection, while others are used as a dumping ground for leftover goods. According to statistics quoted in the Seattle Times, inventory can be divided into four categories: (1) 50% first-quality, current-season goods; (2) 23% from prior seasons; (3) 14% irregulars and seconds; (4) 12% made especially for the outlet.

We've heard people express disappointment over the lack of real bargains. Prices touted as 20% to 75% below retail seem to average first markdowns in department stores. But you can find terrific deals, especially on the sale racks. You just have to look a little harder than you might expect.

FACTORY OUTLET CENTER — NEW LISTING
Centralia: I-5, 82 miles south of Seattle, Exit 82
Hours: Mon-Fri 9-8, Sat 9-6, Sun 11-5

Every day over a thousand shoppers from Portland to Seattle visit the 26 outlets that line the highway beside this formerly quiet little town. Many visitors make a weekend of it, taking in the Centralia Square Antique Mall and Mt. St. Helens, which is about an hour's drive away.

GREAT NORTHWEST FACTORY STORES — NEW LISTING
North Bend: I-90, 40 miles east of Seattle, Exit 31
Hours: Mon-Sat 9-9, Sun 10-6

The newest of the off-price malls, Great Northwest plans to have 42 stores in operation when it's completely built-out. At present, you'll find a pleasant mix of shops and a still-peaceful atmosphere in the foothills of the Cascades near beautiful Snoqualmie Falls.

Something For Everyone, Factory Outlet Malls

PACIFIC EDGE OUTLET CENTER — NEW LISTING

Burlington: I-5, 60 miles north of Seattle, Exit 229
Hours: Mon-Sat 10-9, Sun 10-6

Less than a year after it opened in 1989, this upscale, fashion-oriented mall was already among the top five in the country in gross sales. Their first Labor Day weekend attracted 100,000 shoppers, half of them from Canada. At last count, 34 stores were clustered within these California-style structures set in the pastoral Skagit Valley.

Here's a list of stores in the Factory Outlet malls as we went to press: Centralia's Factory Outlet Center **(F)**   North Bend's Great Northwest Mall **(G)**   and Burlington's Pacific Edge Mall **(P)**.

ADOLPHO II
Famous-maker apparel for women. **(P)**

AILEEN'S
Moderately priced ladies sportswear. **(F,G,P)**

AMERICAN TOURISTER
Luggage, business cases, sports and travel bags. **(F,G,P)**

ARGENTI
Silk apparel for women in Misses, Petite and Large sizes. **(P)**

ATHLETIC SNEAKER & APPAREL
Fifteen major brands of athletic footwear, plus clothing. **(P)**

BANNISTER SHOES
Forty famous brands of men's women's and athletic shoes. **(F,G)**

BARBIZON LINGERIE
Quality lingerie. **(P)**

BASS SHOE
Classic casual and dressy shoes for men and women. **(F)**

BOOK WAREHOUSE
Remainders at low, low prices. **(G)**

CAMPUS SPORTSWEAR
Casual and traditional sportswear for men and boys, plus Tall and Large sizes. **(F)**

CAPE ISLE KNITTER
Contemporary fashion, 100% cotton sweaters and knits for men and women. **(F,G,P)**

CHURCHILL GLOVES
Leather and semi-dress gloves for men and women. **(F)**

Something For Everyone, Factory Outlet Malls

CORNING/REVERE
Cookware, ovenware and dinnerware in sets and open stock. **(F,G,P)**

EVAN-PICONE
Tailored career clothing and sportswear for men and women. **(P)**

FACTORY BRAND SHOES
Name-brand casual and dress shoes for men and women **(G)**

FASHION FLAIR-GANT
Traditional men's, women's and children's apparel from *Izod, Gant, Ship 'n Shore* and jewelry by *Monet*. **(F,P)**

FRAGRANCE WORLD
Name-brand cosmetics and perfumes. **(G)**

GITANO
Trendy, fun clothing for men, women & children. Active and casual sportswear, plus a full line of accessories. **(F,G,P)**

HANES ACTIVEWEAR
Activewear for men and women. **(F,G,P)**

HARVÉ BERNARD
Designer women's apparel & accessories, men's furnishings. **(F,G,P)**

HAWAIIAN COTTON
Women's cotton knit separates. **(G)**

I.B. DIFFUSION
Contemporary women's apparel and trendy sportswear. **(P)**

IDEAS APPAREL
Girls, Junior's and Women's sportswear. **(F)**

J.G. HOOK
Classic sportswear for Misses, Petite and Large sizes. **(P)**

JINDO FUR
Furs & leathers direct from the world's largest manufacturer. **(P)**

JONES OF NEW YORK
Contemporary women's apparel. **(P)**

JORDACHE
Streetwear, accessories and shoes for men, women and children. **(G)**

KITCHEN COLLECTION
Proctor-Silex appliances, *Wear-Ever* cookware, *Bissell* floor care, *Anchor Hocking* glassware and microwave dishes, *Wilton* cake decorating and baking supplies, kitchen utensils and gadgets. **(F,G,P)**

LEATHER LOFT
Luxury leather handbags, luggage, briefcases, jackets and designer accessories. **(F,G,P)**

L'EGGS, HANES, BALI
Lingerie and hosiery. **(G)**

LIZ CLAIBORNE
Contemporary misses and petite dresses, sportswear, handbags and fashion accessories, men's furnishings and sportswear. Some children's clothing. **(P)**

LONDON FOG
Men's and women's rainwear, jackets, outerwear, wools, shirts, sweaters and accessories, all at 50% off retail. **(F)**

MAIDENFORM
Complete selection of lingerie and undergarments. **(P)**

MANHATTAN JEWELRY MANUFACTURERS
Diamonds (loose and mounted), 14K and 18K gold jewelry, gem stones, pearls, watches, etc. **(F,P)**

MIKASA CHINA
Place settings, glasswear, fine crystal & china. **(P)**

MUSHROOM SHOES
Dress, casual and athletic shoes for women by *Selby, Cobbie and Red Cross*. **(F)**

OLD MILL
Women's fashions by *Country Suburban and Old Miss*. **(F)**

OMID INTERNATIONAL RUGS
Oriental rugs. **(G)**

ONEIDA
Flatware by *Rogers, Buffalo and Oneida*. **(F)**

PRESTIGE FRAGRANCE
Men's and women's fragrances and cosmetics. **(F,P)**

RIBBON OUTLET
Three-thousand varieties of first-quality ribbon and trim, craft supplies, seasonal items, bridal and party accessories, gifts, wrapping paper. **(F,G,P)**

SOCKS GALORE
Wall-to-wall socks— over 60,000 pair. **(F,G,P)**

SHOE PAVILION
Name-brand footwear for women. **(P)**

Something For Everyone, Mass Merchandise Discounters

SPERRY/DUFFEL/IN-SPORT
Quality traditional-style men's shoes, men's and women's sportswear. **(F,G)**

TABLE DE FRANCE
Name-brand kitchenware. **(G)**

TANNER FACTORY STORES
Classic apparel for ladies. **(G,P)**

TOY LIQUIDATORS
Milton Bradley, Hasbro, Tonka, Playschool and other name-brand toys. **(F,G)**

TOYS UNLIMITED
Thousands of nationally advertised toys at discount prices. **(F,P)**

VAN HEUSEN
Fashion apparel for men and women. **(F,G,P)**

WALLET WORKS
Men's and women's leather wallets, luggage, handbags and briefcases. **(P)**

WELCOME HOME
Country-style home furnishings. **(F,G,P)**

WESTPORT LIMITED
Women's dresses and separates. **(G)**

WICKER FACTORY
Silk plants, wicker home furnishings and decorative accessories. **(F,G,P)**

☑**Consumer Tip:** ☞ Leave the driving to the Buffy Bus.

Mass Merchandise Discounters

Mass merchandisers sell an incredible variety of goods, so we decided to list them separately, but include only those that offer discounted prices on everything all the time. That doesn't mean that big chains and supermarkets don't offer rock-bottom prices on advertised specials. It pays to comparison shop, especially on big-ticket items.

You never know what you'll find at surplus, salvage and liquidation outlets. Half the fun is discovering something unexpected. Prices will be incredibly low, but examine items carefully for defects since sales are final at most outlets. Food products are regulated by the Health Department, but if something looks questionable, don't buy it. Some surplus operations look like retail stores with everything neatly displayed. Others, operating on a lower overhead, resemble secondhand stores. Inventory changes frequently, so visit often, as the good stuff goes first. Or call every week to find out what's new.

continued >

Something For Everyone, Mass Merchandise Discounters

Shoppers in the greater Seattle area are fortunate to have general merchandisers like Target, K-Mart, Fred Meyer and Pay Less close at hand. Although we have not listed them individually, these stores can be counted on to save you money day in and day out— and all of them stand behind their products. When they run a deeply discounted special on name-brand products, they'll usually beat the prices of all but the used and salvage brokers. Also check into their private-label merchandise, which may save you even more.

AAA LIQUIDATING
Des Moines: 22325 Marine View Dr. ☎ 824-3686
Normandy Park: 19801 1st Ave. S. ☎ 824-2625
Hours: Mon-Sat 9-6, Sun 12-5

The owner of this company started years ago with a truck load of unclaimed freight and built one of the largest liquidating companies in the Pacific Northwest.

There's always a good selection of toys, tools, clothing, sporting goods, luggage, housewares and gift items. Sign up on the mailing list to receive flyers about every six weeks announcing the latest specials. The Normandy Park store is by far the larger of the two.

Checks, Credit cards

ABC SALES
Seattle: ☎ 722-6303
By appointment only

This bare-bones warehouse operation wholesales to retail stores that specialize in surplus and salvaged goods. Inventory usually consists of groceries, mainly canned goods, plus health and beauty aids, drugs and sundries. Clothing and tools were also in stock the day we shopped. Some items must be purchased by the case or carton. Selection may be limited, but the prices are great.

Checks

BEST
Bellevue: 888 116th N.E. ☎ 454-5696
Everett: Broadway N. & Tower ☎ 258-4251
Federal Way: 2200 S. 320th ☎ 941-5000
Lynnwood: 19801 40th Ave. W. ☎ 775-9311
Seattle: 520 Westlake N. ☎ 464-1424 *East of Seattle Center*
Tacoma: 2921 S. 38th ☎ 474-0771
Tukwila: 17500 Southcenter Pkwy. ☎ 575-2540
Hours: Generally, Mon-Fri 10-9, Sat 10-6, Sun 10-5

Very few retailers can beat Best's everyday low prices or selection on name-brand small appliances, kitchenwares, sporting goods, athletic equipment, electronics for home and office, baby furniture, fine jewelry and gift items. Their toy department is a "must" at Christmas. And when they have a sale, even the big discounters get left behind. Shoppers alert: check the clearance rack located near the merchandise pick-up desks for bargains on returns or defective goods.

Checks, Credit cards

CHUBBY & TUBBY

Seattle: 9456 16th S.W. ☎ 762-9791 *White Center*
7906 Aurora Ave. N. ☎ 525-1810 *Green Lake*
3333 Rainier Ave. S. ☎ 723-8800 *Mt. Baker*
Hours: Mon-Sat 9-9, Sun 9-6

Do we call this a sporting goods, hardware, or variety store? The company has been around since 1945, and the shelves are filled with merchandise of all kinds, some of which is close-outs or discontinued styles purchased from distributors or manufacturers. We found consistently low prices on *Dutch Boy* paint, leading-brand athletic shoes, fishing tackle, work clothing and boots (*Levis 501* are always in stock), and *Revere Ware*. The garden center has some of the best buys in town on fertilizer, peat moss and bark. Toys brought in for the holidays are super cheap, as are Christmas trees. Don't miss the "Sneaky Sunday Coupon" sale held the last week in February. *Checks, Credit cards*

DIRECT BUYING SERVICE

Seattle: 915 4th Ave. ☎ 623-8811 *Downtown*
Hours: Mon-Fri 9:15-6, Sat 9:30-4

Although the showroom stocks mainly small kitchen appliances, jewelry, cameras, clocks and luggage, literally anything you want to buy can be ordered factory-direct at savings of 15% to 20%. Staff says they can beat Silo's prices on major appliances and home and office electronics. Many people make this their first stop when shopping for name-brand furniture, household items and decorative accessories. Direct Buying provides manufacturers' catalogs to peruse or suggests you visit other retail outlets to get the brand name, model number, color, size, fabric, plus any other identifying features you'll need to place your order. *Checks, Credit cards*

FUCHS   NEW LISTING

West Seattle: 4526 S.W. California Ave. ☎ 935-7137 *J.C. Penney Bldg.*
Hours: Mon-Sat 10-6, Sun 12-4

Merchandise from bank liquidations ends up here. When we visited, shipments had just come in from the Plaid Pantry, Paris Beauty Supply and a women's boutique. Toys, hardware, arts and craft supplies, band and music accessories, clothing, jewelry and accessories were priced 30% to 60% below retail. *Checks, Credit cards*

HILLSTEAD'S SURPLUS

Seattle: 14802 Pacific Hwy. S. ☎ 241-0303 *Sea-Tac*
Hours: Mon-Sat 9-6, Sun 10-4

Even swap meet dealers shop at Hillstead's, which bills itself as "the store that discounts the discounters." You'll find many of the same items that fill the shelves of a Fred Meyer or Pay Less, but everything is marked down 30% or more everyday. *Rubbermaid* products and household paper supplies are always going to be sold at the lowest price in town, since Hillstead is the local outlet for overstock and close-outs.

continued >

Something For Everyone, Mass Merchandise Discounters

Watch for good deals on furniture, toys, clothing, housewares, tools, pet supplies, health and beauty aids, car accessories and used merchandise of all kinds.

Checks, Credit cards

LIQUIDATION SALES — NEW LISTING
Spanaway: 14968 Pacific Ave. S. ☎ 475-7897
Tacoma: 38t02 S. Cedar St. ☎ 536-8816
Hours: Mon-Sat 9-9, Sun 10-6

These big warehouses hold name-brand merchandise neatly displayed and in good condition. Some items, especially furniture, are purchased factory-direct and sold at discount prices. You'll also find tools, clothing, housewares, camping equipment, automotive accessories and stationary products purchased from stores going out of business.

Checks, Credit cards

SEARS OUTLET
Burien: 500 S.W. 150th ☎ 241-7000
Kent: 26020 104th S.E. ☎ 854-9300
Seattle: 1st Ave. S. & S. Lander ☎ 344-4801 *South of Kingdome*
Tacoma: 8720 S Tacoma Way ☎ 584-8160
Hours: Generally, Mon-Fri 9:30-9, Sat 10-6, Sun 11-6

These stores are the final resting place for surplus, discontinued items and returns from the Sears catalogs. Irregulars and damaged goods should be labeled, but flaws are not always apparent. Inventory varies store-to-store. You'll always find a big selection of housewares, domestics and clothing for the whole family. Furniture, appliances, automotive supplies, audio-video equipment and sporting goods come and go. Some items may be one-of-a-kind. Savings range from 30% to 50%; prices sometimes drop to 1/4th the original value. The Burien store stocks the best selection.

The Seattle location includes a huge liquidation warehouse for furniture and appliances on the north end of the building (344-4476). The second floor of the main store (344-3123) houses discounted apparel for the whole family from the retail stores. Frequent sales at the Seattle location turn up some of the best buys in town. You'll find the catalog outlet store in the basement of the main store. Warranties and return policies are the same as for regular merchandise, but prices are "you-haul" on large items.

The best way to familiarize yourself with the products at Sears Catalog Outlets is to add the Sears catalogs to your reading list. Call 800/366-3000 for a free copy.

Checks, Credit cards

SESSIONS DISCOUNT/VARIETY
Burien: 15415 Ambaum Blvd. S.W. ☎ 248-3399
Renton: 809 S. 4th ☎ 271-5555
Hours: Generally, Mon-Fri 9:30-6, Sat 9-5

continued >

210 Something For Everyone, Mass Merchandise Discounters

Save 25% or more on packaged, frozen, or canned food simply because the case was opened or a can dented. Furniture ranges from moderately priced to expensive name-brands. The staff points out any minor defects that they were not able to repair. Inventory includes famous-name clothing, drug store merchandise and household cleaning supplies purchased from factory overstock and liquidations. Everything is neatly displayed in a retail environment.

Checks, Credit cards

SIX STAR FACTORY OUTLET NEW LISTING
Bellevue: 15015 Main St. #109 ☎ 747-0578
Bremerton: 4213 Wheaton Way ☎ 373-0153 *K Mart Plaza*
Everett: 1001 N. Broadway ☎ 259-4260
Kent: 26016 104th Ave. S.E. ☎ 859-8409
Lynnwood: 19800 44th Ave. W ☎ 672-3144
Puyallup: 733 River Road ☎ 840-2284
Renton: 16930 116th Ave S.E. ☎ 277-1833 *Cascade Center*
Snohomish: 1207 Ave. D ☎ 568-9355
Tacoma: 10223 Gravelly Lake Dr. S.W. ☎ 581-7349
  2661 N. Pearl St. ☎ 756-6790
  804 E. 72nd St. ☎ 475-8819
Hours: Generally, Mon-Fri 9-9, Sat 9-6, Sun 10-6

Nothing sells for over $10 at Six Star, and you'd pay twice as much for the same items at a drugstore or gift shop. Stand-out bargains include hundreds of earrings priced at $1, a big selection of fancy hair ornaments, party goods and gift wrap. Printed T-shirts and sweatshirts are big sellers at $6-10 each. You'll also discover good buys on toys, housewares, makeup, decorative accessories and seasonal merchandise. Customers can participate in a Bonus Book program where $1 in play money (given out for every $1 you spend) can be used in $10 increments to purchase items worth $20 to $40. Lynnwood, the largest store, carries a lot of clothing.

Checks, Credit cards

UNIVALCO BARGAIN MART NEW LISTING
Seattle: 15211 Military Road S. ☎ 244-4182 *Sea-Tac*
Hours: Generally, Mon-Sat 12-7

Univalco buys merchandise from stores going out of business and then wholesales it to dealers or other retailers. Overflow ends up here. Inventory leans toward the general gift variety. Paintings, prints and posters from the 1920s and later (some rare and original) are a specialty. Among the 15,000 assorted items in stock, you'll find picture frames, jewelry, accessories, sunglasses, key chains and collectibles.

When we called, the owner had just acquired 8,000 pairs of shoes. Flags from all over the world are best sellers. Catalogs, available for wholesale buyers and preferred customers, can be purchased in the store or mailed for a fee.

Checks

Something For Everyone, Membership Buying Clubs

WORLD WIDE DISTRIBUTORS, INC.
Kent: 8211 S. 194th ☎ 872-8746
Annual sale
 World Wide is a buying co-op for independent retail stores all over the U.S. They hold a big warehouse sale to clear out samples and leftovers, including toys, shoes, clothing, domestics, luggage, sporting goods and lawn furniture. Merchandise is name-brand and private-label goods. Call to get on the mailing list.

Checks, Credit cards

Membership Buying Clubs

 There are two large buying clubs in the Seattle area, Costco and Price Savers. To become a member of either, you must have a business license or non-profit status, work for a State or Federal agency, or belong to a credit union. You may pick up application forms at any of the warehouses. If you know someone who is already a member, you can go in as their guest, but you must pay cash for your purchases. For those thinking about joining, one-day passes are available if you show proof you can qualify for membership. Fees are similar at both warehouses.

 Membership buying clubs combine low prices with the convenience of shopping at one location for goods you'd normally have to visit a dozen different stores to find. Thousands of products are stacked on shelves that reach to the ceiling, and members spend hours wandering through buildings the size of a city block. Selection may be limited to one or two items, especially in the electronics, furniture and appliances category, but you're getting the best value for your money, and everything is from well-known manufacturers.

 Many people join to take advantage of terrific savings on food, which accounts for over 1/3 of the inventory. Anything you can buy at a grocery store is available, but because restaurants, delis and caterers shop here, canned, frozen, packaged and prepared foods often come in institutional sizes. Small containers are shrink-wrapped together and sold as a unit. Most labels will be familiar, but every once in a while you'll encounter something normally found only in the food service industry.

 Janitorial supplies, paper products, film, batteries, health and beauty products are also sold in quantity. The clothing department carries basic sportswear for the whole family by well-known manufacturers. Housewares, audio-video equipment, office supplies, sporting goods, tools, hardware and automotive represent major departments.

 Price Savers and Costco look the same, operate under the same basic concept and carry the same merchandise mix, but brand names will vary, particularly on one-of-a-kind and special-purchase items. Costco warehouses are larger, so they have a better selection in some categories. Prices are competitive on similar items.

COSTCO WHOLESALE
Federal Way: 35100 Enchanted Pkwy. ☎ 874-1888
Kirkland: 8629 120th Ave. N.E. ☎ 828-6767
Lynnwood: 19105 Hwy. 99 ☎ 775-3577
Seattle: 4401 4th Ave. S. ☎ 622-1144 *South of Kingdome*
Silverdale: 1000 Mickelberry Rd. ☎ 692-9213
Tacoma: 11013 Pacific Hwy. S.W. ☎ 581-2081
Tukwila: 1160 Saxon Drive ☎ 575-3311
Hours: Mon-Fri 12-8:30, Sat 9:30-6, Sun 11-5.
    Business members only, Tues-Thurs 10-12

Costco boasts an in-store bakery, fresh meat counter and big produce area. Apples, oranges and potatoes sold by the case are among the lowest priced in town. Carpet and window coverings can be special-ordered in the home decorating center. We also noted a big selection of vacuum cleaners, TV's, tape recorders and stereo equipment. Automotive supplies include tires by leading manufacturers plus free in-store mounting. Auto buying programs with local dealers can shave 5% to 10% off the cost of your next vehicle. Costco warehouses include their own pharmacy and optical departments.

Members Note: For a fee, Cost Less Express provides a shopping and delivery service for Costco members. Call 763-2735 and they'll mail you a catalog listing the majority of products available at Costco. Put your order in by 3 a.m., and it will be delivered the following day.

Checks

PRICE SAVERS WHOLESALE WAREHOUSE
Seattle: 13550 Aurora Ave. N. ☎ 362-6700 *Haller Lake*
Fife: 3900 20th Street E. ☎ 922-1265
Hours: Mon-Fri 11-8:30, Sat 9:00-6, Sun 10-6. Business members only,
    Mon-Fri 9-11

The food department stocks fresh bakery products and frozen meat, fish and poultry. Cereal, tuna fish, juices, pop, cheeses, deli meats, cleaning supplies and paper products are always a good buy. Many items come in small quantities. The automotive section offers the same products as well as services as Costco. Three things we really like about Price Savers are: **1** big signs in the warehouses clearly designating different departments; **2** price quotes will be given out over the phone as long as you have the manufacturer and model number; **3** an informative brochure and membership application will be mailed on request.

Checks

Thrift Shops

Some secondhand stores operate to benefit a charity, and some are privately owned establishments that buy outright or consign goods. The latter are usually more selective about what they sell, but prices are higher. Space limits us listing all thrift shops, and since most carry a wide variety of ever-changing merchandise in varying degrees of quality, it would be impossible to accurately describe them. For a complete listing by location, check the yellow pages under both "Secondhand Stores" and "Thrift Shops."

Shoppers with the time and inclination to forage through cast-offs know that perfectly usable goods and even brand-new items are just waiting to be discovered. It's amazing what people throw away in our consumer-oriented society. Retailers donate clearance merchandise and businesses send old office furniture and equipment. Some stores even buy new stock from liquidators. Inventory attracts not only families on a budget, but also nostalgia buffs and dealers who snap up the best buys for resale in their own or other stores.

Clothing is the biggest volume item, and prices have gone up as more people discover that secondhand clothes are both economical and socially acceptable. Cindy Lauper made thrift shop attire fashionable again with the younger set.

Housewares, appliances, and new and used furniture are favorites with newlyweds, students and people furnishing rec rooms, rental properties, or vacation homes. Deseret Industries sells brand-new sofas, couches, love seats, dressers and mattresses made in their factory in Utah. Large reconditioned appliances are available at Deseret, all St. Vincent de Paul stores, the Salvation Army in Seattle, Kent and Mt. Vernon, and at Volunteers of America in Everett. St. Vincent provides free delivery, plus a 6-month guarantee.

Some stores display collectibles, vintage and designer clothing separately. St. Vincent de Paul has a special section set aside in its main store for antiques. Odds and Ends in Renton takes antiques in on consignment. Treasures and Trinkets on Capitol Hill has a nice selection of dishes and small collectibles. Union Gospel Mission sends their best stuff to their shop in The Pike Place Market.

Frequent sales ensure a fast turnover on the huge quantity of goods brought into these stores. Value Village takes in about 5,000 items a day, so prices are cut in half on anything that doesn't sell in five weeks, another 50% after three weeks. On Sundays, all used merchandise goes for 20% less. Clothing is marked down 50% during major holidays. St. Vincent de Paul drops clothing prices 50% every weekend. The Wise Penny in the U-District, run by the Junior League of Seattle, hands out flyers and maintains a mailing list announcing great sales throughout the year, including their famous "Bag Day" when customers pay $1 to fill a grocery sack. Call 524-8634 for the exact date.

214 Something For Everyone, Thrift Shops

City of Hope hosts a "Brand X" sale in the fall when men's wool clothing by a well-known manufacturer in Oregon arrives. Call 784-0298 or become a member and receive a monthly newsletter announcing special sales. Many clothing reps donate samples to this shop. You'll find rock-bottom prices at the Salvation Army's "as is" store in the basement of the main store at 1010 4th Ave. S. in Seattle. Most thrift shops do not allow returns or accept credit cards.

Items donated to secondhand stores run by charitable organizations are tax deductible. Just be sure to get a signed receipt for your records. Other benefits include the good feeling you get knowing that your cast-offs help those in need.

GOODWILL

Seattle: Rainier S. at S. Dearborn ☎ 329-1000
Hours: Mon-Fri 10-8, Sat 9-5, Sun 10-5

Seattle boasts the largest Goodwill store in the nation, with over a million items in stock. Their unique monthly sales of special merchandise collected throughout the year represents the cream of the crop. Here's a monthly lineup of these special events, which usually take place on weekends from 10 a.m. to 4 p.m. in a room separate from the main sales floor: (Call the store or sign up on the mailing list for specific dates. In-store displays of seasonal merchandise start 30 days prior to the holiday. While you're in the store, check the bulletin board as you enter for daily specials, and visit the vintage clothing museum before you leave.)

January: Record Sale: stacks of oldie goldies and vintage collectibles. Disney Sale: memorabilia ranging from puzzles and plastic toys to clothes, cartoon viewers and plush animals.

February: Classy art sale: paintings, prints, lithographs, photos and art books. Costumes for Fat Tuesday are displayed in the main store.

March: Hooray for Hollywood!: paraphernalia associated with movie stars and the silver screen— books, films, buttons, posters, photos, etc. Formal wear on display in the main store includes prom dresses and tuxes for the high school social season.

April: Name Droppers Sale: big-time designer clothes. Computer Sale: hardware, software, books and components. Most items donated by businesses upgrading office systems. Some are no more than two years old.

May: Book Sale: over 15,000 volumes— new, used and rare.

June: Funky Sale; wild, wacky party clothes, unusual accessories.

August: Ski Sale: good buys on boots, poles, outerwear and related accessories for the whole family.

September: Name Droppers Sale, repeated. Book Sale, repeated if sufficient inventory.

October: Fur Sale: vintage, as well as expensive furs in current styles. Halloween costumes are displayed in the main store.

Something For Everyone, Rummage Sales and Flea Markets

November: All that Glitters: fancy holiday clothing for men and women. Bare Essentials: men's and women's lingerie and lounging apparel.

December: Kid's Shop: toys for Christmas.

Checks, Credit cards

Swap Meets, Rummage Sales and Flea Markets

There's an art to shopping at these periodic sales. The prices are often negotiable, and they drop drastically at the end of the day, but the good stuff gets snatched up early. The classifieds list dozens of weekend, quarterly and annual events. Publications like "Buy and Sell" and "Little Nickel Want Ads" are especially good resources. Here are a few of our favorites. Call for specific dates and locations.

LAKESIDE SCHOOL RUMMAGE SALE
Seattle: ☎ 368-3600
Semiannual sales

This is a biggie! The March sale, usually held in the Seattle Center Exhibition Hall, lures over 50,000 shoppers who come to sift through literally tons of donations. You'll find brand-new merchandise, collectibles and designer clothing. All items are half-price on Sunday. Monday shoppers can fill grocery bags for $4. The October sale, which is held at the school, is smaller.

Checks, Credit cards

SEATTLE REPERTORY THEATRE'S ELEGANT ELEPHANT SALE
Seattle: Bagley Wright Theatre Scene Shop ☎ 443-2210 *Seattle Center*
Annual sale

Every June for over a decade, this rummage sale has been attracting classy patrons and upscale merchandise. Look for great buys on clothing, china, glassware, books, records, art and kitchenwares, plus a special section for antiques and jewelry. To get first pick, buy a ticket for the preview party the night before. Call to get on their mailing list.

Checks, Credit cards

SWAP AND SHOP ASSOCIATION OF THE NORTHWEST
Seattle: ☎ 588-8621, 800/562-0340
Periodic sales

This organization sponsors the big swap meets and Bargain Fairs that take place periodically at the Puyallup Fairgrounds and in the Kingdome. Sales are usually advertised via display ads in major newspapers. Call if you want to rent a space or find out when and where the next one will be held.

WHOLESALE HEAVEN
Seattle: 2601 Elliott ☎ 885-5827 *Seattle Trade Center*
Periodic sales

Call to get on the mailing list, then shop 'til you drop at this bargain hunter's paradise! Over 100 booths are filled with merchandise brought in by local manufacturers, sales reps, retail stores and wholesale distributors, many of which are listed in our pages.

Everything is brand-new overstock, discontinued, or clearance items, with the main emphasis on apparel and accessories. Selection varies from the latest fashion to casual attire for the whole family. Best buys are on jeans, outerwear, sweatshirts and costume jewelry. You'll also find toys, giftware, sporting goods, housewares, luggage and decorative accessories. The admission fee was up to $5 the last time we attended but, mailings include a $1 off coupon.

Buyers and sellers gather at these locations for old-fashioned swap meets:

GRANITE CURLING CLUB FLEA MARKET
Seattle: 144 N. 128th ☎ 362-2446 *Haller Lake*
Hours: Fri 4-9, Sat 11-5, May through September 15th

PUGET PARK SWAP-O-RAMA DRIVE-IN THEATER
South Everett: I-5 at 128th St. Exit ☎ 337-1435
Hours: Sat & Sun 9-4 April through October

STAR-LITE SWAP & SHOP DRIVE-IN THEATER
Tacoma: S. 84th & S. Tacoma Way ☎ 588-8090
Hours: Tues-Fri 10-6, Sat & Sun 9-4

Auctions

To find out when and where auctions are taking place, look under Auction Notices in "The Commerce Business Daily," "The Seattle Daily Journal of Commerce," or subscribe to the "Auction Greensheet," the only publication of its kind in the country. Weekly editions list over 100 auctions in Western and Central Washington and Oregon sponsored by private, commercial, government and community organizations, or businesses. Subscription fee is $95/yr or $55/6-months. Call 486-5444 for a complimentary copy.

Government auctions usually offer the best bargains because they do not use professional auctioneers or spend a lot of money on advertising. Goods will be surplus or used, the latter sometimes in "like new" condition. School districts sell anything you'd find in a school except books. Unclaimed, stolen, or lost and found property sold at police auctions include cameras, jewelry, clothing, TV's, VCR's, tools and household items. Many people attend just to pick up super buys on bicycles. Vehicles are sold at The City of Seattle, IRS, GSA, and sometimes at police auctions. Government agency vehicles are sold off every three years, so they're often still in good condition. IRS auctions include land and buildings. All sales are final, "as is," and many require cash or cashier's checks. Here's a list of a few area auctions. Call for information; some have mailing lists.

GENERAL SERVICES ADMINISTRATION/ PERSONAL PROPERTY SALES
Auburn: ☎ 931-3979

INTERNAL REVENUE SERVICE
Seattle: ☎ 442-0702

KING COUNTY POLICE AUCTION
Seattle: ☎ 296-4078

SEATTLE POLICE AUCTION
Seattle: ☎ 684-8187

SCHOOL DISTRICT AUCTIONS:
Seattle: ☎ 298-7560
Tacoma: ☎ 596-1290

U.S. CUSTOM SERVICES AUCTION
Seattle: ☎ 442-4678

Shopping Tours

For the same reasons we elected to print this book on recycled paper, the publishers wish to urge readers to take advantage of public transportation whenever possible. Here's one final listing to save time, money and gasoline:

THE BUFFY BUS
Kirkland: 611 Market St. #C ☎ 827-6328
Hours: Daily, 10-5

Sign up for tours with great titles like "Bargain Binge," "Junky Jaunt" or "Fashion Fling" and spend the day visiting factories, discount outlets and liquidators. The $30 fee includes breakfast and lunch, and sometimes special discounts from participating stores. Other choices include Wholesale Heaven, factory outlet malls, or out-of-state destinations. Private bookings and custom-designed tours are available for groups. Call for a free brochure listing prices, departure dates and detailed descriptions. Become a member of Buffy's Frequent Rider Club for access to special events and free tours. Seats sell out fast, so we recommend making a reservation a month in advance.

Checks, Credit cards

218 Greater Seattle Area, Locator Map

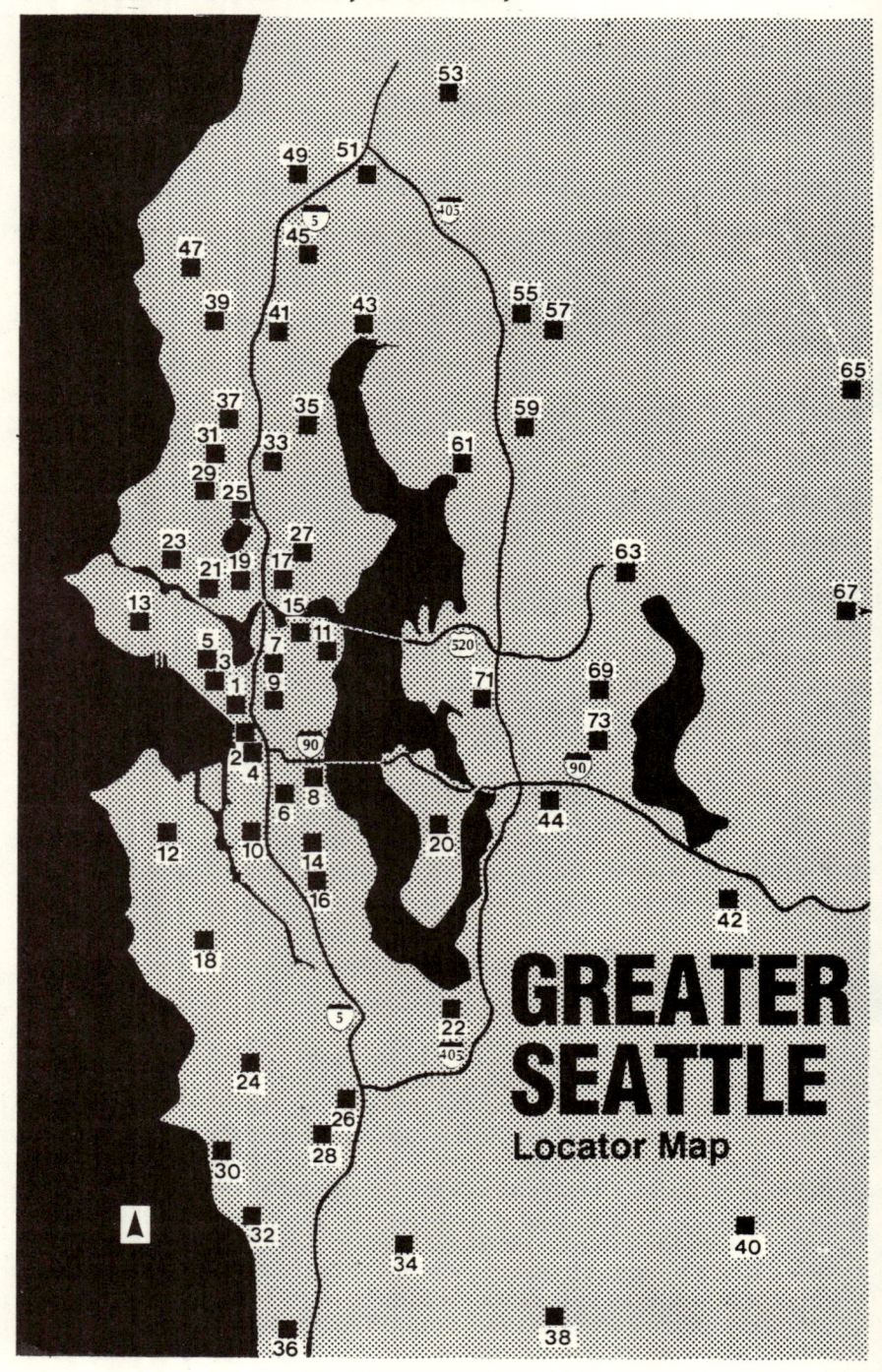

Greater Seattle Area, Locator Key 219

Shopping destinations North of Downtown Seattle are indicated by odd numbers, those South by even numbers. The numbering starts with (1) in Downtown Seattle.

Locator Map Key

Alderwood Manor, 51
Ballard, 23
Beacon Hill, 6
Bellevue, 71
Bothell, 55
Broadway, 7
Burien, 24
Carnation, 67
Crossroads, 69
Des Moines, 32
Downtown, 1
Duvall, 65
Eastgate, 44
Echo Lake, 39
Factoria, 44
Federal Way, 36
Firdale, 47
First Hill, 9
Fremont, 21
Georgetown, 10
Greenlake, 25
Greenwood, 29
Haller lake, 37
Holly Park, 16
Interbay, 13
International District, 2
Issaquah, 42
Juanita, 61
Kenmore, 43
Kent, 34
Kingdome, 4
Kingsgate, 59
Lake City, 35

Lake Hills, 73
Lynnwood, 49
Madison Park, 11
Magnolia, 13
Maple Valley, 40
Mercer Island, 20
Meridian, 38
Mill Creek, 53
Montlake, 15
Montlake Terrace, 45
Mount Baker, 8
Normandy Park, 30
North City, 41
North Park, 31
Pioneer Square, 2
Queen Anne, 5
Rainier Valley, 14
Ravenna, 27
Redmond, 63
Renton, 22
Richmond Highlands, 39
Roosevelt, 27
Sea Tac, 28
Seattle Center, 3
Totem Lake, 59
Tukwila, 26
University, 17
Victory Heights, 33
Wallinford, 19
West Seattle, 12
Westgate, 47
White Center, 18
Woodinville, 57

Locator Index

Clothing

Factory & Manufacturer's Outlets Locator Index

Bothell 3
Downtown 2, 4, 5
Eastgate 3
Everett 2
Fife 4

Georgetown 5
Kent 4, 6
Mercer Island 6
Pioneer Square 2
Puyallup 2

Renton 1
Seattle 1-6
Seattle Center 3-5
Sunset Village 3
Tacoma 1, 3, 4

Off-price Stores Locator Index

Auburn 13
Aurora Fashion Plaza 6, 8, 11
Bellevue 9, 11, 12
Capitol Hill 8
Cascade Plaza 12
Century Square 9, 12
College Plaza 10
Downtown 8, 9
Edmonds 7
Everett 10-12
Everett Mall 11, 12
Factoria Square 6-11
Federal Way 7, 12
Greenwood 12
Haller Lake 12
Kent 10, 13

Kent Hill Plaza 10
Kitsap Mall 9
Loehmann's Plaza 10
Lynnwood 8, 11-13
Northgate 6, 8, 13
Northgate Village 6, 8, 13
Overlake 8, 11
Overlake Fashion Plaza 8, 11
Park Row 9
Parkway Plaza 12
Pavilion Mall 6-8, 11
Puget Park 10
Puyallup 13
Queen Anne 12
Redmond 8, 11
Renton 10, 12, 13

Renton Shopping Center 10
Ross Plaza 8, 11, 12
Seattle 8-14
Seattle Center 12
Silverdale 8, 9, 11, 12
Southcenter 7, 8, 11, 12
Tacoma 7, 8, 10-13
Tacoma Center 11
Tacoma Central Plaza 13
Tukwila 7, 8, 11, 12
U-District 8, 14
Villa Plaza 12
West Seattle 10
Westwood 10

Clearance Centers Locator Index

Bellevue 15
Downtown 15
Everett 14, 15
Everett Mall 15
Kirkland 14

Lynnwood 15
Northgate 14
Parkland Mall 14
Pavilion Mall 15
Renton 15

Seattle 15
Sixth Avenue Plaza 14
Southcenter 15
Tacoma 14
Tukwila 15

Women's Consignment Shops Locator Index

Bainbridge Island 18
Bellevue 16, 19, 20, 22, 23, 25
Bellevue Lake Mall 19
Bellevue Square 20
Bothell 17, 24
Burien 22
Capitol Hill 24
Crown Hill 17
Downtown 17
Edmonds 17, 24
Everett 17, 18
Federal Way 17

Fircrest 24
Greenwood 24
Issaquah 19
Jefferson Square 21
Kirkland 18, 19, 22
Lake Hills Shopping Center 23
Lynnwood 20, 25
Madison Park 20
Mercer Island 19
North Creek Center 17
Northgate 16, 21
Queen Anne 23

Ravenna 16
Redmond 23
Renton 19, 20
Seattle 16, 17, 19-21, 23, 24
Seattle Center 23
Spectrum Business Park 17
Tacoma 18, 20-22, 24
U-District 16, 21
West Seattle 21
Westgate Shopping Center 18

Locator Indexes, By Category 221

Menswear Locator Index

Aurora Fashion Plaza 28
Bellevue 27, 28
Burien 29
Downtown 28
Federal Way 28
Federal Way Shopping Ctr. 28
Fremont 30
Kent 29
Kirkland 29
Kitsap Mall 28

Lincoln Center 28
Lynnwood 28, 29
Madison Park 27
Northgate 28
Overlake 28
Overlake Fashion Plaza 28
Queen Anne 27
Redmond 28
Sea-Tac 28
Sea-Tac Mall 28

Seattle 27-30
Seattle Center 27
Silverdale 28
Southcenter 28
Tacoma 28
TJ Maxx Plaza 28
Tukwila 28, 29
U-District 29

Maternity & Children's Locator Index

Aurora Fashion Plaza 31
Bellevue 36
Burien 35
Centerplace 32
Century Square 31
Edmonds 31, 37
Everett 31, 32, 34
Everett Mall 31
Factoria Square 31
Federal Way 31, 35
Fife 32
Greentree Plaza 31

Issaquah 32
Kent 32, 34, 36
Kirkland 32, 38
Lake Forest Park 35, 36
Lake Hills Shopping Ctr 36
Loehmann's Plaza 36
Lynnwood 31, 32, 34
Madison Park 33
Northgate 35-37
Overlake 31
Overlake Fashion Plaza 31
Redmond 31, 32, 38

Ross Plaza 31
Seattle 31, 33, 35, 37
Shoreline 35
Silverdale 31
Southcenter 32
Tacoma 31, 36, 37
Tacoma Central Plaza 31
Totem Lake West 38
Tukwila 32
Wallingford 35

Shoes & Accessories Locator Index

Alderwood Towne Ctr. 39
Bellevue 39, 40
Cascade Plaza 40
Downtown 39, 40
Lakewood Mall 40
Loehmann's Plaza 40
Lynnwood 39, 41

Northgate 40
Northgate Village 40
Parkway Center 39
Pavilion Mall 39, 40
Renton 40
Renton Center 40
Ross Plaza 40

Seattle 39-41
Seattle Center 39
Southcenter 39, 40
Tacoma 40
Tukwila 39, 40
U-District 39

Formal Wear, Bridal Attire & Furs Locator Index

Ballard 44
Bellevue 42
Burien 45
Downtown 43
Greenwood 45

Kent 42, 45
Lynnwood 42, 45
Madison Park 44
Newport Square 45
North City 45

Queen Anne 43, 44
Renton 43
Seattle 43-45
Tacoma 45

Fine Jewelry Locator Index

Ballard 47
Bellevue 46-48
Downtown 46-48
Federal Way 48

Koll Center 48
Pavilion Mall 46
Puyallup 46
Seattle 46-48

Southcenter 46
Tacoma 46, 47
Tukwila 46

# Food

Food Service Warehouses, Locator Index

Ballard 51
Everett 50-52
Everett Mall 51
Fife 51
Kent 52
Rainier Valley 50
Renton 52
Seattle 49-52
Snoqualmie 51
Tacoma 50, 51
Tukwila 51

Bakery Goods, Locator Index

Ballard 53
Bellevue 53, 54
Bremerton 53-55
Capitol Hill 52, 55
Crossroads Mall 54
Downtown 55
Everett 53-55
Everett Mall 54
Georgetown 53
Greenwood 55
International Dist. 53
Kent 52-55
Lynnwood 53
North City 55
Seattle 52-55
Tacoma 53-55
University Village 54
Woodinville 53

Eggs & Dairy Products, Locator Index

Everett 56
Federal Way 57
Kent 57
Puyallup 56
Redmond 56, 57

Fruits & Vegetables, Locator Index

Capitol Hill 59
Downtown 60
Everett 59, 60
Federal Way 58
International District 58
Kent 58
Puyallup 58, 60
Ravenna 59
Renton 60
Renton Center 60
Seattle 58-60
Snohomish 60
Woodinville 59

Meat, Poultry & Seafood, Locator Index

Ballard 61
Duvall 61
Edmonds 61
International District 62
Kent 62
Kent Hill Plaza 62
Kirkland 62
Richmond Highlands 61
Seattle 61, 62
Snoqualmie 61
Tacoma 62

Beverages, Locator Index

Bothell 65
Des Moines 64
Everett 63
Georgetown 63
Kirkland 66
Lake Union 65
Madison Park 65
Rainier Valley 65
Ravenna 65
Renton 63
Seattle 63-66
Snohomish 63, 64
U-District 66
University Village 65
Vashon Island 64
Wallingford 64

Sweets & Treats, Locator Index

Burien 67
Capitol Hill 68
Issaquah 67
Kent 70
Lake City 68
Lynnwood 67, 68
Rainier Valley 69
Ravenna 67
Seattle 67-69
Tacoma 67, 69
Tukwila 69

Ethnic Foods, Locator Index

Downtown 72
International District 70-72
Lynnwood 70
Rainier Valley 71
Seattle 70-72
White Center 71

Locator Indexes, By Category 223

Natural Foods & Health Products, Locator Index

Alderwood Village 75
Capitol Hill 73
Downtown 75
Federal Way 75
Fremont 76
Georgetown 73
Greenwood 76
Kirkland 75, 76
Lynnwood 75
Northgate 74, 75
Ravenna 76
Renton 74
Seattle 73-76
Snohomish 76
Tacoma 75
Tacoma Mall 75
U-District 75
West Seattle 75

Personal Care

Drugs & Sundries, Locator Index

Ballard 78
Burien 79
Everett 78
Federal Way 78, 79
Greenwood 78
Kent 78, 79
Kirkland 78, 79
Lynnwood 78, 79
Northgate 78
Northgate Village 78
Parkway Plaza 78
Queen Anne 78
Seattle 78, 79
Silverdale 78, 79
Southcenter 78
Tacoma 78, 79
Tukwila 78
Wallingford 79

Cosmetics & Grooming Products, Locator Index

Bellevue 81
Everett 80, 81
Federal Way 81
Kirkland 81
Lynnwood 82
Pavilion Mall 82
Redmond 82
Sea-Tac 81
Southcenter 80, 82
Tukwila 80, 82

Grooming Services, Locator Index

Bellevue 84
Downtown 84
Everett 85
Greenwood 85
Northgate 85
Redmond 83
Seattle 84, 85
Shoreline 85

Home Building and Remodeling

Building Materials, Hardware & Tools, Locator Index

Auburn 88, 89
Bellevue 88
Des Moines 93
Downtown 88, 90
Everett 87, 88, 91-93
Georgetown 92, 94
Kenmore 88
Kent 86, 87, 91, 93
Kirkland 93
Lake City 93
Lynnwood 87, 89
Northgate 92
Pioneer Square 87
Queen Anne 90
Renton 88, 94
Seattle 87-94
Seattle Center 93, 94
South Park 94
Tacoma 87, 88, 91-94
U-District 92
Woodinville 88

Floor Coverings, Locator Index

Ballard 97
Bellevue 93-97
Bremerton 95
Burien 95
Des Moines 98
Downtown 98
Everett 93, 94, 97
Federal Way 94-96
Georgetown 95
Greenwood 94, 95
Issaquah 95
Kent 95, 97
Kirkland 95
Lake City 93, 95, 96
Lynnwood 94-97
Northgate 95
Parkway Plaza 94
Redmond 93, 95, 96
Renton 95, 96
Seattle 94-98
Silverdale 94
Southcenter 94
Spanaway 97
Tacoma 93-95
Tukwila 94

Locator Indexes, By Category

Paint & Wallpaper, Locator Index

Bellevue 99, 100
Burien 100
Everett 100
Federal Way 99, 100
Greenwood 100
Kent 99

Kirkland 99
Lynnwood 99, 100
Parkway Plaza 100
Puyallup 99
Redmond 99
Seattle 99, 100

Southcenter 100
Tacoma 99, 100
Tukwila 99, 100
Wallingford 99

Window Coverings, Locator Index

Bellevue 102
Federal Way 102
Greenlake 103
Kent 101
Lynnwood 102
Mill Creek 101
Queen Anne 103
Renton 102

Seattle 102, 103
Southcenter 102
Tukwila 102
Bellevue 102
Federal Way 102
Greenlake 103
Kent 101
Lynnwood 102

Mill Creek 101
Queen Anne 103
Renton 102
Seattle 102, 103
Southcenter 102
Tukwila 102

Home Furnishings

Furniture, Locator Index

Bellevue 106, 107, 109
Bremerton 108
Downtown 108-110
Everett 107, 108
Everett Mall 107
Federal Way 104
Georgetown 106

Issaquah 108
Kent 105, 108
Kirkland 107
Lynnwood 104
Parkway Plaza 104
Seattle 105, 106, 108-110
Seattle Center 105, 109

Southcenter 104, 105, 107
Tacoma 107-109
Tukwila 104-107, 110
U-District 106
West Seattle 108

Household Appliances, Locator Index

Bellevue 110, 113, 114
Bothell 111
Capitol Hill 111
Downtown 110, 112, 114
Everett 113
Everett Mall 113
Federal Way 112, 113
Kent 111

Kirkland 114
Lynnwood 113
Northgate 113
Parkway Plaza 113
Queen Anne 111
Renton 112, 113
Ross Plaza 113
Seattle 110-114

Seattle Center 111
Silverdale 113
Southcenter 113
Tacoma 110, 113
Tukwila 113
U-District 113
Woodinville 113

Kitchen Equipment, Locator Index

Kent 114
Lake Union 115
Pavilion Mall 115

Seattle 115
Seattle Center 115
Southcenter 115

Tacoma 115
Tukwila 115

Locator Indexes, By Category

Bedding & Linens, Locator Index

Ballard 117, 121
Bellevue 117, 119-121
Bothell 119
Capitol Hill 118
Downtown 120
Duvall 120
Edmonds 118
Everett 119
Federal Way 119
Fremont 121
Greenwood 120
Haller Lake 117, 119
Holly Park 118
Kent 119, 121
Kent Hill Plaza 119
Lake Forest Park 119
Loehmann's Plaza 116
Lynnwood 116, 119
Parkway Plaza 117, 119
Pavilion Mall 118, 119
Puyallup 116, 119
Redmond 121
Richmond Highlands 121
Seattle 116-121
Seattle Center 118
Silverdale 119
Southcenter 117-119
Tacoma 116, 119-121
Tukwila 117-119
U-District 121
Woodinville 116, 120

China, Crystal & Silver, Locator Index

Downtown 121
Ravenna 122
Seattle 121, 122

Decorative Accessories, Locator Index

Auburn 124
Georgetown 125
Kirkland 123
Lake City 124
Normandy Park 123
Pavilion Mall 123
Renton 124
Seattle 123-125
Southcenter 123
Tacoma 123, 124
Tukwila 123

Plants, Flowers and Greenery

Nurseries, Locator Index

Bellevue 126
Des Moines 126
Edmonds 125
Issaquah 126
Lynnwood 125
Puyallup 125, 126
Redmond 126
Renton 126, 127
Seattle 127
Snohomish 125, 127, 128
Stanwood 125
Woodinville 125

Garden Ornaments, Locator Index

Seattle 128
Tukwila 128

Florists, Locator Index

Bellevue 130
Burien 130
Federal Way 129
Issaquah 130
Lynnwood 129
Mercer Island 130
North City 130
Queen Anne 130
Seattle 129, 130
Seattle Center 130
Tacoma 128, 129
U-District 129
University Village 130
West Seattle 129, 130
White Center 130

Holiday Greenery, Locator Index

Seattle 130
Snohomish 130
Tacoma 130

Office Needs

Office Furniture, Machines & Supplies, Locator Index

Bellevue 132-134
Capitol Hill 135
Downtown 132, 133
Georgetown 136
Kent 131, 133
Pioneer Square 131
Queen Anne 133
Seattle 131-136
Seattle Center 132
Tacoma 134
Tukwila 133
U-District 135

Locator Indexes, By Category

Computer Hardware & Software Locator Index

Ballard 136, 137
Bellevue 137-142
Burien 140
Downtown 139, 141
Duvall 141
Everett 141
Federal Way 141
Fife 138
Kent 136

Kirkland 137
Lake Union 138
Lynnwood 140
Mercer Island 142
North Park 141
Northgate 141
Parkway Plaza 141
Pavilion Mall 138
Redmond 138, 139

Renton 139
Richmond Highlands 138
Sea-Tac 141
Seattle 137-143
Seattle Center 140
Southcenter 138, 141
Tacoma 137, 138, 140, 141
Tukwila 138, 141
U-District 141, 142

Paper Products for Home & Office, Locator Index

Bellevue 144
Everett 145, 146
Haller Lake 146

Lynnwood 145
Redmond 146
Seattle 144, 146

Tacoma 146
Tukwila 147

Recreation and Hobbies
Sporting Goods & Recreational Clothing Locator Index

Ballard 149
Bellevue 148, 149, 153-156
Burien 149
Capitol Hill 151, 156, 157, 159
Cascade Plaza 154
Downtown 151, 152, 155, 157
Everett 148, 149, 152-154
Everett Mall 148, 149
Factoria Square 148, 149
Federal Way 148, 149, 156
Fife 158
Haller Lake 151
Kent 150

Kirkland 149, 152
Lake City 148, 155
Lake Union 159
Lakewood Mall 148
Lynnwood 149, 154, 155, 158
North Park 156
Northgate 155
Overlake 148
Overlake Fashion Plaza 148
Pioneer Square 154
Queen Anne 158
Redmond 148, 155
Renton 149, 154

Sea-Tac 148, 149
Sea-Tac Mall 148, 149
Seattle 148-152, 154-159
Seattle Center 157
Silverdale 154
South Park 159
Tacoma 148-151, 153-155
Tukwila 150, 151, 155
U-District 149, 156
West Seattle 149
Woodinville 152

Audio & Video Equipment Locator Index

Bellevue 159-161
Burien 160
Cascade Plaza 161
Downtown 161
Federal Way 161

Green Lake 160
Lake City 160
Lake Union 161
Magnolia 159
Ross Plaza 161

Sea-Tac 161
Seattle 159-161
Southcenter 161
Tacoma 159, 161
Tukwila 161

Audio & Video Recordings Locator Index

Ballard 162
Bellevue 163, 164, 166, 167
Bellevue Square 163
Bothell 161
Burien 166
Capitol Hill 164, 165, 167
Crossroads Mall 164
Downtown 164
Everett 164, 167
Everett Mall 167
Federal Way 166, 167

Kent 162
Kirkland 164
Lynnwood 163, 164, 167
Pavilion Mall 165
Pioneer Square 162
Puyallup 163
Queen Anne 165
Ravenna 162, 164
Renton 163, 164
Ross Plaza 163
Sea-Tac 166

Sea-Tac Mall 166
Seattle 161-167
Seattle Center 165-167
Silverdale 163
Southcenter 165
Tacoma 163-167
Tukwila 165
U-District 161, 163, 166, 167
Wallingford 164

Photographic Equipment & Supplies Locator Index

Ballard 168
Bellevue 168
Denny Regrade 169
Downtown 168, 170
Green Lake 168, 169
Rainier Beach 169
Seattle 168-170
Seattle Center 169

Arts and Crafts & Sewing Locator Index

Bellevue 172, 173, 177, 179
Burien 177
Capitol Hill 175
Downtown 174, 176-178
Everett 172, 174, 178, 179
Fremont 176
Georgetown 176
Greenwood 174
Juanita 176
Kent 172
Kirkland 172, 174, 176
Lakewood Mall 175
Lynnwood 172-174, 176
Renton 173-175
Richmond Highlands 177
Seattle 173-178
Seattle Center 176
Shoreline 173
Silverdale 173
Sixth Avenue Plaza 175
Snohomish 179
Spanaway 173
Tacoma 173, 175-177, 179
U-District 176, 178
West Seattle 175
Woodinville 178

Used Books Locator Index

Auburn 180
Bellevue 181
Capitol Hill 180, 182
Downtown 179, 183
Edmonds 180
Kirkland 181
Lake City 182
Lake Union 180
Northgate 180
Sea-Tac 180
Seattle 179-183
Tacoma 181, 183
U-District 179, 181, 182
West Seattle 182

Museums, Films & Performing Arts Locator Index

Bellevue 184
Capitol Hill 185
Seattle 184, 185
Tacoma 184

Dining Out Locator Index

Edmonds 186
Everett 186
Lynnwood 186
Seattle 186, 187
West Seattle 187

Luggage Locator Index

Bellevue 190
Downtown 190
Kitsap Mall 190
Lynnwood 190
Northgate 190
Pavilion Mall 190
Redmond 190
Seattle 190
Silverdale 190
Skyway 190
Southcenter 190
Tacoma 190
Tukwila 190

Children's Toys Locator Index

Bellevue Square 191
Federal Way 191, 192
Issaquah 191
Lynnwood 192
Mercer Island 193
Pavilion Mall 193
Redmond 192
Sea-Tac 191
Sea-Tac Mall 191
Seattle 192, 193
Silverdale 192
Southcenter 191-193
Southcenter Mall 191
Tacoma 191, 192
Tukwila 191-193
Wallingford 192
Woodinville 191

Locator Indexes, By Category

Automotive

New & Used Automobiles, Locator Index

Bellevue 197
Des Moines 197
Downtown 196
Edmonds 194
Green Lake 197
Redmond 197
Sea-Tac 196, 197
Seattle 195-197
Wallingford 196

Parts & Accessories, Locator Index

Auburn 197
Ballard 197-199
Bellevue 197
Bothell 197, 198
Bremerton 198
Burien 198
Edmonds 199
Everett 198
Federal Way 198, 200
Fife 198
Georgetown 198-200
Issaquah 198
Kirkland 199
Lake City 198, 199
Lynnwood 198, 199
Northgate 199
Rainier Valley 198
Richmond Highlands 197
Seattle 198-200
Tacoma 198

Something for Everyone

Factory Outlet Malls, Locator Index

Burlington 202, 203
Centralia 202, 203
North Bend 202, 203

Mass Merchandise Discounters, Locator Index

Bellevue 207, 210
Bremerton 210
Burien 209
Des Moines 206
Downtown 208
Everett 207, 210
Federal Way 207
Green Lake 207
Kent 209-211
Lynnwood 207, 210
Normandy Park 206, 207
Puyallup 210
Renton 209, 210
Sea-Tac 208, 210
Seattle 207-210
Seattle Center 207
Snohomish 210
Southcenter 207
Spanaway 209
Tacoma 207, 209, 210
Tukwila 207
West Seattle 208
White Center 207

Membership Buying Clubs, Locator Index

Federal Way 212
Fife 212
Haller Lake 212
Kirkland 212
Lynnwood 212
Seattle 211, 212
Silverdale 212
Tacoma 212
Tukwila 212

Thrift Shops, Swap Meets & Auctions, Locator Index

Auburn 216
Capitol Hill 213
Everett 213, 216
Haller Lake 216
Kent 213
Puget Park 216
Puyallup 215
Renton 213
Seattle 213-217
Seattle Center 215
Tacoma 216, 217
U-District 213

Greater Seattle Shopping Center Location Guide

Bellevue
Park Row, 4th Ave. at Bellevue Way
Bellevue Square, N.E. 8th at Bellevue Way
Lake Hills Shopping Center, 156th S.E. at Lake Hills Blvd.
Bellevue Lake Mal, 11810 N.E. 8th
Crossroads Mall, 156th N.E. at N.E. 8th
Bellevue Plaza, 124 105th N.E.
Bellevue Village, 104th N.E. at N.E. 8th

Bothell
Canyon Park Shopping Center, Bothell Everett Hwy. at 226th St. S.W.

Everett
Everett Mall, I-5 at Everett Mall Way
Puget Park, 12800 4th Ave. W.
College Plaza, 1000 N. Broadway
Greentree Plaza, 505 S.E. Everett Mall Way

Factoria
Factoria Square, I-90 & I-405
Loehmann's Plaza, I-90 & I-405

Federal Way
Federal Way Center, S. 312th Pacific Hwy. S.
Century Square, S. 320th at Pacific Hwy. S.
Sea-Tac Mall, S. 320th at Pacific Hwy. S.

Kirkland
Parkland Mall, 529 Park Place Center
Totem Lake Mall, 12537 116th N.E.

Kent
Kent Hills Plaza, 25824 104th Ave S.E.

Lynnwood
Alderwood Towne Center, 3100 Alderwood Mall Blvd
TJ Maxx Plaza, Alderwood Mall Blvd. at 184th St. S.W.
Alderwood Village, 3800 196th St. S.W.
Alderwood Mall, 184th St. S.W. at 36th Ave.

Redmond

Overlake Fashion Plaza, 2172 148th N.E.

Renton

Renton Shopping Center, Ranier Ave. S. at Sunset Blvd.

Seattle

Aurora Fashion Plaza, N. 160th at Aurora
Aurora Village, N. 200th at Aurora
University Village, N.E. 45th St. & 25th Ave. N.E.
Northgate Village, 8th Ave. N.E. at N.E. Northgate Way
Northgate Mall, I-5 at N.E. Northgate Way

Silverdale

Kitsap Mall, 10300 Silverdale Way N.W.
Ross Plaza, Silverdale Way N.W. & Bucklin Hill Rd.

Tacoma

Sixth Avenue Plaza, 5401 6th Ave.
Cascade Plaza, 2919 S. 38th
Lakewood Mall, 10659 Gravelly Lake Dr. S.W.
Villa Plaza, 10401 Gravelly Dr. S.W.
Tacoma Central Plaza, 19th at Union
Tacoma Mall, 47th at Pine
Westgate Center, N. 26th St. at Pearl St.
Tacoma Place, S. 74th St. at Alaska Place
Lincoln Plaza, 2900 S. 38th

Tukwila

Pavilion Mall, 17900 Southcenter Pkwy.
Parkway Center, 16880 Southcenter Pkwy.
Southcenter Mall, I-5 at I-405 South
Parkway Plaza, 17900 Southcenter Pkwy.

West Seattle

Westwood Village, S.W. Barton at 25th Ave. S.W.
Jefferson Square, 4700 42nd S.W.

Greater Seattle Super Shopper, General Index

Index Note:

Firms with full listings appear in this index in ALL CAPS. Firms mentioned in the text appear in upper and lower case type. Some of the listed companies will appear both ways.

A

A & B FOOD MARKET 50
A CLASS ACT 16
A to Z 33
A-AMERICA WHOLESALE OAK FURNITURE 105
A-JACK COMPANY 132
AA RENTALS 149
AAA LIQUIDATING 206
AAA NEW & USED RESTAURANT EQUIPMENT 115
AARDBOOKS 179
ABC NAIL & SKIN COLLEGE 84
ABC SALES 207
ABCO PIZZA SUPPLY CO. 70
ABODIO CLEARANCE CENTER 106
ABOUT FACE 34
ACCENT ON FASHION 17
ACE BOX COMPANY 148
ACE NOVELTY CO. 190
ACME OFFICE FURNITURE 132
ACT II CONSIGNMENT BOUTIQUE 17
ACT II CONSIGNMENTS 17
ACTION DISCOUNT WALLCOVERINGS 102
ACTION OFFICE INTERIORS 132
ACTION SMALL APPLIANCE SERVICE 111
ADOLPHO II 203
AILEEN'S 203
AIRCRAFT PARTS EXCHANGE 91
AJ's 34
AJAX ELECTRIC, INC. 111
ALBERT LEE APPLIANCE 112
ALL STAR RENT-A-CAR 197
ALLIED CUSTOM DRAPERY STORES 103
ALMOST NEW 34
ALPINE HUT 149
AM COMPUTER SWAP MEET 137
AMARANT BLINDS 103
AMBERSON EGG FARM 56
AMERICAN APPLIANCES 112
AMERICAN AUTOMOBILE ASSOCIATION 200
AMERICAN DISCOUNT WALLCOVERINGS 102
AMERICAN DRAPERY & BLINDS 103
AMERICAN SHAREWARE 141
AMERICAN TOURISTER 203
AMERICOAST 1
AMWAY MOTORING PLAN 201
answering machines 161
ANTHONY RICHARDS 26
ANTIQUE LIQUIDATORS 106
antiques 106, 213, 215
APEX WHOLESALE 78
appliance repair 114
appliances, kitchen 50, 70, 88-90, 113, 115-116, 204, 208, 212
appliances, general household 94, 105, 111-115, 120, 160, 161, 207-209
ARBORETUM FOUNDATION 128
architectural and engineering supplies 107, 134
ARGENTI 203
ARNIE'S DISCOUNT TOYS 191
ARONSON-CAMPBELL INDUSTRIAL SUPPLY, INC. 92
ARRAY OF THE RAINBOWS WEDDINGS 45
art prints 124, 125, 183, 214
art supplies 146, 147, 172, 174, 192
arts and crafts 172-178
ARTY'S CUSTOM-BILT MATTRESS AND UPHOLSTERY 121
ARVEY PAPER & OFFICE SUPPLIES 145
ATHLETIC EXPRESS 149
Athletic Express 38
athletic shoes 38, 149, 151, 203, 205, 208
ATHLETIC SNEAKER & APPAREL 203
auctions 213, 217
audio equipment 114, 160-162, 164, 212
audio equipment, auto 198
AURORA MEATS 61
AUTO ADVISOR, INC. 195
AUTO AMERICARD 201

232 Greater Seattle Super Shopper, General Index

AUTO INSIDER 195
automobiles 194-197
automotive supplies 92, 93, 197-199, 209, 211, 212
AVIS USED CARS SALES 197

B

B & B HOBBIES AND CRAFTS 172
B & I SPORTS SHOP 150
baby furniture 23, 34-37, 192, 207
backpacking clothes and equipment 149, 157
BACKTRACK VIDEOS AND RECORDS 164
BACKWOODS SUPPLY CO. 150
BADER'S DUTCH BISCUIT COMPANY 52
BAKER & CHANTRY ORCHIDS 126
BAKER'S CANDY COMPANY 67
bakery goods 50, 52-56, 59, 73, 74, 186, 212
Ballard Camera 170
Ballard Computer 137
BALLARD COMPUTER 138
balloons 131, 147
balls 152, 156, 158
BANK AND OFFICE INTERIORS WAREHOUSE OUTLET 133
BANNISTER SHOES 203
BARBIZON LINGERIE 203
BARGREEN COFFEE 63
BARGREEN'S RESTAURANT SUPPLY, INC. 50
BARGREEN-ELLINGSON, INC. 116
Bartell's 49
baseball 158
BASS SHOE 203
bathroom accessories 117
bathtubs 90
batteries 78, 211
batteries, auto 198, 199
batting 119, 176
BAY CREST MATERNITY FACTORY OUTLET 32
BAYSIDE SUPPLY CO. 94
BEATTY BOOK STORE 179
BEAUTY AND THE BOOKS 179
beauty schools 84
beauty supplies 82
BEDAZZLED EVENING WEAR RENTAL 45
bedroom furniture 104-110, 116-121, 213
BEDS, BUNKS & MATTRESSES 117

BEDS NORTHWEST 117
BEDSPREAD & LINEN WAREHOUSE 117
bedspreads and comforters 103, 117-119, 121, 151, 152
beer 64-66
BEL-BOUTIQUE 1
BELLEVUE OFFICE FURNITURE 133
belts 10-12, 17, 21, 22, 38, 41, 176
BENOY'S CARPET WAREHOUSE 95
BERGMAN LUGGAGE 190
BEST 207
BEST FABRIC OUTLET 172
BEST RENT-A-CAR 197
BETWEEN FRIENDS 17
BEVERAGE HOUSE 64
BEVERAGE HOUSE, THE 65
beverages 50, 62-66
BI-LO CLOTHING 7
BIBELOTS AND BOOKS 180
BIG 5 38, 150
BIGFOOT OUTDOOR OUTLET 151
biking equipment and clothing 4, 151, 153, 157, 158, 159
BILL'S TIRE EXCHANGE 199
birthday party supplies 146, 191
BLACK AND DECKER 111
BLACK TIE MEN'S FORMAL WEAR 42
blinds 101-104
Blockbuster Video 163
boating and marine supplies 90, 153, 156, 160, 162, 176, 206
BOB STAFFORD 106
BOEHM'S 67
Boeing Surplus 194
BOEING SURPLUS 86
bolts 175
BON CLEARANCE STORE 14
BON MARCHE HOME FURNISHINGS AND ELECTRONICS 106
BOOK AFFAIR 180
BOOK WAREHOUSE 203
books 163, 179-185
booties 35, 152
boots 39-41, 151, 153, 158, 208, 214
BOP STREET RECORDS AND TAPES 164
BOTHELL APPLIANCE AND TV 112
boxes 148
BRB MANUFACTURING INC. 2
bread 52-56, 73

Greater Seattle Super Shopper, General Index 233

BRENCO 151
bricks 56, 88
BROADLOOM NORTHWEST 95
BROWN AND HALEY 68
brushes 80, 82
BUBBLE RECORDS & VIDEOS 164
BUD'S JAZZ RECORDS 164
BUDGET BATTERIES 198
BUDGET BOUTIQUE 17
BUDGET OFFICE FURNITURE 133
BUDGET RENTAL CAR SALES 197
BUDGET TAPES AND RECORDS 164
BUFFALO BILL'S SPORTING GOODS AND TOYS 191
Buffy Bus 206
BUFFY BUS 217
building materials 86-92
BUR-BANK DOMESTICS, INC. 118
BURLINGTON COAT FACTORY 7
Burlington Coat factory 38, 119
BURLINGTON'S BABY ROOM 31
buttons 174, 176
buying clubs 211, 212

C

C. RHYNE & ASSOCIATES 46
cabinets 86, 88-91, 112
cakes 53-55, 186, 204
CALICO CORNERS 173
CALVERT MANUFACTURING CO., INC. 151
camcorders 161
CAMERA SHOW 170
cameras 161, 169-172
Cameras West 170
camping equipment 149-151, 154, 156, 159, 160, 191, 200, 209
CAMPUS SPORTSWEAR 203
candles 42, 125, 172
candy 50, 67-69, 71
CANNED FOODS STORE 50
canned goods 49, 50, 207, 210, 212
canoes 152
canvas 174, 177
CAPE ISLE KNITTER 203
CAPTAIN SAM'S 37
car stereos 198
CAR/PUTER INTERNATIONAL 195
carpet 94-99, 101 212
CARPET EXCHANGE 95
CARPET REMNANT OUTLET 96
CARPETERIA 95
CARROLL AND ASSOCIATES 122

CARTER'S FACTORY OUTLET 31
CARTON SERVICE 148
CASCADE CO. 118
CASCADE COFFEE, INC. 63
CASCADE COOKIE COMPANY 52
CASCADIAN SPORTSWEAR 2
Cascadian Sportswear 27, 147, 148
CASE LITTELL 121
CASH & CARRY WHOLESALERS 51
CATCHPENNY BOOKS 180
CELLOPHANE SQUARE 165
CENTRAL CO-OP 73
ceramic pottery 123
ceramic tile 96, 99
CERBONE'S 58
CHADWICK'S OF BOSTON 26
chairs 105-112, 132-137
CHAMPAGNE TASTE 18
cheese 53, 56, 57, 62, 72
CHILDREN S ATTIC 34
children's books 32, 180, 182
children's car seats 33-36, 38
CHILDREN'S ORTHOPEDIC HOSPITAL 128
children's shoes 11, 13, 14, 33, 35, 38-41
china 121, 122, 205
CHINA SILVER & CRYSTAL SHOP 122
CHINOOK DOOR 87
CHIPPER'S 46
chips 56, 70
chocolates 67-69, 186
Christmas trees 131, 207
CHRISTOPHER PALLIS & ASSOCIATES 39
Chubby & Tubby 126, 131
CHUBBY & TUBBY 207
CHURCHILL GLOVES 203
cider 63, 64
CIDER SHED 64
CINDERELLA'S CLOSET 18
CITY PRODUCE CO. 58
CLASS ACT CONSIGNMENT BOUTIQUE 18
CLAY ART CENTER 123
cleaning supplies 51, 78, 115, 146, 147, 210-212
clocks 110, 208
CLOSE OUT 151
CLOSET TRANSFER 18, 27
CLOTHES CONNECTION 19
CLOTHESTIME 7, 8
clothing catalogs 26

Greater Seattle Super Shopper, General Index

clothing, children's 4, 11, 18-20, 31-38, 192, 204
clothing, men's 4, 5, 7, 9, 12, 13, 16, 19, 22-24, 26-30, 41-44, 203-206, 214-216
clothing, recreational 149-160
clothing, women's 1-26, 38-48, 203-206, 213-216
CLOTILDE 173
Clyed's Cameras 170
COAST TOOLS, INC. 92
coats 38, 44, 7, 18, 23, 119 (also see outerwear)
coffee 63, 75
COFFEE BREAK SERVICE CO. 63
coffee makers 111, 117
COHO SUPPLY INC. 112
coins 46, 47
COLD MOUNTAIN JUICE CO. 64
collectibles 213-215
COLLEGE COUPONS, LTD. 187
color enlargements 171
COLOR TILE 96
COMMISSARY CASH & CARRY, INC. 51
COMPACT DISC CONNECTION 165
compact disc recordings 164, 165, 167
COMPU-TECH 138
COMPUADD 143, 144
COMPUTER CITY 139
COMPUTER EXCHANGE NORTHWEST 138
computer books 136, 214
computer furniture 134-136
computer games 169
computer hardware and software 137-145, 162, 214
computer supplies 133, 146, 147
COMPUTERS 'N' THINGS 138
COMPUTERS & APPLICATIONS 138
COMSTOCK'S BINDERY AND BOOKSHOP 180
CONSIGNMENT CLOSET 19
CONSOLIDATED CARPET WAREHOUSE 96
CONSUMER REPORTS AUTO PRICE SERVICE 194
contraceptives 79
cookbooks 179-184
COOKIE CONSPIRACY 53
cookies 52-54, 56, 70, 71-72, 186
cookware 50, 114-117, 204
copy paper 136
CORNING/REVERE 204
CORT FURNITURE RENTALS CLEARANCE CENTER 107
cosmetics and makeup 76, 78, 80-82, 204, 205, 210
COST LESS 79
COST PLUS RX 79
COST SAVERS, LTD. 198
COSTCO WHOLESALE 212
Costco Wholesale 160
COSTCO WHOLESALE PHARMACY 79
costume jewelry 6, 7, 10-13, 17-24, 38, 109, 172, 204, 210, 215, 216
coupon books 73, 187-189
COWTOWN BOOTS FACTORY STORE 39
crafts 172-178, 192
Critic's Choice Video 163
croquet 158
cross country ski equipment 150, 151, 200
Crown Camera 170
crystal 121-123, 205
CRYSTAL THREADS 19
CURRENTS 146
CURRIER & CO. 2
cut glass 123
CUT-THE-CORNER FRAME SHOP 124
cutlery 114, 116

D

DAHNKEN OF TACOMA 46
dairy products 51, 56-60, 72-74, 76, 212
DAISY KINGDOM/ DK SPORTS 173
DAN HOWARD'S MATERNITY FACTORY 32
DANIEL SMITH 174
DARK HORSE 19
darkroom supplies 171
darts 158
DATA PRINT RIBBONS 133
DAVE BELL BOOKSELLER 182
DAVE'S APPLIANCE REBUILD 112
DAVIES PRODUCE CO., INC. 58
decorative accessories 21, 22, 87, 107, 108, 110, 115, 122-124, 147, 172, 206, 208, 210, 216
Definitive Audio 160
deli foods 51, 56, 61, 62, 70, 212
DELL COMPUTERS 144
Deseret Industries 213
DESIGN CENTER NORTHWEST 107

Greater Seattle Super Shopper, General Index 235

DESIGNER DIRECT 26
desks 104-110, 132-137
diamonds 46-48, 205
DICK'S CAMERA AND VIDEO 161
DICK'S RESTAURANT SUPPLY 116
DILETTANTE CHOCOLATE, INC. 68
dining out 185, 186
dining room furniture 104-110
dinnerware 50, 51, 115, 116, 118, 203, 215
DIRECT BUYING SERVICE 208
DIRECT CARPET SALES 97
DIRECT TRADE INTERNATIONAL 152
DISCOUNT BRIDAL SERVICE, INC. 42
DISCOUNT COMPUTER SOFTWARE 141
DISCOUNT OFFICE FURNITURE MART 133
DISCOUNT PAPER PRODUCTS 146
DISCOUNT SPORTS 152
DISCOUNT WATERBEDS, INC. 118
DISCOUNT WINDOW COVERINGS 104
DISHRACK 116
DOLLAR RENT A CAR SALES 197
DON'S HOUSE OF RECORDS 165
doors 86-91
DOWN FACTORY 152
draperies 101-104, 172, 178
DRASTIC PLASTIC RECORDS 165
DRESS BARN 8
DRUG EMPORIUM 78
drugs 77-79, 148, 207, 210, 212
DUCKY'S OFFICE FURNITURE 134
duplicate slides 171

E

earrings 12, 19, 46, 47, 210
EASTSIDE CHEESE 56
EASTSIDE MATTRESS CO. 122
EASY RIDER CANOE & KAYAK CO. 152
EDDIE BAUER 152
Eddie Bauer 5, 153, 156
EDMONDS COMMUNITY COLLEGE 126, 186
EDMONDS OLDE BOOKSTORE 180
EEJAYS HAIRCUTTER & BEAUTY SUPPLY 83
EGGHEAD DISCOUNT SOFTWARE 141
eggs 56, 57, 62, 73

EIGHTH AVENUE WOOLENS 2
ELÉGANCE FABRICS 174
electrical supplies 86, 87
ELEGANTE FORMAL WEAR, INC. 45
EMMANUEL RUG & UPHOLSTERY CLEANERS 97
EMPEROR'S NEW CLOTHES 43
ENCORE CONSIGNMENTS 20
Encore Consignments 27
ENER-G FOODS 73
ENTERTAINMENT PUBLICATIONS, INC. 187
envelopes 146, 147
Ernst 86
ethnic foods 70-73, 189
EVAN-PICONE 204
evening wear 10, 16-19, 21, 24, 26, 27, 33, 41-45, 175, 214
EVERETT BEAUTY SUPPLY 80
EVERETT COMMUNITY COLLEGE 85, 186
EVERETT STEEL 153
EVERETT TENT & AWNING CO. 174
EVERETT WHOLESALE PAPER COMPANY 146
EVERGREEN FRUIT & PRODUCE 58
EVERREST MATTRESS 122
exercise apparel 4, 32 149-160
EXIT WEST CLOTHING CO. 2
EXOTIQUE IMPORTS 165

F

FABRICLAND, INC. 174
fabrics 101-103, 172-178, 208
FACTORY BRAND SHOES 204
FACTORY DIRECT DRAPERIES 104
FACTORY DIRECT TIRE SALES 199
FACTORY OUTLET CENTER 202
FACTORY OUTLET L'EGGS BRANDS, INC. 39
factory outlet malls 27, 202-206, 217
FAIR SHARE 142
FALLOUT RECORDS & SKATEBOARDS 166
FANTASTIC SAMS 83
FARWEST PAINT 100
FASHION DIRECTIONS 8
FASHION FACTORY LIQUIDATORS 3
FASHION FLAIR-GANT 204

FASHION GALAXY 26
FASHION QUEST 20
fax machines 132, 134, 135, 146, 160-162, 170
fertilizer 71, 208
50 HOUR CLUB 185
FILLIPI BOOK AND RECORD SHOP 181
film 78, 148, 166, 169-172, 211
fish 51, 60-63, 75, 76, 212
fishing equipment 27, 41, 152, 154, 156, 160, 191, 208
fleece 2, 178
FLO COMPUTING 139
floor coverings 94-101
FLOOR DESIGN WEST 97
FLOORS TO GO 97
florists 129-131
flotation systems 121
flowers 125-131
FLOWERS PLUS 129
foam 107, 176
FOAM SHOP 107
FOOD CUPBOARD 74
Food Giant 49
food service warehouses 50, 51, 63, 111, 115
FOOD SERVICES TACOMA 51
FOR FAMILIES AND FRIENDS 188
FOR YU FURNISHINGS 107
formal wear 10, 16-19, 21, 24, 26, 27, 33, 41-45, 175, 214
FORRESTER FURS 43
FORTUNA BOOKS 181
47TH STREET PHOTO 170
47th Street Photo 144, 160, 169
FOSTER'S USED OFFICE FURNITURE 134
4 DAY TIRE STORES 199
FOX BOOK COMPANY 181
fragrances 12, 82, 204, 205
FRAGRANCE WORLD 204
Fred Meyer 49, 86, 162, 206
FREDERICK AND NELSON RED TAG CLEARANCE CENTER 14
FRIENDS OF THE SEATTLE PUBLIC LIBRARY 181
fruit 56, 58-60, 212
FUCHS 208
fur scraps 178
FURIE, LTD. 20
furniture, children's 23, 33-38, 192, 207
furniture, household 90, 104-112, 115-121, 208-210, 213
furniture, lawn 211
furniture, office 132-137, 145, 146
furs 7, 17, 19-24, 41-45, 204, 214
FUTON FACTORY OUTLET 118
FUTON OF NORTH AMERICA WAREHOUSE 119
futons 116, 118, 119

G

GAFFNEY SUPPLIERS, INC. 56
GAI'S SEATTLE FRENCH BAKING CO., INC. 53
games 27, 33, 162, 169, 191, 193
GARDEN FRESH FOODS 59
garden ornaments 128, 129
garden supplies 87, 126-130, 208
GEMINI SHAREWARE 142
GEMOLOGIST, INC. 46
gemstones 45-48, 122
GENA'S RESALE FASHIONS 20
GENE JUAREZ ADVANCED TRAINING CENTER 84
GENERAL COIN DISTRIBUTERS 193
GENERAL SERVICES ADMINISTRATION PROPERTY SALES 216
GENESIS FINE ARTS 124
GENTLEMEN'S CONSIGNMENT 27
GERRY SPORTSWEAR 153
GIFT CHECKS/WARDCO, INC. 188
gift wrapping 146-148, 192, 205
giftware 13, 46, 122-125, 216
GITANO 204
GLAD RAGS BOUTIQUE 20
glassware 46, 50, 115-117, 123, 191, 204, 215
Glazer's Cameras 170
GLOBE BOOKS 181
GOLD "C" SAVINGS SPREE 188
GOLDEN AMERICAN 188
GOLDEN EGG SKI AND SPORT 153
GOLDEN OLDIES RECORDS & TAPES 166
GOLDEN PHEASANT NOODLE CO. 70
golf equipment 154-158
GOLFLAND DISCOUNT PRO SHOP 154
GOODWILL 214
GRANDMOTHER'S HOUSE 34
GRANITE CURLING CLUB FLEA MARKET 216

Greater Seattle Super Shopper, General Index

GRANTREE FURNITURE RENTAL CLEARANCE CENTER 107
GREAT HAIRCUTS 33
GREAT NORTHWEST FACTORY STORES 202, 203
GREEN EARTH NUTRITION 74
GREEN RIVER CHEESE AND DAIRY PRODUCTS CO. 57
GREENBAUM'S CLEARANCE CENTER 108
Greenshield's 194
GREENSHIELD'S INDUSTRIAL SUPPLY 92
grooming products 77-82
grooming services 83-85
GROW & SONS LUMBER 87
GROWING GREEN INTERIORS 127
gumballs 69

H

hair care 78, 80-82, 84
HAIR PERFORMERS 80
HAIRCRAFTERS 83
HAIRMASTERS 84
HALF PRICE BOOKS RECORDS MAGAZINES 182
HALF PRICE SOFTWARE 142
HANCOCK FABRICS 174
handbags 10-12, 17-19, 22, 23, 38, 40, 190, 204, 205
handcrafted items 6, 33, 35, 37
HANES ACTIVEWEAR 204
hardware 86-94, 100, 153, 208, 211
HARDWICK'S SWAP SHOP 92
HARLAN-FAIRBANKS CO. 68
HARRIS CONLEY DISCOUNT GOLF SHOP 154
HARVÉ BERNARD xyz
HAWAIIAN COTTON 204
Hawthorne Stereo 160
health products 51, 60, 64, 69, 72-76, 206-208
HEALTH-TEX SAMPLE SALES 31
HEAVEN SENT 35
Henry Bacon 86
herbs 73, 75
HERTZ USED CAR SALES 97
HI-TECH RENTALS 139
HIGHLANDS CLEANERS 43
hiking equipment 41, 150, 151, 154
HILLSTEAD'S SURPLUS 205
HIS 27
holiday greenery 131

home building and remodeling 86-103
HOME CLUB 87, 88
home furnishings 14, 26, 104-119, 121-124, 206
honey 68, 69, 76
HORIZON BOOKS 182
hosiery 12, 38, 39, 205
HOUSE OF PIES THRIFT STORE 53
housewares 11, 51, 86, 106, 113, 116, 121, 207-211, 213, 216
HOVEN FOOD CO. 71
HUNTER'S FURNITURE OUTLET 108
hunting 154
HYDE'S NORTHWEST CANDY, INC. 68

I

I.B. DIFFUSION 204
ice cream 57, 64, 68, 69
IDEAS APPAREL 204
IKEDA AND COMPANY 71
IMPERIAL MATTRESS CO. 122
INTERIOR ART AND FRAME 124
INTERNAL REVENUE SERVICE AUCTION 216
INTERNATIONAL NEWS JUNIORS 3
INTERNATIONAL WORLD OF WEDDINGS 43
invitations 42, 177
Italian food 62, 70, 71, 72
ITEM HOUSE 3

J

J & S SEWING AND HOUSEWARES 113
J. THOMPSON 9
J.C. PENNEY'S FURNITURE WAREHOUSE 108
J.G. HOOK 204
J.G. STYLES 15
JACLYN'S 9
jams, jellies and preserves 37, 64
JAN SPORT FACTORY OUTLET 154
JANE'S BOOKS 182
janitorial supplies 51, 146, 147, 211
JANTZEN FABRIC OUTLET 175
jeans 3, 4, 9, 13, 15, 20, 25, 27, 29, 32, 216

Greater Seattle Super Shopper, General Index

JEANS TO GO 9, 27
JEN-CEL-LITE CORP. 119
JERRY'S SURPLUS 154
jewelry boxes 1
jewelry, costume 6, 7, 10-13, 17-24, 38, 109, 172, 204, 210, 215, 216
jewelry, fine 44-48, 122, 205, 207, 208
JINDO FUR 204
JJ's ON CALIFORNIA 21
JOHN'S FURNITURE FACTORY 108
JOHNSON CANDY CO. 69
JONES BROTHERS MEATS 61
JONES OF NEW YORK 204
JORDACHE 204
JOSEPH M'S 7
juice 63, 64
JUMP SPORTSWEAR 3
junior-size clothing 1, 3, 4, 7, 8, 10-14, 20, 21, 204, 213
JUST FOR YOU 35

K

K AND K COMPANY 124
K'S BEAUTY SUPPLY & SALON 81
K-Mart 206
KARIN'S BEAUTY SUPPLY 81
KATHY'S KLOSET 21
Kathy's Kloset 5
KAY-BEE TOYS, INC. 191
kayak 152
KEEFER DESIGN GALLERY 47
Ken's Cameras 170
KEY DISCOUNT DRUGS 79
KID'S KLOSET 35
KIDS CRAFT 192
KIDS ON 45TH 35
KIDS' MART 31
KIMURA NURSERY 127
KING & BUNNY'S DISCOUNT APPLIANCE & TV 113
KING COUNTY POLICE AUCTION 217
KING'S DEN 84
KISKI CABINETS 88
KITCHEN COLLECTION 204
kitchen equipment 74, 111-117, 204-206
Kits Cameras 170
knitting 177, 178
knives 114, 116
KOKESH CUT GLASS CO. 123
KUPPENHEIMER MEN'S CLOTHIERS 28
KUSAK CUT GLASS WORKS 123
KYM'S KIDDY CORNER 35

L

L.A. CONNECTION 10
L.A. FRAMES 124
L'EGGS, HANES, BALI 205
LA MEXICANA 71
LAKE CITY PICTURE FRAMING 125
LAKESHORE MINUTE MART 65
LAKESIDE SCHOOL RUMMAGE SALE 215
laminated counter tops 87-91, 96, 100
LAMPAERT MEATS 61
LANGENDORF BAKERIES 54
LARGE & TALL OUTLET 28
large and tall sizes, men's 7, 19, 26, 28, 29, 203
large sizes, women's 7, 11-15, 18-20, 22, 23, 25, 26, 33, 204
LARRY'S MARKET 131
Larry's Market 64
layette 31-38
leather accessories 39-41, 151, 198, 203-205
leather clothing 3, 9, 10, 21
leather fabric 175, 177, 178
LEATHER LOFT 205
LEE'S VIDEO-AUDIO-FAX-CELLULAR 161
LEISURE BOOKS 182
LENORA SQUARE SHOWROOM 109
LET'S EAT ETHNIC 189
LEWIS & HART NATIONAL INFORMATION & REFERENCE SERVICE 210
light bulbs 88, 112
lighting fixtures 86-88, 90, 91, 112
LIGHTING SUPPLY, INC. 88
LINCOLN SAVE-RITE PHARMACY 79
linens 13, 116-121
lingerie 12, 13, 18-20, 22, 25, 26, 36, 203-205, 215
LIPPS BEAUTY SUPPLY 81
LIQUIDATION SALES 209
liquor 52, 64, 66
LITTLE ANGEL BOUTIQUE 36
LIZ CLAIBORNE 205
LOEHMANN'S 10
LONDON FOG 205
luggage 190, 203-205, 207, 208, 211, 216

Greater Seattle Super Shopper, General Index

lumber 86, 87, 89, 90
LUXURY LINENS 119

M

M & L ASSOCIATES 166
M & L INTERNATIONAL 32
M. GENAUER & CO. 4
MACPHERSON LEATHER CO. 175
Magnolia Hi-Fi & Video 160
MAGUS BOOKSTORE 182
MAIDENFORM 205
MAJOR BRAND APPLIANCES 113
MAJOR BRANDS 100
makeup and cosmetics 76, 78, 80-82, 204, 205, 210
MANHATTAN JEWELRY MANUFACTURERS 205
MANNA MILLS, INC. 74
marble 101
MARCI JEWELRY 47
marine and boating supplies 90, 153, 156, 160, 162, 176, 206
MARKET SPICE 75
MARMOT MOUNTAIN WORKS 154
MARQUIS BEAUTY PRODUCTS & SALON 81
MARSHALL'S 11
Marshall's 27, 38
MARY'S POP-INS 44
MASTER GARDENERS 128
maternity clothing 11, 16, 17, 19-23, 30-38
MATTRESS OUTLET 120
mattresses 110, 112, 117, 120, 121, 198, 213
MATTREST 120
MAXINE'S BABY WORLD 36
McCARTHY & SCHIERING WINE MERCHANTS 65
McLENDON HARDWARE, INC. 88
meat 49, 60-62, 74, 76, 212
MEAT DISTRIBUTORS INC. 62
MEDICINE MAN 73
membership buying clubs 211, 212
MEN'S WEARHOUSE, INC. 28
menswear 4, 5, 7, 9, 12, 13, 16, 19, 22-24, 26-30, 41-44, 203-206, 214-216
MERLINO'S FINE FOODS 71
METRO PASS SAVERS 189
Mexican food 57, 71, 72
MEXICAN GROCERY 72
MIDLAKE'S FLOOR COVERINGS 98
MIKASA CHINA 205

milk 72-74
MILLER'S INTERIORS, INC. 98
millwork 86-91
MJ MEATS 61
mobile phones 161
MOBILI LTD. 109
MODERN WOMAN 11
MOM 'N ME 36
MOM'S N TOTS 36
MONDO'S WORLD 65
MONTE VISTA DISTRIBUTORS BULK WAREHOUSE SALES 51
MORNING SUN OUTLET 4
MOSS BAY MERCANTILE 29
MOTTO 4
mountain climbing 149, 154
MOUNTAIN PRODUCTS 155
MOUSE CLOSET 36
MOVIE MASTERS 166
MR. TALL & BIG 29
MT. PILCHUCK SKI & SPORT 155
museums 184
MUSHROOM SHOES 205
MUSIC VEND DISTRIBUTING CO. 193
MUTUAL MATERIALS 88

N

nails 80-84
napkins 116, 124, 146, 148
NATIONAL CAR RENTAL 197
NATIONAL FURNITURE RENTALS AND SALES, INC. 109
NATIONAL KITCHEN SALES 89
NATURAL FOOD SUPPLEMENTS 75
natural foods 73-76
NEARLY NEW CONSIGNMENT SHOP 21
NEVADA BOB'S DISCOUNT GOLF 155
NEVER ENDING FANTASY 45
NEW ATTITUDE BEAUTY SUPPLY & SALON 81
new look 7
NEW YORK BAGEL BOYS 54
newsprint 178
NINE TO FIVE BUSINESS FURNITURE 135
NORDSTROM RACK 15
NORDSTROM SHOE RACK 39
NORMANDEE ROSE 4
NORTH SEATTLE COMMUNITY COLLEGE 186
NORTHWEST GROCERS 52

NORTHWEST HANDBAG
  COMPANY 40
NORTHWEST HORTICULTURAL
  SOCIETY 128
NORTHWEST ICE CREAM NOVELTIES 57
NORTHWEST LIQUIDATION &
  SALES 134
NORTHWEST RECORD &
  COMPACT DISC CONVENTION 167
NORTHWEST VENDING SUPPLY
  69
NOTHING TO WEAR 45
NOWELL & ASSOCIATES SAMPLE SALE
  5
NU YU FASHIONS 29
nurseries 126-129
NUTRA SOURCE 75

O

O'LEARY'S BOOKS 183
OBERTO FACTORY OUTLET
  STORE 62
Odds and Ends 213
OFF CENTER FURNITURE
  WAREHOUSE 109
OFFICE CLUB 134
Office Club 160
office furniture and equipment 105,
  108-110, 132-137, 145, 213
OFFICE FURNITURE CO-OP 135
OFFICE FURNITURE
  DISCOUNTERS 135
OFFICE FURNITURE EXPRESS 135
office supplies 132, 134-136, 145,
  146, 190, 211
OLD MILL 205
OLD TECHNOLOGY SHOP 161
OMID INTERNATIONAL RUGS 205
ONEIDA 46, 122, 205
OPTECHS CAMERA SUPPLY 170
optical products 79, 189, 212
orchids 126, 131
organic 61, 74, 76
Oriental food 70-72, 185
ORIENTAL FURNITURE
  WAREHOUSE 110
OROWHEAT BAKERS, INC. 54
ORPHEUM 167
outdoor clothing 150, 156, 158, 160
OUTDOOR CLOTHING OUTLET 156
OUTDOOR EMPORIUM 156
outerwear 1-3, 5, 7, 12, 26-28, 32,
  119, 150, 152, 153, 173, 205,
  214, 216

P

P.J.'S BEAUTY SUPPLY 82
PACIFIC AIR TOOL 94
PACIFIC COLOR, INC. 171
PACIFIC COMPUTER EXCHANGE,
  INC. 139
PACIFIC COMPUTER NORTHWEST
  139
PACIFIC EDGE OUTLET CENTER 203
PACIFIC FABRICS WAREHOUSE
  OUTLET 175
PACIFIC FLOWER MARKET 130
PACIFIC FOOD IMPORTERS 72
PACIFIC INDUSTRIAL SUPPLY 89
PACIFIC IRON'S BUILDING
  MATERIALS 90
PACIFIC LINEN OUTLET 120
PACIFIC ROSE HOUSE 130
PACIFIC TRAIL SPORTSWEAR 5
PACIRIM 40
packaging 146-148
PAGE ONE DESIGNS 45
paint 87, 95, 99-101, 208
PAMBIHIRA ORIENTAL FOOD
  MART 72
PANDORA'S BOX 22
Pandora's Box 27, 41
PANDORA'S CASTLE 44
pans 115, 116
PAPER FACTORY OUTLET 147
PAPER MERCHANT 147
PAPER PICK-UP 147
paper products, kitchen 50, 51, 63
paper products, office 136, 144-147,
  190, 191, 211, 212
PARK AVENUE RECORDS 167
party goods 146-148, 177, 191, 210
pasta 59, 70, 71-72
pastries 52-55, 186
PAVILION MALL SUPER SHOPPER
  189
Pay Less 49, 86, 206
Pay'n'Pak 86
Pay'N'Save 49
PC CONNECTION 144
Peaches Music and Video 162
PENNER GOLF PRODUCTS, INC.
  156
PENNY LANE RECORDS & TAPES
  167
PEOPLE'S FURNITURE RENTAL
  110
PERFECT FIT/McDONALD CO. 176
perfume 12, 82, 204, 205

personal care products 77-84
pet supplies 79, 208
PETE'S SUPERMARKET 65
PETERSON FRUIT CO. 59
petite-size clothing 2-4, 7, 11, 12, 14, 19, 25, 26, 33, 203, 204
photo albums 171
photo copiers 132
photographic equipment 144, 160, 169-172
PICKERING APPLIANCE & TV 113
picture frames 124, 125, 210
Picway 38
pies 54, 56
PIKE PLACE FURNITURE CLEARANCE CENTER 110
pillows 107, 117-119, 151, 152, 172, 176, 178
pizza 57, 62, 70, 73, 187
plant sales 127
PLANTS & PLANTING GREENHOUSES 127
plants 125-131
PLAY IT AGAIN TOYS 192
PLENTY OF TEXTILES 176
plumbing supplies 86, 87, 90, 91
popcorn 50, 68
PORTER-CABLE 94
POST WALLCOVERING DISTRIBUTORS 102
posters 123-125, 147, 210
POTTERY SALES NORTHWEST 129
poultry 60-62, 212
pre-teen sizes 20, 31, 34, 36
PRECISION HAIR CUTTERS 84
prescriptions 77-79
PRESTIGE FRAGRANCE & COSMETICS 82
PRESTIGE FRAGRANCE 205
PRICE SAVERS WHOLESALE WAREHOUSE 212
Price Savers Wholesale Warehouse 160
printers 139-141, 145, 147
PRO GOLF DISCOUNT 156
PRO-BEAUTY 84
PROCREATIONS MATERNITY LEASEWEAR 33
PROCTOR'S CONSIGNMENT 37
produce 49, 50, 58-60, 73, 74, 212
PROUD PEACOCK 22
PUETZ GOLF CENTERS 157
Puget Consumer's Co-op 73
PUGET CONSUMERS CO-OP 76
PUGET PARK SWAP-O-RAMA 216

Q

QFC 65, 131
QUALITY CLASSICS SPORTSWEAR 5
QUANTITY PHOTOS, INC. 171
QUEEN ANNE THRIFTWAY 131
QUEEN SIZE BOUTIQUE 15
QUEEN'S CLOSET 22
QUIET COMPANION BOOKS 183

R

R & E 2ND GEAR 157
R AND S SALES, INC. 136
radar detectors 161
RAGAMOFFYN'S 22
RAINBOW BOUTIQUE 37
raincoats 3, 5, 7, 9, 205
RAINIER PHOTOGRAPHIC SUPPLIES 171
RAINWARE SOFTWARE 143
Razz M' Tazz 5
RAZZ M'TAZZ 23
READ PRODUCTS, INC. 90
REBELLIOUS JUKEBOX 167
RECORD PLANET 167
recordings 162-169, 181-183, 185, 192, 214, 215
recreational clothing 149-160
REDRESS 23
REI 157
REMINGTON SHAVER SERVICE 113
REMNANT KING 98
restaurant equipment and supplies 114-116
RESTAURANT MART 116
RESTMORE MATTRESS AND FURNITURE FACTORY 122
ribbon 78, 205
RIBBON OUTLET 205
rice 60, 71-73
RICK'S TIRE & CHEVRON 199
RISING SUN FARMS & PRODUCE 59
RITZY RAGS BUDGET BOUTIQUE 37
road services 200, 201
RODDA DECOR CENTER 100
ROGER'S CANDY COMPANY 69
ROOS MARKET 55
ROSE HEARTS 130
roses 129, 130
ROSS DRESS FOR LESS 12
RUBATO'S 168
RUBBER TREE 79
RUG BARN 98
rugs 97, 98
rummage sales 215
RUTH ASHBROOK BAKERY THRIFT SHOP 55

S

S.T. PRODUCE 59
Safeway 144
Safeway 49
SAFEWAY 66, 131
SAGERS' GEORGETOWN TIRE & RETREAD 200
salvage 87, 90, 91, 147, 206
SALVAGE BROKER 147
Salvation Army 213
SAMPLE FASHIONS 12
SAMPLE SALES 31, 32
SAMUEL MARTIN LTD. 5
SARCO 114
SATIN HANGER 23
Satin Hanger 27
sausage 61, 62
SAV-ON DRUGS 79
SAVVY 23
scarves 10-12, 24, 38, 124
SCHOENFELD'S 110
SCHOOL DISTRICT AUCTIONS 217
scissors 80, 82, 114
SCOTT MICHAEL'S FINE JEWELRY 47
SEAFIRST BANK VEHICLE SALES FACILITY 196
seafood 51, 60-63, 75, 76, 212
SEARS OUTLET 209
SEATTLE BUILDING SALVAGE, INC. 90
SEATTLE CENTRAL COMMUNITY COLLEGE 85, 186
SEATTLE FABRICS 176
SEATTLE FURNITURE FACTORY 111
SEATTLE MASTER BUILDERS ASSOCIATION 91
SEATTLE MICRO 140
SEATTLE OFFICE FURNITURE 133
SEATTLE PACIFIC INDUSTRIES 6
Seattle Pacific Industries 27
SEATTLE POLICE AUCTION 217
SEATTLE REPERTORY THEATRE'S ELEGANT ELEPHANT SALE 215
SEATTLE SUPPER CLUB 189
SEATTLE TELECOM & DATA, INC. 140
SEATTLE TILTH ASSOCIATION 128
SEBASTIAN'S CLOSET 24
Sebastian's Closet 42
SECOND AVENUE CONSIGNMENTS 24
SECOND BASE 158
SECOND TIME AROUND RECORDS, STEREO & VIDEO 168
SECURITY PACIFIC BANK VEHICLE LIQUIDATION WAREHOUSE 196
senior citizens 55, 56, 73, 76, 113
SESSIONS DISCOUNT/VARIETY 209
75¢ Video 163
SEWING MACHINE SERVICE CO. INC. 114
sewing supplies and equipment 113-115, 152, 172-178
SHAKESPEARE & MARTIN 183
SHAMEK'S BUTTON SHOP 176
shampoo 78, 82, 83
SHANE CO. 47
shareware 141-143
SHAREWARE OUTLET 143
shavers 111, 113, 114
SHEEPSKIN STATION FACTORY OUTLET 198
sheets and towels 116-120
SHERMAN SUPPLY 91
SHOE PAVILION 40, 205
shoes, athletic 12, 38, 41, 149-152, 157, 158, 203-205, 208
shoes, children's 11, 13, 14, 33, 35, 38, 39, 41
shoes, family 11, 13, 14, 33, 38-42, 150-152, 158, 203-205, 211
shoes, men's 26, 27, 38-42, 204, 206
shoes, women's 17-19, 20-23, 26, 38-41, 204, 205
shopping tours 217
SHORELINE COMMUNITY COLLEGE 85
SHOREY BOOKSTORE 183
SHUTTERBUG 171
SIERRA TRADING POST 158
SILK AND FLORAL EXCHANGE 125
silk flowers 125, 129, 177
SILK GREENHOUSE, INC. 176
SILO 114
Silo 160, 208
SILVER BOW HONEY COMPANY 76
silverware 22, 50, 115-117, 122, 205
SINGER REGIONAL FACTORY SERVICE CENTER 115
SIT 'N' SLEEP 121
SIX STAR FACTORY OUTLET 210
skateboards 165

Greater Seattle Super Shopper, General Index

ski apparel and equipment 5, 19, 25, 27, 149-153, 155, 158, 173, 200, 214
SKI BONKERS 158
SKI RACK SPORTS 158
SKIL CORP. 94
SLEEP-AIRE MATTRESS CO. 122
SMART SIZES 12
snack foods 49, 50, 52, 55, 70
SNIAGRAB and SPORTS BLAST 158
soap 82
soccer 152, 158
SOCKS GALORE 205
soda 50
SOFT COVERINGS 177
SOFTWARE CONNECTION 43
SOUND VIEW FLOORS 99
SOUNDWAVES 168
SOUTH SEATTLE COMMUNITY COLLEGE 85, 130, 186
SPECIALTY CANDLES BY LUNDS 125
SPERRY/DUFFEL/IN-SPORT 206
spices 56, 72, 73, 75
SPORTCO 159
sporting goods 27, 38, 114, 149-160, 172, 191, 207-209, 211, 216
SPORTS EXCHANGE 159
SPORTS REPLAY 159
sportswear 1-5, 8-10, 12-14, 16-18, 22, 23-28, 32, 149-160, 203-205, 211
SPORTSWEAR EXPRESS DISCOUNT JEANS & TOPS 13
SQUAK MOUNTAIN GREENHOUSE 127
SQUIRE SHOP 29
St. Vincent de Paul 213
STANDARD BATTERIES 199
STANDARD BRANDS 101
STAR-LITE SWAP & SHOP 216
stationery 146, 147
stereo equipment 114, 160-162, 168, 198, 212
Stereo Shoppe 160
Stock Market 49
STONEFELT AND COMPANY 57
STRICTLY BUSINESS/CROSSINGS 30
suede 10, 175
SUN COAST VIDEO 168
SUN COMPUTERS 140
SUN WEST CARPETS 99
sundries 77-79, 148, 207
sunglasses 153, 159, 210
SUPER CUTS 84
SUPER YARN MART 177
SUTLIFF'S CANDY COMPANY 69
SWAP AND SHOP ASSOCIATION OF THE NORTHWEST 215
sweaters 1, 3, 5, 9, 10, 13, 17, 20, 26, 29, 30, 37, 175, 203, 205
SYSCO CASH & CARRY / CONTINENTAL FOOD SERVICE 52

T

T.J. MAXX 13
T.W. CARROL & CO. 190
T-DEE APPLIANCE 161
T-shirts 1, 2, 4, 5, 13, 29, 151, 210
TABLE DE FRANCE 206
TACOMA BOOK CENTER 184
TACOMA LUGGAGE & OFFICE SUPPLY 190
TACOMA SCREW PRODUCTS ANNEX 92
TACOMA TENT & AWNING 177
TACOMA TOOL 93
TAKE TWO 5, 24, 27
Tall's Cameras 170
TANDY LEATHER 177
TANNER FACTORY STORES 206
Target 162, 206
tea 63, 122
televisions 106, 111, 161, 162, 168, 170, 212, 216
tennis clothing and equipment 19, 25, 151, 156
tent 150, 156, 174, 177
TEXTILE NETWORK MARKETING 178
The Wise Penny 213
theaters 184, 185
THREE BEARS 37
thrift shops 213
THRIFTY CAR RENTAL 197
TICKET TICKET 185
tickets 184-187
ties 38, 44
tile 88, 95-101
TIMBER WINDOWS 91
TINA'S 24
tires 194, 199, 212
TIRES PLUS 199
TITLEWAVE BOOKS 184
tofu 71

244 Greater Seattle Super Shopper, General Index

TOM CHRISTIE & ASSOCIATES 40
TOOL TOWN 93
tools 86-88, 90-94, 141, 161, 175, 194, 198, 207-209, 211, 216
tools, air 198
tools, mechanic's 90-94, 194, 198
tools, building 86-88, 90-94, 161, 207-209, 211, 216
TORINO SAUSAGE CO. 62
TOTEM FOOD PRODUCTS, INC. 70
towels and sheets 116-120
TOWER RECORDS & VIDEO 168
TOY LIQUIDATORS 206
TOY WORLD 193
TOYS 'R' US 192
toys 21, 32-38, 188, 190-193, 206, 207, 208, 210, 211, 214-216
TOYS UNLIMITED 206
Treasures & Trinkets 213
tree 38, 79, 131, 139
TREE HOUSE 38
TRINITY TECH INC. 140
TROPICAL FOLIAGE 128
TRU-ART PICTURE FRAME CO. 125
TSUE CHONG CO. 72
tuxedos 41-44
TUX SHOP 44
TV tubes 162
TV's 106, 111, 161, 162, 168, 170, 212, 216
TWENTY-FIFTH STREET MARKET 60
TWICE IS NICE BOUTIQUE 24

U

U.S. CUSTOM SERVICES AUCTION 217
U.S. MICRO EXPRESS 141
U-pick 60
ULTIMATE OUTLET 26
UNDER-WARE ELECTRONICS 144, 162
underwear 12, 13, 18-20, 22, 25, 26, 28, 31, 36, 153, 203-205, 215
UNICORN BOUTIQUE 38
Union Gospel Mission 213
UNITED PRODUCTS 141
UNIVALCO BARGAIN MART 210
UNIVERSITY OFFICE PRODUCTS 136
UNIVERSITY ROSE GARDENS 130
UNIVERSITY SOFTWARE 143

upholstery supplies 176
used cars 194, 196, 197
USED TIRE & WHEEL CO. 199
USED TIRE WHEREHOUSE 200

V

V.J.'S VINTAGE BRIDAL PARLOR 44
VAAR-M BEAUTY SUPPLY & SALON 82
VALERIE'S 14
VALLEY HARVEST 60
Value Village 213
VAN HEUSEN 206
VAULT, THE 48
VCR's 106, 111, 161-163, 216
vegetables 58-60, 73, 212
vehicles 194, 196, 199, 202, 212
video equipment 115, 144, 160-170, 193, 209, 211
VIDEO ONLY 162
video tapes 162-168
video tape duplicating service 171
VIKING DISCOUNT OFFICE PRODUCTS 136
vinyl flooring 94-97
vitamins 74
VIVIAN'S PRIDE GOURMET ICE CREAM 57
Volume Shoe Source 38
VOLUNTEER PARK CONSERVATORY 128
Volunteers of America 213

W

WACKY WAREHOUSE 136
WAISTED BELT CO., INC. 41
WALLET WORKS 206
wallets 38-40, 178, 190, 205
wallpaper 87, 95, 96, 99-102
WALLPAPERS TO GO 101
WARSHAL'S SPORTING GOODS AND PHOTOGRAPHIC SUPPLY CO. 172
Warshal's Camera Department 170
washers and dryers (see appliances)
WASHINGTON POTTERY CO. 129
WASHINGTON SHOE COMPANY 41
WASHINGTON STATE LIQUOR STORES 66
water heaters 86, 113
waterbeds 118

waterski equipment 160
WAX ORCHARDS 64
WEARABLE ART SALE 6
WEAVING WORKS 178
wedding gowns 23-25, 33, 42-44
WEDDINGS, ETC. 45
WELCOME HOME 206
WELL-MADE BED 21
WELLWORTH'S 173
WESSCO 104
WEST COAST DIAMONDS & GEMS 48
WEST MARINE PRODUCTS 160
WESTERN FISH AND OYSTER CO., INC. 62
WESTERN TOOL SUPPLY 93
WESTLAKE OFFICE FURNITURE 133
WESTPORT LIMITED 206
wheels 198, 199
WHEREHOUSE, THE 169
Wholesale Heaven 1, 32
WHOLESALE HEAVEN 215
WICKER FACTORY 206
WILEY'S WATERSKI SHOP 160
WILL-WOOD PREFIT, INC. 91
WILLIAMS & SON, INC. 48
window coverings 95, 100-104, 172, 212
WINDOW WARES 102
windows 86-91
wine 64-66, 73, 187
WINE WAREHOUSE 66
WINTER'S OFFICE FURNITURE 137
women's apparel 1-26, 38-48, 151, 156, 203-206, 213-216
WONDER BREAD HOSTESS CAKE THRIFT STORES 55
wood flooring 95, 96, 99
work clothes 18, 208
WORLD WIDE DISTRIBUTORS, INC. 211
wrapping paper 146-148, 192, 205

XYZ

yarn 99, 177, 178
YESTERDAY'S 25, 42
YORKTOWNE WALLPAPERS 102
young men's sizes 3, 4, 6, 7, 29
YOUR HIDDEN CLOSET 25
YOUR TOOL HOUSE, INC. 94
Your Tool House, Inc. 194
ZOBRIST CONSUMER ELECTRONICS 162

Greater Seattle Super Shopper, Personal Shopping Notes